TOWN HOUSES

TOWN HOUSES

Urban Houses from 1200 to the Present Day

Marcus Binney

Whitney Library of Design
an imprint of Watson-Guptill Publications/New York

For my wife

TOWN HOUSES
by Marcus Binney

Specially commissioned photography by Nicholas Kane

First published in the United States in 1998 by
Whitney Library of Design, an imprint of Watson-Guptill
Publications, a division of BPI Communications Inc.,
1515 Broadway, New York, NY 10036

First published in Great Britain in 1998 by Mitchell Beazley,
an imprint of Reed Consumer Books Limited,
Michelin House, 81 Fulham Road, London SW3 6RB
and Auckland

Executive Editor Alison Starling
Executive Art Editor Vivienne Brar
Senior Editor Anthea Snow
Designer Adrian Morris
Editor Richard Dawes
Editorial Assistant Stephen Guise
Picture Research Anna Kobryn
Production Rachel Staveley
Illustrations Maltings Partnership, Joy Fitzsimmons and
Stefan Chabluk
Index Hilary Bird

ISBN 0-8230-6962-1
First printing, 1998
1 2 3 4 5 6 7 8 9/06 05 04 03 02 01 00 99 98

Binney, Marcus.
  Town houses: urban houses from 1200 to
the present day/ Marcus Binney.
    p. cm.
  Includes bibliographical references and index.
  ISBN 0-8230-6962-1
  1. Row houses—History. I. Title.
NA7520.B56 1998
728'.312'09—dc21   98-4148
                                CIP

Set in Caslon 224, Scotch Roman, Serifa
Produced by Toppan Printing Co., Ltd
Printed and bound in China

FRONT JACKET **Nineteenth-century brownstones, New York**

Contents

Lost and Saved

Tragically, these overhanging medieval houses in Lisieux were destroyed during the Allied invasion of Normandy in 1944. This photograph, taken at the beginning of the 20th century, shows the timber-frame construction with one storey jettied out over that below. The detail above shows herringbone bricks set between the timbers, and rare "flame-headed" ogee arches.

Almost every city in Europe had distinctive types of town house, built in rows along streets to take advantage of limited space and the high land values that came with prosperity. For centuries these houses were so common that they rarely attracted study. Yet all over Europe and North America they yield fascinating first-hand evidence of the way people lived, as well as providing adaptable homes for today. During the 20th century, many town houses have been lost or damaged through thoughtless development or insensitive alteration. The losses make painful reading, but the survivals are no less remarkable.

Rhinelander Gardens was an impressive row of houses at 110–24 West 11th Street, New York. Built in 1854 to the design of James Renwick, it was torn down in the late 1950s. The tiers of richly ornamental cast-iron balconies gave dignity and unity to the street front, leaving only the steps leading up to the front doors to mark the individual houses.

This book is prompted by a race against time, a quest to save from destruction the traditional house in a street. Thousand upon thousand have gone from our cities and towns; even more have been disfigured by alterations, stripped of original features. In England's Georgian city of Bath alone, 2,000 artisans' cottages built of beautiful Bath stone were demolished in the 1960s. Half of New York's brownstones have gone, as have half of San Francisco's delightful painted wooden houses known as "Painted Ladies."

For nearly a century preservation efforts have concentrated on the exceptional, on the peaks of human architectural creativity: cathedrals, temples, castles, grand public buildings and country houses. More recently there has been a widespread awakening of interest in the typical, a realization that more modest buildings and interiors can yield a wealth of fascinating information both about building techniques and about social history in the way people lived in the past.

The great engines of civilization and economic growth in Europe and North America have been the towns and cities. And to a surprising and fascinating extent many communities have developed their own particular patterns of living, which can sometimes be traced back hundreds of years – for example, in Cluny, France (see pages 16–17), to the 12th century.

Terrace houses, as they are called in Britain, or row houses, as North Americans know them, have benefited from the new emphasis on the protection of groups of buildings and whole neighbourhoods that has developed since the 1960s. New legislation has continued to safeguard the character of whole streets, even though, in many cases, the emphasis has been on preserving external features.

In recent decades there has been a growing realization that even the plainest façade may shield a remarkable interior, and that no historic building should be condemned simply because of a decrepit exterior. In much of Europe, for all the great rebuilding of Baroque times, the typical town house was remodelled rather than torn down and rebuilt. One result of this is that above Rococo and Neo-classical ceilings an increasing number of painted wooden ceilings are being discovered.

Similarly, in English market towns many a Georgian brick façade is found laid over a 15th- or 16th-century timber frame. Many old houses have a story to tell. For a long time it was believed that house bricks arrived in 18th-century Philadelphia as ballast from England, whereas it now seems clear that, from an early date, they were in fact baked in local kilns. Nor were Sydney's fanciful wrought-iron balconies and verandahs shipped out from England, but made in local foundries that were established at the time of the gold rush.

During the Second Empire in France (1852–70) the heart of Paris was transformed by Napoleon III's chief planner, Baron Georges-Eugène Haussmann (1809–91), who swept away countless streets of old houses and replaced them with wide boulevards lined with apartment blocks for a growing middle class. The great age of many of the houses is evident from views expressed at the time of their destruction, which was the subject of much lament.

AVERTING THE THREAT

My eyes were opened to the hidden beauties of the terrace house when I wrote a university thesis on the English architect Sir Robert Taylor (1714–88) who, as surveyor to the Grafton Estate, built numerous houses that are only slowly being identified. In Grafton Street, in London's Mayfair (see pages 74–9), behind the plainest of façades I discovered one of the most beautiful staircases I had ever seen, with daringly undercut stone steps that projected from the wall in a way that seemed to defy gravity. In the same house I found below the basement another storey, completely submerged, of vaulted cellars, installed to keep the whole house dry. The exquisite plasterwork of Georgian houses has long been admired. Yet Home House, in Portman Square, Robert Adam's finest

London house, has a remarkably little-touched basement, stone-flagged with built-in dressers – a rare and important survivor. It is equivalent to the basement in Brunswick Square, Hove (see pages 94–7), which was saved by the initiative of the Brighton historian Nick Tyson and friends, who went on to restore the whole house to its original state.

In 1975 I and a group of contemporaries formed SAVE Britain's Heritage. That year was European Architectural Heritage Year, and we were concerned that the official campaign would be "yet another occasion for Britain's architects, town planners and local authorities to pat each other on the back and give themselves awards."

Our anger was exacerbated by the news that the Department of the Environment had just given permission for the demolition of an entire railway village in Buckinghamshire, at Wolverton, consisting of row after row of simple terrace houses – 200 in total. The extent of destruction in those bulldozer-happy years of "comprehensive redevelopment" and "neighbourhood clearance" was underlined by the horrendous statistic that 60–75 percent of the housing demolished by the Greater London Council between 1966 and 1971 was in fair to good condition and capable of renovation.

Street after street of usable homes was razed for lack of plumbing that could have been installed for a fraction of the cost of the high-rise blocks that were built to replace them and that rapidly became the slums of today. Even worse was the forced

These tall merchants' houses in Hamburg, many with overhanging upper storeys, were demolished soon after 1900. Had they survived, they would be one of northern Europe's architectural treasures.

This photograph of a delightful Rococo house, built in 1729, in Brussels' Rue Cantersteen, was taken shortly before it was demolished in 1897, and appeared in the magazine *L'Emulation*.

Archaeologists believe that the 14th-century Vicars' Close in Wells, Somerset (below), is the earliest example of terrace housing in Britain. The houses were built for the vicars choral, the deputies of the cathedral's canons, and appear to have been finished by 1363. Excavations have shown that the land was carefully terraced to create an even slope. The footings were constructed piecemeal and by several different masons, which indicates that the houses were built in groups, like terrace houses of the 18th century.

dispersal of whole communities that had regarded these houses as their homes for several generations.

Just as terrace houses were being swept away by the thousand, the great revival began. In Britain, London led the way; in America, Baltimore. Terrace houses were bought up and restored by individual owners and sometimes, although often with less success, by local authorities. Among the great champions are enterprising conservation organizations such as the Spitalfields Trust, which has saved dozens of 18th-century houses in the East End of London, and, in the USA, Historic Savannah.

For some time it looked as if the sheer pressure on land in many cities – and the consequent pressure to build ever higher – would spell the end of the terrace house. For example, during the 18th century Paris embraced the *immeuble*, or apartment block, in preference to the house, and most European cities followed suit in the 19th and 20th centuries.

In our cities – where row housing is seen as the most basic kind of accommodation – the desire to move up the housing ladder to a semi-detached or free-standing house is powerful and understandable. However, in many cities a limit is imposed by the sheer price, and availability, of land. The advantage of terrace housing is that it can be built to remarkable densities. With free-standing houses, eight to an acre (0.4ha) is dense, but in San Francisco's Fulton

During the Second World War the Old Market Square in Warsaw was the victim of systematic destruction by German troops as they evacuated the Polish capital. After the war the Poles, determined that the memory of their beautiful city should not perish, rebuilt the square and surrounding streets from the evidence of paintings and photographs. Every detail of ornament and colour has been painstakingly reproduced, as the photograph on the right illustrates.

Grove two enterprising developers have built 22 houses on half an acre (0.2ha). This is equal to the density that can be achieved with high-rise public housing, where tower blocks must stand some distance apart to provide enough light and air to make living conditions tolerable.

In pursuing the story of the terrace house up to the 1990s, it is fascinating constantly to find novel and imaginative variations on a familiar theme. The Berlin houses of Bruno Taut, Nicholas Grimshaw's metal houses in Camden, London, and futuristic steel and glass houses in Konstanz, Germany, all show that a traditional form can offer exciting new possibilities. Within its box of four enclosing walls the classic terrace house is infinitely adaptable. For example, living rooms may be on the ground floor, or on the first floor, as in Savannah, or even in airy, studio-like spaces at the top, as in San Francisco's Fulton Grove.

Town houses, far more than country houses, have been the victims of modern warfare. The panic induced by Hitler's vicious raid on the Spanish town of Guernica led Nazi leaders to believe that civilian populations could be subdued by carpet bombing. Hitler's "Baedeker raids" – the inspiration for the name was Germany's famous guidebooks – of April 1942 were intended to demoralize Britain by destroying its most beautiful cities. Unsurprisingly, they provoked Churchill to an overwhelming response, and night after night Germany's major cities were pounded by bombing of a previously unknown intensity. Neither the Germans nor the British were subdued by these horrific exchanges,

but the devastation of history, above all of town houses, blasted chapter after chapter of history from the face of Europe. The Allied invasion of Normandy brought the destruction of Caen and, sadder still, of beautiful Lisieux, which had one of the finest and most intact streets of medieval timber houses in northern Europe.

And yet there is inspiration here too, in the way that Europe's heritage rose from the ashes. Perhaps most encouraging of all is the story of Warsaw. Poland's capital city was left in complete ruins by the Nazis, bombed, shelled and torched, but after the Second World War the old square and surrounding streets were painstakingly recreated. A guide to reconstruction was provided by photographs and by the late-18th-century paintings of Bernardo Bellotto, which depicted garrets, chimneys, windows and frescoes in superb detail. Warsaw may now be virtually a film set, but it is inspiring to step back in time and see in three dimensions how a famous square looked in the late 18th century. Here is a living lesson in the perfection of classical proportions. Intriguingly, it is these carefully recreated layers of history that help produce a sense of the picturesque – the element that gives Europe so much of its best townscape.

Often it is loss, or imminent loss, that sparks a study of historic architecture. The study of town houses is very different from that of country houses and castles, for numerous examples of both the latter are preserved and accessible to the public. This book is about typical town houses, not the grand family *palazzi* found in every Italian town or the *hôtels particuliers*, with their fine courtyards, of noble Parisian families. A number of the houses discussed are open to visitors.

In London the study of typical town houses was pioneered by the *Survey of London*, whose volumes on individual parishes show how streets were developed by successive landlords and speculators. Much architectural history has been written from the sources left by architects – drawings, plans and letters – but with town houses, in the building of which architects have played a smaller role, the dates of houses have more often been traced by the study of parish rates books (payments would cease during rebuilding) and town records.

In Germany the remarkable series *Das Deutsche Bürgerhaus*, which currently numbers 30 volumes, provides details of typical houses from medieval times. This is important because architecture has often been no respecter of frontiers, and the clues to a new development in one country may be found in another. Randolph Delehanty, in one of the very best books ever written on American domestic architecture, *In the Victorian Style*, shows how the terrace house was taken to San Francisco by a London-born entrepreneur, George Gordon, employing an architect and surveyor from England, George H Goddard.

In Cluny, in Burgundy, British scholars working with French colleagues have produced a remarkable volume illustrating Romanesque row houses of the 12th century. Now that the hunt is on, one of these scholars hopes to find as many as 3,000 Romanesque houses in France. In Britain, by contrast, there are barely a dozen. In Venice superb work has been done on the city's Gothic houses by the English architect Richard Goy.

BACK FROM THE BRINK
In 1987 I settled with my family on the British island of Jersey, off France's Normandy coast. Here we founded the organization Save Jersey's Heritage and became embroiled in a battle to save a terrace of

In the 1970s the 29 houses in this attractive Georgian terrace in Shepherdess Walk, Shoreditch, London, were scheduled for demolition by Hackney Council. However, a fierce campaign against their destruction reversed the decision, and the houses went on to be restored for residential use by a local housing association.

These largely 18th-century houses in Hue Street were the oldest in St Helier, in the British Channel Island of Jersey. They had been empty for nearly 20 years, and rain poured in through the roofs, when Save Jersey's Heritage saved them from imminent demolition. Less than a month after the restoration was complete, prospective purchasers had made offers for all the houses and the corner shop.

No.6 Palace Street (right), which stands on the main street leading to Caernarfon's great medieval castle, was four days from demolition when, in January 1995, SAVE Britain's Heritage obtained a High Court order preventing its destruction. The house, along with its characteristic Caernarfon bay windows, is now completely restored.

seven houses in the main town, St Helier. These, the town's oldest houses, were in a desperate state and widely derided as an eyesore. For many years the only inhabitants had been hundreds of pigeons, and the floors and staircases were thick with guano. We mounted a campaign to save them, secured a 99-year lease, drew up plans, found a sympathetic investor and repaired the houses.

In 1995 SAVE intervened to stop the demolition of a house in Palace Street, Caernarfon, north Wales. The house, believed to be the oldest building in the town after the great castle built by King Edward I in the 13th century, had been compulsorily purchased by the local council to ensure that it was restored, but then it decided that this was too difficult an undertaking and declared the building to be in a dangerous condition. Demolition was scheduled for January 3, 1995. We went to the High Court, obtained a stay of demolition and undertook to buy the house from the council and repair it. During the restoration we found a handsome 15th-century hall on the first floor.

ROW UPON ROW

This book is mostly about terrace houses with a shared character and layout. These range from large and expensive town houses to small artisans' cottages. No less interesting are the occasional mavericks: terrace houses designed to stand out from their neighbours.

Toward the middle of the 19th century, there was a reaction against the sameness of Georgian streets. John Ruskin, the English art critic and social reformer, delivered a famous broadside against London's Gower Street, which was begun in 1790 and had long, unadorned brick terraces that he denounced as "the *ne plus ultra* of ugliness in street architecture." Later the distinguished historian Sir John Summerson, asked to come to the defence of a row of Georgian houses in Dublin's Fitzwilliam Street, wrote scornfully of "acres of Georgian rubbish."

Chambers' *Encyclopaedia* complains in 1904: "Under the Renaissance, town-houses in streets lost their distinctive qualities, being all designed so as to form as it were one flank of an extensive palace or single edifice. This monotonous arrangement is now being gradually departed from, and each house is beginning to be designed, as it should be, independently." The house of the operatic librettist Sir William Schwenck Gilbert in Harrington Gardens, London (see pages 122–5), although built as one of a group, is one such example. The extraordinary Gothic house built for the painter Mario De Maria in Asolo, Italy (see pages 134–5) is another. Row houses that go against the trend, like those at Port Grimaud (see pages 146–7) on France's Côte d'Azur, can be as interesting and successful as the latest in high tech.

My intention here is not to write a history of the terrace house but to explore this vast subject and convey some of the exciting revelations being provided by historians, archaeologists and architects throughout the Western world. This book is a personal selection of buildings that I know, and there are many more equally interesting examples that could have been included. Further suggestions of buildings worth investigation are welcome, as well as those titbits of information that so often provide unexpected insights and bring history alive.

MEDIEVAL MASTER
Builders

During the 13th and 14th centuries the Flemish town of Bruges enjoyed a position of wealth and power that was almost unrivalled in Europe. Effectively self-governing, it grew rich on the manufacture and sale of Flanders cloth. In the 15th century, when Bruges had a population of more than 200,000, the Dukes of Burgundy made it one of the centres of their splendid court. The decline that set in during the following century, as the river to the sea silted up, helped many of the town's numerous medieval houses survive to this day.

Despite the ravages of war and successive waves of rebuilding in times of prosperity, medieval town houses survive in great number in Europe, built of brick, stone and timber. The earliest are Romanesque, as at Cluny in France, while Venice boasts the largest number of Gothic houses anywhere. Many towns flourished on trade, and numerous medieval houses also served as warehouses. The limited space within defensive city walls led, from an early date, to the building of houses that abutted on their neighbours. The Rows in Chester, England, are a fine example of this dense, linear style of urban building.

Since the late 1980s a team of British and French archaeologists and historians has discovered 150 Romanesque houses in Cluny, in Burgundy, eastern France. The results of its work have been published in a remarkable volume, *La ville de Cluny et ses maisons XI–XV siècles* (1997). "We believe this is the largest collection of Romanesque houses to survive anywhere in Europe," says Professor Michael Jones of England's University of Nottingham.

In the 10th and 11th centuries the monastery at Cluny, the largest ever built in the West, towered above all others and grew to be the capital of a monastic empire. By the 12th century it controlled some 1,500 abbeys and priories all over Europe, and more than 10,000 monks. Cluny flourished under a dynasty of four great abbots and pioneered a new spirit of monasticism. As a result it became a major centre of pilgrimage, which prompted the growth of a substantial town below it. However, in later centuries the monastery declined steadily, and it was destroyed after the French Revolution.

the church of Notre Dame, in the centre, are the houses of the professional class. Those of the craftsmen are at the west end, almost certainly a cheaper location because the river here flooded.

Professor Michael Jones has pieced together documentation from original charters in the Bibliothèque Nationale in Paris and from inventories of documents that existed in the 17th century but which are now lost. A number of the houses were evidently built for the abbey, others speculatively: "You find repeating motifs, for example with windows, as if builders' yards were turning out standard motifs," Jones says. Almost all the houses were of mixed use (*maisons polyvalentes*), having shops and workshops on the ground floor and residential accommodation from the first floor upward. It is not known whether they were single-family houses or if, as is more probable, a family lived on each upper floor. Nor is it clear whether each floor was subdivided, and, if so, how; only the upper floor enjoyed real privacy. Professor Meirion-Jones believes that "many houses were let short term to people of rank, to knights and middling

Romanesque Cluny
BURGUNDY

In this 12th-century house (above) at Rue d'Avril 12 the large arch would originally have contained a shop or workshop. The door to the right led to the upper floors. Only two of the first-floor window arches survive.

A lithograph (right), probably dating from the 1870s, shows three Romanesque houses at Petite-rue Lamartine 5–9. These tall, narrow houses were demolished about 1880. In medieval times Cluny's popularity among pilgrims made it one of the richest monasteries in Europe. The town's prosperity is reflected in the many handsome stone houses, displaying carved detail as rich as that of contemporary churches.

Late-19th-century aquatints depict groups of tall, narrow, stone-fronted houses with rows of characteristically Romanesque round-arched windows that are supported on stout columns with carved capitals. The tiled roofs overhang the street by three or four feet (1–1.2m), and the ground floors have larger arches with wooden shutters opening into shops and workshops. It is sad to see early photographs of some of these houses being demolished. Presumably they were destroyed because, in Cluny at least, they seemed commonplace. Today, thanks to the work of the archaeologists, the town takes great pride in its new-found heritage.

The initiator of the Cluny survey, Professor Gwyn Meirion-Jones, explains that "the ground floor of the houses takes the form of a stone undercroft, vaulted with round or two-centred arches. Beside the main arched opening is a narrower door, sometimes with a shouldered arch, opening onto a straight stone staircase, leading to the first floor, with a further flight above leading to the second floor."

The town comprises three almost distinct sections. The grander, three-storey houses are near the abbey and the church of St Marcelle. Concentrated around

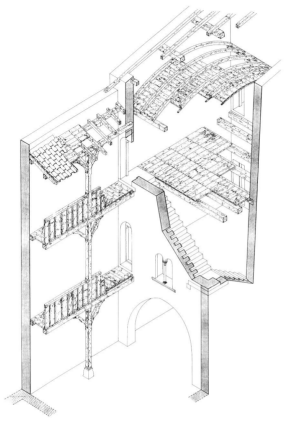

A diagram (below) of the reconstruction of Rue de la République 25 shows the open wooden galleries that led across the internal court to the wing at the back of the house. The stone staircase rises from the street entrance to the first floor in a straight line, then continues at a right angle to the upper floor.

Rue de la République 25 (above), built in the 12th century, was restored about 1912. The arcade has the paired arches often found in Romanesque architecture. This example has paired columns alternating with single columns. Such deep, overhanging roofs are a common feature of Cluny's 12th- and 13th-century houses.

and minor aristocrats." All the windows had wooden shutters and at least some had glass, "as much to be seen as to see." While some rooms had fireplaces, others had none, which poses the question of how rooms were heated in winter. Possibly the inhabitants used braziers, but it is debatable whether these were adequate in the corner houses, which have rows of windows on two sides. The external stone carving around these windows was purely for show, although there are also fine stone seats within.

The survey has discovered fragments of brightly coloured wall paintings, as intensely coloured as modern fabrics, with bold contrasting stripes and stylized leaf patterns. In one house a painted 13th-century timber ceiling was recently revealed beneath later plasterwork.

Often Romanesque stone fronts have stood concealed behind 19th-century stucco; ironically, it was sometimes peeling plaster that revealed the medieval stonework – including window jambs, arches and string courses – or timber framing behind. At first it was thought that the Cluny houses were 12th-century, but now it appears that these were second-generation houses replacing wooden houses of the previous century. Most of the gardens behind the houses had wells and outdoor privies, and in Rue Merdesson the latter were conveniently sited by a stream at the gardens' ends. Later documents mention orchards and hemp in these gardens.

As work continues at Cluny, Professor Meirion-Jones believes that in France as a whole up to 3–4,000 surviving Romanesque houses will be found. In England, by contrast, it would be difficult to find as many as 20 examples.

Venice boasts more substantial, well-preserved Gothic houses than any other city in Europe. The Ca' d'Oro, on the Grand Canal, is one of the most famous sights, but there are hundreds of smaller Gothic houses. The distinguishing features are the flame-headed, or ogee, arches of the windows, which are often grouped in threes or fours in the middle of the façade. Like the great palaces on the Grand Canal, these houses are often symmetrical, with a single window on either side of the central group. Most are of two or three storeys.

We possess extensive information on the design and construction of Venice's Gothic houses thanks to a book by Francesco Sansovino, *Venetia Città Nobilissima et Singolare*, published in 1663. By the late Middle Ages Venice was one of the largest, most prosperous cities in Europe. Increasing property values and the problems of building in the lagoon forced occupants of all houses except the grandest palaces to share party walls with their neighbours. Large buildings were built on closely packed oak piles, and then a raft of timber planks, the *zatterón*, was laid to form the first part of the footing. Smaller houses were often built without piled foundations. Walls of soft orange brick rose directly from the *zatterón*; these were bedded in a soft lime mortar, to allow for differential settlement, and were rendered externally to protect them against the weather.

The typical symmetrical Venetian house has four parallel structural walls. In the middle, running from front to back, is the *androne*, or hall. If the house is on a canal, the main entrance is a timber watergate on the canal side, while on the other side there is a landgate, which, in most cases, gives onto a small central courtyard.

Medieval Gothic houses
VENICE

The bold ogee arch of the land-gate to the Casa Goldoni is characteristic of late-Venetian Gothic. The stylized flower on top and three-lobed tracery suggest a date of around the 1440s. Window and door surrounds were almost all of white Istrian stone, here with a typical notched edge to the arch.

Merchants and merchant nobles occupied many of the small Gothic houses, using the ground or mezzanine floor for business and living above. They traded mainly in highly profitable goods, notably cloth, including cloth of gold, which was used for clothes and wall hangings, and spices. Goods were displayed to visitors in the *androne*, while the rooms on both sides were used for storage. (In larger houses there was sufficient height for a mezzanine above these side rooms.) Each upper floor had, above the *androne* and likewise running from front to back, a *portego*, a large central hall with windows at either end to promote a flow of cooling air. Many plans of three-storey houses show identical first and second floors, which suggests that each floor was a self-contained apartment for different members of the family. In some houses there is evidence of a kitchen on each upper floor, but otherwise rooms were employed for various purposes at different times.

The upper floors were supported on beams of oak (or sometimes larch or pine). Spans in medium-sized houses were rarely more than 16–20 feet (5–6m), to allow for the weight of the characteristic Venetian floor, made of terrazzo. This compound of marble chips and cement mortar, Sansovino wrote, "is coated with linseed oil, with which it achieves such a lustrous finish that a man may see himself reflected in it, as in a mirror."

In buildings such as the Casa Goldoni (right), goods were taken in through the watergate and stored in rooms on either side. The square windows on the mezzanine are later additions. The main apartment was above, on the *piano nobile* (with the tallest windows).

The flame-headed windows on the mezzanine (above) give onto the canal. The window surround is of solid stone and bears the marks of the centuries. When shut the window fits snugly in a recess.

Many medieval houses had outside staircases that rose to the first floor from a courtyard. Internal stairs, when they were introduced, were set halfway along the *androne*, rising sideways in two flights.

Thanks to the famous glass furnaces of nearby Murano, Venice was to enjoy the luxury of plentiful window glass far earlier than other cities. Sansovino records that "the windows are glazed not with waxed linen or paper, but with beautiful clear white glass, held in frames of wood and kept in position with iron and lead, not only in the palaces and apartment buildings but everywhere else, even in humble places, which causes visitors to marvel."

Rainwater from the roofs was conducted by pipes into underground clay-lined cisterns filled with sand to filter it. Sansovino wrote: "There are no rivers, no basins underground where one might find sweet water, and thus cisterns are used, the water of which is purer and better for the digestion than fresh running water." In larger houses rainwater was channelled downward by pipes built into the thickness of the walls. In small houses it simply discharged into a nearby *campo*, to drain into a communal cistern. From the 16th century, or earlier, latrines discharged into a vertical pipe which then curved sideways with a steady fall, to empty into a nearby canal.

Casa Goldoni

The wooden open-beam ceiling (top), with painted decoration, in one of the rooms flanking the main hall, or *portego*.

The windows of the first floor *portego* overlooking the canal (middle). A grille is set in the floor to provide a view of people arriving at the watergate below.

The courtyard with external marble staircase ascending to the *piano nobile* (bottom). Water was drawn up a bricklined shaft from the cistern below the courtyard.

KEY

① The watergate, where goods were unloaded from boats on the canal

② The landgate is in typically flamboyant late-Gothic style

③ Ground-floor rooms flanking the watergate, usually used for storage

④ The wellhead, made of white Istrian stone, stood in the private courtyard over an underground cistern that collected rainwater from the roofs

⑤ External stair leading from the courtyard to the main apartment on the first floor; visitors arriving on foot usually went straight up without going through the trading quarters

⑥ Gothic windows lit the low-ceilinged mezzanine where the owner probably conducted business

⑦ The tall *piano nobile* containing the main apartment. The four central windows lit the *portego*, a room that typically runs from front to back of a large ventian house or *palazzo*

⑧ The second floor, slightly lower in height, contained the private apartments (mainly bedrooms) and probably the original kitchen

⑨ A typical Venetain chimneypot (*fumaiolo*), incorporating a cinder-trap to catch flying embers

GROUND FLOOR

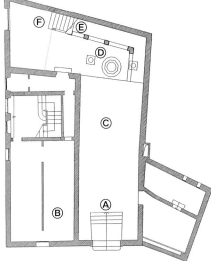

Ⓐ Watergate
Ⓑ Storage room
Ⓒ *Androne*, or hall
Ⓓ Wellhead in central courtyard
Ⓔ External staircase to first floor
Ⓕ Landgate

Nineteenth-century romantics thought of Chester as the archetypal medieval town. Ironically, it was their enthusiasm for its restoration that turned it into a predominantly Victorian and Edwardian creation, albeit of outstanding architects such as TM Lockwood and John Douglas. The great exception is the Rows. These medieval houses have covered galleries on their first floors that were built for use as shops and are without exact parallel in Europe. The best preserved of the Rows are found in Watergate Street; this runs west from the High Cross, which marks the junction of the two main streets.

Historians and archaeologists discovered that, because Chester's bedrock was just beneath the surface, the builders of the Rows chose not to excavate deep cellars but instead to construct undercrofts slightly below street level and place the shops above. It then became more practical to link all the shops by a first-floor gallery than provide a separate flight of

God's Providence House (right) – so named because a family living there escaped the plague during the Middle Ages – was rebuilt in 1862. The reconstruction, loosely based on an earlier building, incorporated one of the first-floor arcaded shops characteristic of Chester's medieval Rows.

The Rows
CHESTER

In medieval times there were stalls displaying goods on both sides of the arcades. The floor was raised up when the Rows were built to provide headroom over the stairs descending to the cellars.

steps to each. Another reason for the creation of these galleried shops was that from Roman times the land behind the main streets had silted up with debris, so that, at the back, the first floor was at ground level.

Although Chester was one of the principal towns of Roman England, little of substance from that period is still to be found there today. However, the main

streets substantially follow the rectangular plan of the Roman *castrum*, or military camp, which gives the city its name. Chester acted as the mustering point for Edward I's campaigns against the Welsh in 1277 and 1282, and for the subsequent building of the great medieval Edwardian castles and walled towns in North Wales. Hundreds of craftsmen, carpenters, masons and labourers were summoned from all over the country to carry out the work.

William of Doncaster, the leading local merchant during Edward I's reign (1272–1307), had property in Watergate Street, as did some of the richest families in Elizabethan times: the Bavands, Mainwarings, Challenors and Alderseys. Later, Cheshire families with large country estates, like the Grosvenors of Eaton Hall, the Cottons of Combermere and the Booths of Dunham Massey, had town houses in the street. In the 1620s Watergate Street was described by William Webb, a local antiquarian, as "well-furnished with buildings, both ancient and new."

Watergate Street broadly follows the longer of the two main streets bisecting the town. The Rows in this street have survived thanks to decline and neglect. When the River Dee became seriously silted up in the 18th century, Watergate Street's appeal lessened and other streets offered more fashionable places to live

This reconstruction (right) shows the Leche House, 17 Watergate Street, as it was around 1725. The undercroft, dating from the late 14th century, was used for storage. The timber-framed house above dates from the latter part of the following century. There was a shop behind the open walkway along the front, and behind it a Great Hall rising to the roof. A passage with a gallery above led to bedrooms and a kitchen at the back of the house. The street façade and the large upper chamber behind it date from the early 17th century, as do the fireplace, decorative plasterwork and wooden panelling in the hall.

and shop. There was little demolition in the 19th and 20th centuries, although as late as 1985 permission was given to demolish a decrepit butcher's shop, just before its well-preserved 13th-century undercroft was recognized. Nearly 50 such houses survive, many with shops still occupying the galleries. The heroes of Watergate Street are the Chester Archaeological Society, which has pioneered its systematic study, and the city's assiduous conservation officer, Peter de Figuereido, who has promoted repair through a partnership grant scheme with English Heritage.

In Watergate Street the undercrofts, typically set just a few steps below street level, were often partly or wholly built of stone – that is, with stone walls and sometimes a stone vault supported on columns. Some examples have decorative timber roofs, which suggests that they were intended to impress. The undercrofts were barely lit at the front and, because of the build-up of silt at the back, windowless on that side. They seem to have had no direct stairs to the houses above and, in many cases, to have remained in separate ownership from the timber-framed buildings above. This suggests that, as at Krakow and Sterzing (see pages 26–7 and 28–9), the undercrofts were used by merchants to store valuable goods for sale or to keep foodstuffs cool.

The layout of the houses is shown by the cutaway drawing of the Leche House above. Like almost all surviving medieval town houses it has been overlaid with alterations, but the late-15th-century Great Hall still survives, with its large fireplace and decorative plasterwork, both from the 17th century. Outside, the first-floor gallery has sloping stalls at the front, the slope allowing vital extra headroom over the outside steps leading down to the undercroft.

The main spaces in the house followed the line of the roof trusses. At the front, looking out onto the Row, was the shop, with a spacious solar or upper chamber above, open to the roof. Behind the shop a passage leads past the hall to the back of the house, but this may be of later date. The hall, like the solar, is open to the roof. Behind it a stair rises dogleg fashion to the first floor. This connects to the solar at the front by way of a gallery running along the side of the hall. At the back of the house is a parlour with a chamber above. The kitchen was probably housed in a separate building at the back to reduce the fire risk.

When the Leche House came up for sale in 1994, Peter de Figuereido alerted Britain's National Trust, which was interested but unable to raise the funds for its care. However, today the house is a furniture shop – so it is still possible to glimpse the Great Hall.

Rennes, the capital of the ancient Duchy of Brittany, illustrates well how, against the odds, medieval houses can survive. The approach to the city is not promising, for huge modern factories and warehouses swamp the surrounding countryside. Moreover, in 1720 much of the old quarter was destroyed by a savage fire that lasted a week and destroyed more than 850 houses, making 8,000 people homeless. And yet, possibly because the fire destroyed so much history, what survived did so in a more complete state over subsequent centuries. Significantly, in the church of St-Sauveur is a votive painting commissioned by the inhabitants of the streets behind the church, grateful that the fire stopped just before it could engulf their houses. The new centre, a classic grid of straight streets, was laid out on a standardized plan by the engineer Isaac Robelin, aided by Jacques Gabriel.

Lining the narrow streets here are wooden houses jettied out in successive stages, almost to the point where neighbours may shake hands across the street. Everywhere there is evidence of settlement, most of

In Rennes the tradition of timber-framed houses continued unbroken from the Middle Ages until the great fire of 1720. Houses built in the latter part of this period, like those in the Place du Champ-Jacquet (right), which in the main date from the 17th century, lack the overhang of medieval and Renaissance examples.

Half-timbered houses
RENNES

it historic, with the subsidence pushing doors and windows dramatically out of shape. Some of the taller houses lean sideways, as if they were left without lateral support while a neighbour was rebuilt, so that the whole timber frame lurched to one side. Good examples of this are the houses overlooking the Place du Champ-Jacquet.

Many of Rennes' ancient timber-framed houses (in France they are referred to as "*maisons du pan de bois*") are to be found in the streets behind the cathedral and the church of St-Sauveur, in the Rues du Chapitre, St-Yves, Rallier-du-Baty, St-Malo and St-Georges, the Place Ste-Anne, and also across the river in the Rue Vasselot.

The oldest houses date from the 15th century and are characterized by the advance of the upper storeys and the simple robustness of the woodwork, which displays little carved ornament. Examples are Rue de la Psalette 12 and the house in the Rue du Chapitre opposite the 18th-century Hôtel de Blossac. The Renaissance often appears as a break with medieval traditions, but in Rennes, because houses continued to be built with timber frames, there is continuity

and gradual evolution. The Renaissance arrived in Brittany later than it did in the Loire region to the south, and an early sign is the appearance of heads in profile – a reflection of Renaissance humanism, which prompted a strong interest in classical studies as well as in portraiture and portrait heads.

The second phase of the Renaissance led to the incorporation of scrolls, strapwork, volutes, putti, dolphins and classical cornices; for example, at the corner of the Rues de la Psalette and de Chapitre, or at Rue des Portes Mordelaises 3.

The third period of the timber frame is marked by a flat vertical façade without projections, and beams lacking carving or decoration. The façade becomes a play of chevrons, herringbones, crosses or lozenges, such as are found at Rue de Chapitre 5, in the Place du Champ-Jacquet or in the *hôtels particuliers* (private houses) in the Place des Lices. These last were built in the 17th century for the nobles of the Rennes Parliament. The fourth period of timber framing introduced plaster or roughcast to conceal the woodwork as a protection against fire spreading from house to house.

These houses (right) in the Rue de la Psalette have timber-framed upper floors that are set on stone bases. The medieval house in the corner, with herringbone pattern woodwork, is jettied out on plain brackets.

Some of the houses can be visited because they are now used as restaurants and cafés, in some cases with second dining rooms above, so one can go upstairs. The Auberge St-Sauveur, which is 16th-century and still Gothic rather than Renaissance, has a large hooded stone fireplace and, at the back, a handsome stair, probably dating from the 17th century. Potentially most interesting of all is the Breton restaurant Ti-Koz (Breton for "old house"), but in 1997 this was awaiting restoration after an electrical fire. It is formed from two canons' houses, dating from the first half of the 16th century, behind the cathedral. The detail is all still Gothic, with heavy chamfering along the beams that support the projecting upper floors. The tradition that suggests it was built for Du Guesclin, the great Breton warrior, would place it in the 14th century, 200 years earlier than the architectural detail would imply.

Daniel Derveaux's book *Les Vieux Logis de Rennes* (1946) shows that at this date the majority of timber-framed fronts had disappeared beneath plaster and, in some cases, vertically hung slates. The systematic re-exposure of the timber framing was stimulated by the creation in 1988 of a *secteur sauvegardé*: a conservation area. It is now obligatory to expose the timber frames, the legislation was prompted partly by the fact that 67 per cent of owners were not living in the houses and took little care of their appearance.

Timber framing has not, however, simply been exposed; in many houses it has also been painted. Usually this is done in one colour – often red, brown or blue – but on some houses the details of the woodwork are picked out in several colours, and one in the Rue St-Malo is a virulent mustard yellow.

The democratic process continued with a questionnaire during European Open House Weekend in September 1997, when people were asked about colour in the town. The majority responded that they wanted to see more colour in the timbers – a few of the results may be as painful as others are delightful.

The detail in this first-floor window of a house on the west side of the Place Ste-Anne is Gothic, which suggests that the house was built in the late 15th century. Typical of this style are the chamfers cut into the beams that support the projecting storey above.

Krakow has long been known as one of the most remarkable historic towns in Eastern Europe, yet the first impression given by its pretty painted façades, its gables and its sober classical detail is of a Baroque and Neo-classical city. It is only as you explore and find houses supported by giant angled buttresses that the much greater age of its buildings becomes apparent. Venture through stone archways and you will find elaborate Gothic vaults, and often handsome stone doorways with finely carved Gothic

Today the old town is a mix of narrow and double fronts. As many of the houses, particularly in the Market Place and surrounding shopping streets, are in multiple occupancy, with numerous small offices and agencies on the upper floors, the casual visitor may explore behind the street frontages to an unusual degree. This has evidently been possible for a long time because there is a delightful book dating from 1908, *Le Vieux Cracovie: Rues, Portals, Vestibules*, by Fr Maczynski, full of drawings, plans and sections of vaulted halls. Most of the surviving

Stone and stucco houses
KRAKOW

In this late-Gothic entrance arch (above) of a house near Krakow's Market Place the mouldings of the arch "die" gently into the sides. Classical windows on upper floors (right) make many of the town's streets look predominantly 18th- or 19th-century, but sloping buttresses indicate that important elements of the medieval fabric survive.

and Renaissance detail. Numerous houses, which from the outside appear to be of one date, turn out to be palimpsests of the centuries. The early features have survived not because of conscious respect for the past, but because the medieval houses were such substantial constructions that they have been largely incorporated in later rebuilding.

The town plan (or *locatio*, to use the original Latin term) of Krakow dates back to 1257. It was centred on the enormous Market Place, which measures just under 660 square feet (61m²). Between the 13th and 15th centuries Krakow was fortified with walls and ramparts and ditches, elements that still contain the old quarter today.

Around the Market Place the streets were laid out on a grid plan, enclosing regular blocks measuring some 275 square feet (26m²). These blocks were subdivided in turn into eight plots of 69 feet by 138 feet (21m by 42m), known as *curiae*. The layout was strictly regular, with plots running back perpendicularly and then turning through 90 degrees to face the main streets leading off the Market Place. In the 14th century the increasing demand for space led the city authorities to allow the *curiae* to be divided into *demi-curiae*. Again the division was carried out on a systematic basis, creating long, narrow plots that typically measure 38 feet by 138 feet (11.5m by 42m). As a result, houses began to develop on long, deep plans, each with a courtyard toward the back of the house overlooked by a rear block connected to the main house by a gallery.

The staircase leading to the upper storeys appears to have been at first an external stair in the courtyard, but from the 15th century it was usually placed in the ground-floor hall.

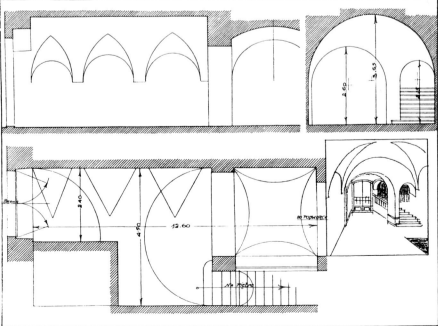

vaults are of stone or brick finished in plaster. Often they simply disappear or "die" into the walls, but occasionally a supporting corbel or Doric capital gives an indication of Gothic or Renaissance origins.

In the wider houses a vaulted passage leads through to a courtyard behind, above which a first-floor gallery leads to still more accommodation. In many of the narrower houses there is a deep vaulted vestibule inside the entrance, with another long, narrow room beside it. Some of the houses have deep and surprisingly tall vaulted basements or cellars, which may be indicated by dugout windows at pavement level.

Just off the Market Place, at Pl Mariacki 3, a 14th-century town house has become a museum and show house open to the public. This provides a delightful vignette of changing interior decoration over the centuries, with some Renaissance and elaborate Baroque plasterwork.

To explore old Krakow, walk eastward out of the main Market Place to the smaller marketplace. Here and in the surrounding streets numerous buttresses project onto the pavement. As you walk south toward the castle, turn off into Kanonicza, which descends gently on a curve. Here there are substantial houses forming a continuous line along the street; several of them are in university or administrative use. Although there is no obvious sign of basements, the house occupied by the school of architecture and planning has an impressive lofty brick-vaulted cellar, now used as a bar.

Ninety years ago Fr Maczynski warned that "these façades, a true mosaic forming a dictionary of architecture, are seriously threatened. New municipal regulations favour demolition." Today the old town is a designated World Heritage site. While some of its shopping streets are still not protected from a rash of neon signs expressing the joys of the free market, nevertheless the old quarter is more complete, and in the past half-century has been less altered behind the façades, than almost any historic town in Western Europe.

The grid of streets around the large Market Place (above left) dates from 1257. Many houses fronting this large square still stand on the original medieval plots – some of them wide, some of them narrow – with courtyards behind. Houses in the streets off the Market Place were built on smaller plots, as may be seen at the bottom left corner.

This plan (left) from Fr Maczynski's book on old Krakow, published in 1908, shows a vaulted ground floor that is typical of the town's medieval and Renaissance houses. The vaults are built without ribs and, as with the arches opposite, disappear into the walls.

In this aerial view of Sterzing (below), the town's main street runs diagonally across the upper half of the photograph. Closely packed houses fill the long, narrow plots, and the only light entering the back of the buildings comes from the occasional rear courtyard. These houses, many of medieval origin, look like warehouses. Indeed, they were built for this purpose, as well as to provide accommodation for the owners. Parapets of a later date conceal the gable ends on the street side.

There is a special pleasure in finding yourself in a place unlike anywhere you have been before. Such a place is the town of Sterzing (also called Vipiteno), just south of the Brenner Pass over the Alps, in Italy's South Tirol or Alto Adige. The area is German-speaking and was ceded to Italy by Austria after the First World War. Sterzing has a delightful main street, with the brightly painted stucco façades characteristic of western Austria. Many of the houses have bay windows on the upper stories, and bold crenellations instead of shaped gables or cornices. In contrast to the fading ochre typical in much of Italy, Tiroleans keep their buildings looking as good as new, and at first glance Sterzing appears to be a well-preserved blend of 17th-, 18th- and 19th-century architecture. It is only as you look inside the ground-floor shops that it becomes clear that many houses are much older, and are indeed of medieval origin.

Many of the archways opening into the shops are pointed, not rounded, indicating a pre-Renaissance date (the 15th century or earlier). Inside, the ground floors consist of vaulted undercrofts running back some way from the street. Many of the undercrofts take the form of a series of separate (and sometimes parallel) chambers, elongated in form and opening into one another, giving the impression that they have been extended in successive stages. The buildings in fact look more like warehouses than places where people might live; they fill every inch of their sites, providing accommodation in the upper storeys but rarely so much as a patch of garden.

The distinctive form of these houses is particularly evident from above, with aerial shots showing long narrow parallel roofs running back from the street. From the front, the high flat façades with their plain or battlemented parapets completely screen the extent of the building behind. With houses built next

Wine lock-ups
STERZING

The key to the unusual design of these houses lies in the town's location. The place is marked on a road map as early as the second century: on the Roman *Tabula Peutingeriana*. In the Middle Ages the town prospered as a staging post on the road up to the Brenner Pass, the principal route linking Germany and Austria, at that time a conglomeration of states and free towns forming the Holy Roman Empire, with the Italian states to the south. Situated at 3,110 feet (948m), Sterzing was an important resting place on the way to the 4,511-feet (1,375m) summit of the Pass, just 9 miles (15km) to the north. Then, as now, the Brenner was the easiest of the great Alpine passes to cross, its relatively steady incline making it an excellent route for merchandise.

Local prosperity increased with the development of silver and lead mines from the 13th century, and many mansions in the main street were built for mining families. Importantly, the owners also profited from certain regulations placed on trade.

In the Middle Ages, transport guilds held a monopoly on the carriage of goods, and their rules required that all wares be unpacked and stored on each night of the journey. If you wished to send a barrel of wine from Tuscany to Munich, a guild master would appoint one of his members to take it to the next town where it could be left overnight. This was never more than half a day's journey away, allowing the man conveying the wine to reach home that evening. The guilds insured the freight against loss, providing a reliable system. (There were, inevitably, disputes regarding the service, and the process is documented in court records.) These "mulekeepers' towns" were often quite distinct in character from nearby market towns, not least because their houses took on the role and design of warehouses.

As late as 1876 the *Imperial Gazetteer* newspaper noted that Sterzing has "a considerable trade in wine." Today, with the autostrada passing close by, merchandise speeds past in heavy lorries, and the town prospers as a resort. The undercrofts, meanwhile, have become shops, but their smooth white vaults remain little changed since the Middle Ages.

The vaulted arcade with pointed arches (above) is characteristically medieval. The façade above it dates from the 18th century.

to each other on long, narrow plots, there is little opportunity to light rooms from the sides, and as you delve deeper inside you discover that many have lightwells, like small courtyards, which draw daylight down through the buildings. A number of these lightwells are surrounded by balconies on the upper floors, and some are combined with staircases.

In this plan (right) of a typical ground floor, a vaulted passage with shops on each side leads to an internal courtyard with a staircase and galleries above. Further back there is a second staircase, and beyond this are four long parallel ranges of vaulted stores that are entered from the back.

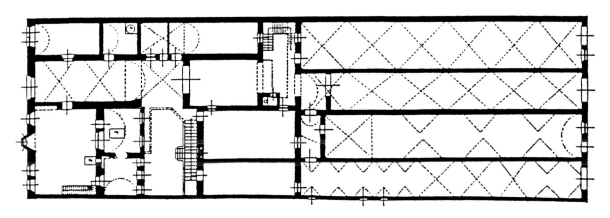

The town of Rouen, in the north of France, retains some extraordinarily unaltered medieval churches and houses, although many are now blackened and decaying. To see them is like stepping into the 19th century, when the care and restoration of old buildings had barely begun.

In the shopping district of the old town, appallingly insensitive development has created modern stores at street level by destroying whole ground floors beneath fine timber-framed fronts. A whole block opposite one of the best runs of these houses, in the Rue Martainville, had been gouged out in spring 1997, to be replaced, according to the developer's hoarding, by a row of post-modern fronts with crude gables and bay windows.

Nevertheless, the town retains ten medieval houses of the late 14th or early 15th century and about 85 from the period between 1470 and 1520. These have been recorded in fascinating detail by Alain

Houses in Rue du Gros Horloge (right). The tradition of timber-framed building continued in Rouen from the late 14th century until the latter part of the 17th century; the cross-shaped mullion and transom windows are a typical feature. Here the low building linking the two houses has shaped classical balusters.

Timber-framed houses
ROUEN

The classical pilasters between the windows of this house date it to the period of Renaissance influence in Rouen. It was was probably built during the latter half of the 16th century or in the early 17th century.

Gasperini in his 36-page booklet *Rouen: Les Maisons à Pans de Bois*. His drawings show the evolution of wooden houses over the centuries.

In the Rue du Petit Mouton a good example survives that shows how the first floor was jettied out over the ground floor, supported by plain tapering corbels or brackets. At Rue St Vivien 61 the windows, each three lights wide, take their proportions from the vertical timbers of the front. Glass was rare, and

the upper lights of the windows were inset with squares of oiled parchment, which admitted daylight. The lower part of the windows had a rising shutter which could be opened to air the room, to allow people to look down on the street, talk to neighbours and pour slops into the gutter below. The roof is parallel with the street and inset with a dormer into which goods were hoisted from the street.

The substantial number of houses dating from 1470 to 1520 bears witness to the recovery that followed the Hundred Years War of 1337–1453. Rue de la Pie 7 has a central door leading to the house above. The two shops flanking it are in fact stalls with counters resting on solid stone bases from which customers standing in the street were served.

The detail of this house is more elaborate than that in the earlier examples. There is a boldly modelled cornice above the ground floor, and the windows above have fluted surrounds descending to sculpted bases. The windows now have diamond-pane glazing in the upper lights, allowing light to enter when the rising shutters below are closed. Diagonal timbers enrich the pattern of the façade. Sculpted details at this date were polychrome, and the plain timbers were painted either ochre red or in colours derived from wine dregs. This house, which has lost its dormers, has a roof parallel with the street, but it was more usual for the gable end to face the street.

A remarkable picture of Rouen's medieval houses is provided in *Le Livre des Fontaines*, a manuscript with plans on parchment. Between 1518 and 1525 the author, Jacques Le Lieur, set out to trace the canals that supplied the town's fountains, providing pictures of houses on the streets where they flowed.

Raymond Quenedey, in his fine book *L'Habitation Rouennaise* (1926), collated fascinating details of the layout of the town's medieval houses from ancient documents. Shops and workshops, for example, were always found on the ground floor, with openings to the street that could be closed by shutters. Beside the shop was a corridor leading to the dwelling above, making it possible to isolate one from the other. The shops never had fireplaces, although the kitchens – also on the ground floor – naturally did. The *seuille*, on the same floor, was a store for salt (then a valuable commodity) or wine. *Caves*, or cellars, also held wine and were ventilated by air holes or light shafts.

Archaeological study has produced evidence of a series of stone houses of essentially square form. Typically these had half-sunken vaulted basements that were entered by steps from the street and, in a few cases, connected with upper floors by tight spiral staircases. No evidence has been found to confirm the basements' purpose, but they probably held goods. On each raised first floor was a *grande salle*, often referred to as an *aula* (Latin for "hall") in medieval documents. Above, on the second floor, were the private living quarters. One stone house had a water supply, contrived within the thickness of the walls on the first floor and above, and a privy.

No tiles of the 11th or 12th century have been found during excavation, which suggests that houses were thatched. Tiles became common from the 13th century, but thatch continued to be widely used. Exteriors of stone houses had fine stone carving, including blind arcades.

Inventories of Rouen's medieval houses describe beds similar to modern beds, although more than two might sleep in them. In addition there were chests or cupboards, tables and chairs. The inventory taken in 1435 of the house of Pierre Surreau, Receiver General of Normandy, lists 17 rooms with 15 beds, 10 dressers or cupboards, 34 wooden and copper chests, 9 tables and desks, 35 chairs and 18 candlesticks.

Timber-framed houses in Rue Martainville (below), showing signs of ground settlement over the archway. Diagonal timbers cutting across two vertical members are found from the 14th century onward, as are the hooded dormers through which goods were hoisted from the street below.

Until the Second World War many German cities were rich in medieval buildings. Germans had been among the first to recognize the importance of what they call the *Stadtbild*, the general townscape produced by a large number of humble domestic buildings. The idea was voiced in 1902 by the Burgomaster of Hildesheim, who asked whether people's spiritual well-being was not enhanced by realizing "how the city has gradually built itself up, and how not only the streets, but every single public building, each individual house, even each piece of carved ornament, has grown in the course of time to be what it is." Although Allied bombers devastated many German cities during the Second World War, Lübeck was fortunate enough to escape extensive damage, and today there are still streets that look little altered from photographs and prints of the late 19th century.

The first small Slavic settlement, Liubice, was founded by Prince Kruto (1066–93). In 1226 Lübeck was made an Imperial Free City by Frederick II, and during the 14th century it became the head of the Hanseatic League, rapidly growing to become one of the largest of German towns.

Medieval Lübeck was built principally of brick, and one example of this style, the Rathaus, is among the finest town halls of that period to survive. As the Hanseatic League prospered, it extended its influence to embrace 80 cities – from Amsterdam in Holland and Cologne in Germany to Wrocław and Krakow in Poland and Novgorod in Russia.

In the 15th century Lübeck is said to have numbered 20,000 inhabitants, but in the following two centuries the growing maritime power of England and Holland steadily eroded its position. Partly as a result of this curb on expansion, large numbers of medieval houses have survived.

Hanseatic merchants' houses
LÜBECK

The medieval brick houses of Hanseatic towns on the Baltic are imposing and memorable. Lübeck has many good examples, built with steep roofs inset with up to three tiers of windows in the gable facing the street.

Medieval houses of various sizes with stepped brick gables may be seen in Dr Julius-Leber-Strasse, at the corner of Königstrasse. Gothic houses have tall pointed arches of moulded brick stepped up to the top of the façades. Inset are pairs of smaller windows with pointed arches.

Lübeck's medieval houses were built on plots that typically measured between 26 and 33 feet (8–10m) in width and between 33 and 98 feet (10–30m) in depth. Behind the houses were gardens and stables.

The bricks used to construct both houses and churches were made in kilns outside the city walls run by the great churches. They were of a design that compelled builders to simplify Gothic forms almost to abstraction, and to dispense with carved ornamental detail. Roofs were covered in clay tiles known here, as elsewhere, as "monks" and "nuns." The latter were laid in "u" fashion down the slope of the roof, with a monk placed like a "n" over the joint between each pair. These tiles were superseded by pantiles during the Renaissance.

Architectural expression was achieved mainly through the powerful tall stepped gables that front the steep roofs of the houses. From an early date the façades were remarkable for an exact symmetry, within which the entrance was usually placed centrally. In most houses the front doors were recessed and reached by climbing a few steps, a design that allowed small, shuttered openings to be placed at pavement level on either side, providing light and access to cellars below. These were usually vaulted in brick and used for storage, particularly of wine.

The entrance arches were tall, and in most houses led into a double-height room, the "Diele," or hall, which had a large fireplace and served as both a living room and a place where goods were sold. Above the ground floor, a string course in moulded brick usually divides the façade. The storeys above are treated as part of the gable even if the façade does not step back until a higher level. This arrangement of floors was to continue well into the 17th century.

A striking characteristic of these Gothic houses is the pointed brick arches framing the windows – these are often stepped up like organ pipes. In many houses the upper façades have between three and five storeys, with no more than a tiny window at the top. In fact, the oldest houses in Lübeck are not Gothic but Romanesque, and have a pair of small round-arched windows, framed by a larger one, set in a plain, sloping gable. It was with the Gothic style that the stepped gable arrived. Good examples can be seen in Mengstrasse, including No.25, Zum Goldenen Hirsch (The Golden Stag). This and others, including those at Wahmstrasse 60 and Grosse Petersgrube 15 and 25, are illustrated in Hans Hübler's book *Das Bürgerhaus in Lübeck*, published in 1968.

The commercial use of ground floors has, in many cases, continued to this day. This has been to the detriment of the town's appearance when modern shop fronts have been inserted into ancient façades. The accommodation above the shop was also used for storage; further living quarters were in a domestic wing to one side of a yard at the back.

In this group of houses, Mengstrasse 23–31, the medieval house second from the left has distinctly Gothic windows. Its neighbour in the middle, although it has a matching stepped gable, has larger windows grouped horizontally rather than vertically, indicating a later date.

RENAISSANCE AND BAROQUE
Splendour

From the Renaissance onward architects used classical motifs with increasing boldness and monumentality. Narrow house fronts were given a forceful presence on a street by emphatic cornices, not only at the top of the building but also between the storeys. The diagonal was a major feature of the Baroque, and the fronts of many 17th-, 18th- and 19th-century town houses in central Europe, such as these on Mostecka in Prague, look best when seen from an oblique angle.

With the Renaissance came the revival of the classical orders of architecture and a new sense of proportion and monumentality. Architects sought to bring regularity to the layout of streets old and new. Handsome houses rose along Amsterdam's newly extended canals and behind the new ramparts at St Malo in France, while a whole quarter of attractive Baroque houses was laid out in London's Spitalfields. Regional differences remained strong. In northern Europe gables still predominated, first stepped and then increasingly curved and scrolled. Sculpture and decoration assumed more importance.

Among the huge outpouring of frescoes in Renaissance Italy, some of the most fascinating are topographical scenes that depict houses and villas in town and country. A group of these is to be found in the Palazzo Vecchio in Florence, in the apartment of Eleanor, the Spanish wife of Cosimo I de Medici. Here the frieze in the Sala di Gualdrada reveals much about the typical houses of the city's squares and streets. These houses are largely of a type, although they vary considerably in detail. The façades are plain, with simple round-arched windows and shallow overhanging tile roofs. In some cases, as can be seen in the Piazza Santa Croce, the upper storeys project over the ground floor as in medieval English houses. Most of the houses are only two or three windows wide, but often differ markedly in height from their neighbours. Others have the stone benches still seen today in front of large *palazzi*; in the frieze, spectators stand on these to get a clear view over those standing in the square.

Many Florentine houses and palaces in the 15th and 16th centuries had painted façades, often showing allegorical figures in allusion to the virtues and accomplishments of the owners. Giorgio Vasari had won a reputation as a painter of façades with the Palazzo Almeni, on the corner of Via dei Servi, and the Palazzo Ramirez in Borgo degli Albizi. Ramirez was Cosimo's chamberlain, and the ground floor included figures of Modesty, Fidelity, Prudence and Constancy – all, of course, desirable in a courtier – with Obedience, Secrecy and Vigilance portrayed for good measure above.

The Palazzo Benci, at Piazza Madonna degli Aldobrandini 4, was described by the diarist Lapin as "the most beautiful of all," and the decoration has been painstakingly restored. Unfortunately most of this painted decoration has been lost from palaces throughout the city, partly because of the vulnerable nature of the materials and partly because 19th-century purists saw Florence as a city entirely of plain stone and stucco.

The minor palaces
FLORENCE

This fresco, which is one of a series in the Palazzo Vecchio portraying the streets and squares of Florence, shows a ball game being played in the Piazza Santa Maria Novella. The large street doors of the houses opened into shops and workshops. For privacy, adjacent windows were set well above eye level. The accommodation was usually on the two top floors, and here the windows are much larger and more numerous.

The stone mostly used for external walls was *pietra forte*, extracted from quarries on the city's outskirts. In 1389 the Governors of Florence decreed that it should be used to face all houses overlooking the Via Calzaiuoli, which runs through the heart of the city. Because it was so hard to work, it gave Florence its solemn, even severe aspect and led to the fashion for rough-cut rustication. The early Renaissance saw the widespread use of *pietra serena*, a favourite material of the architect Brunelleschi (1377–1446). This is a darkish stone, again austere, but because it was much easier to carve it could be used for the most exquisite and precise classical detail. Furthermore, Brunelleschi's use of *pietra dura* for architectural elements, such as columns and entablatures, set off against pale bare stucco walls became a dominant architectural treatment.

The great palaces of the Medici and Strozzi families, with their heavy *bugnato* stonework and powerful cornices, were to provide, in the 19th century, the inspiration for banks, gentlemen's clubs and opulent private houses all over Europe and North America. Florence also gave birth to the classical, sometimes monumental treatment of the smaller town house. The typical terrace house found all over the English-speaking world is usually two or three windows wide, and a group of small Florentine palaces prefigures much of what was to follow subsequently in terms of façade design.

One of the first is the Palazzo Bartolini Salimbeni (1520–23), built for Conte Giovanni Bartolini by Baccio d'Agnolo (1462–1543). The palace, overlooking the Piazza Santa Trinità, stretches back along two flanking streets, but the façade, which overlooks the square, has many of the elements that recur in classical town houses over more than three centuries. The three storeys are firmly demarcated by a string course on which sit the sills of the windows above. The corners are emphasized by quoins, here treated

as a form of pilaster with the suggestion of a capital. The window surrounds take the form of pilasters supporting an aedicule – a shallow pediment. Alternately triangular and arched or segmental, these aedicules create a contrasting rhythm. The window itself is divided into four by a stone cross formed by a vertical mullion and a horizontal transom. This arrangement was to be found in most classical buildings in Britain and the Netherlands until vertically sliding sashes came in towards the end of the 17th century.

A second façade of this type is seen on the Palazzo Cocchi Serristori, which overlooks the Piazza Santa Croce. This palace, dating from the first half of the 16th century, is built in stone with a trio of windows on each floor. The most beautiful of all is the honey-coloured front of the Palazzo Uguccioni (1550–59) in

The Palazzo Uguccioni is a model of the way in which the orders of classical architecture – here Ionic and Corinthian – were used to add gravitas to a house that was, by the standards of the city's mighty Medicis, modest. Classical motifs – columns, entablatures and pediments – leave a minimum of blank wall and the rough-cut stonework on the ground floor is characteristic of Italian architecture in the 16th century.

the Palazzo della Signoria. This has long been thought to be the work of a great architect, and attributed variously to Raphael and Michelangelo, although Raphael had been dead for 30 years, and one of Michelangelo's biographers would surely have mentioned it. This is an astoundingly accomplished design – the paired columns flanking each window with a full entablature above were the motif adopted by John Wood of Bath for his famous Circus in that city, begun in 1754. The ground floor is all in the rusticated stonework found in Regency Edinburgh or on New York brownstones (see pages 106–11). One endearing feature of this house is the projecting tile roof that takes the place of a monumental cornice and harks back to 15th-century houses – perhaps a sign that work was brought prematurely to a halt.

The typical Florentine house may have had a narrow front, but most stretched back a long way from the street. A house that is only three or even two windows wide usually conceals a beautiful courtyard behind, and sometimes a second. Even though there may not be sufficient width for a full open arcade all round, the impression of regularity and symmetry is usually achieved by blind arches on one side. The Palazzo Bartolini Salimbeni has a perfect example decorated with *sgraffito*. This incised ornament had the advantage that it could be carried out quickly and was not spoilt by rain, unlike painted decoration. A metal point was used to scratch through a layer of whitish plaster to a darker layer, which, according to Vasari, was achieved by mixing burnt straw into the lime. The top layer around the drawing was then removed to reveal the dark background.

The most original of all narrow town-house façades is that of the house of the painter Federico Zuccari, which he built in Via Giusti on returning from Rome in 1579 to take over from Vasari the decoration of the cupola of the Duomo. This house looks like a mason's demonstration of the techniques of stone carving, with inset panels showing different treatments and textures, and witty idiosyncratic details such as bells (the family emblem) on the window grilles. It is again the precursor of a series of flamboyant and eccentric houses designed by artists as places to live and work in themselves. Where a large studio window might be expected, instead a plain blank plaque awaits a fresco if not an inscription. The other feature of the design is that it is very high-waisted, with the main storey of high rooms towards the top.

One late-15th-century house that may be explored in some detail is the Palazzo Horne, near the Uffizi, attributed to Simone del Pollaiuolo. The house was acquired and restored early in this century by the English art critic Herbert Percy Horne (1864–1916) and is now open to the public as a museum. The *palazzo* stands on a corner of the Via de' Benci and the Corso dei Tintori. It is of three main storeys and is set over a submerged basement of vaulted cellars. An entrance vestibule opens into a deep arcade that overlooks a delightful small courtyard off which a typical Renaissance stair rises dogleg fashion under tunnel vaults. The first and second floors each have a large *salone* on the street corner, while the third floor, contrived within the slope of the roof, looks out onto a concealed terrace.

From February 1911 Horne kept a detailed diary of his restoration, which was published in a book on the Palazzo by the Horne Foundation in 1993. First he cleared the great *sala* of modern partitions, then revealed the chimney opening onto the second-floor *sala*. He opened up the third-floor terrace, where there was a ledge that he thought had been devised

Alternating triangular and rounded pediments, as seen in the upper windows of the Palazzo Bartolini Salimbeni (right), were a favourite motif in the classical repertoire that inspired the architects of Renaissance Italy. The heavy stone mullions and transoms that divide the windows into four remarkably survive; in most Florentine palaces they have been replaced by larger casement windows.

for drying silk or cloth in the sun (cloth was one of the main sources of Florence's wealth). He also speculated that the second-floor fireplace was "for the exercise of some industrial art" as it was of "a very plain description." In May 1913 he "finished removing old 'graffiti'" from the façade. In September the second-floor windows were reglazed using old round panes of glass (*vetri tondi*) in new patinated leads. Among the most beautiful features are the carved capitals in the courtyard, exquisitely carved in *pietra serena*. A final interesting feature to note, on the second-floor gallery overlooking the courtyard, is a pair of flush-fitting wooden doors opening onto a shaft that descends to the well and allowed water to be hoisted up to the top of the house.

Many Florentine palaces no more than three windows in width have behind them beautifully proportioned arcaded courtyards, treated as symmetrically as the narrow space permitted. The upper walls of the courtyard of the Palazzo Bartolini Salimbeni are embellished with *sgraffito*, a form of decoration that was also often applied to façades.

The Place Royale, known since 1800 as the Place des Vosges, is the creation of Henri IV. When the king triumphantly entered Paris in 1594, France had been rent by civil war and her trade and industry almost ruined. Henri devoted the first years of his reign to driving out Spaniards, making peace with the remaining rebels and establishing religious toleration. From 1598 he and his finance minister Sully worked to rebuild the economy, restore the crown's power and transform Paris.

Among the projects that they undertook was the building of the new Place Royale, which, unusually, was to combine workshops for making silk and gold and silver thread in the fashion of Milan with a series of grand town houses. The king's letters patent of 1605 state: "The square will be appropriate to help the establishment of the silk industry … [and] serve as a promenade for the inhabitants of our town, who are very congested in their houses because of the multitudes of people who flood in from all sides."

The open space was to be vast – 72 toises (468ft or 142.6m) square. Nine pavilions containing houses were planned for the west, south and east sides, and

Place des Vosges
PARIS

workshops for the north. The king gave the first building lots to his political allies, mostly nobles holding financial office. The deeds state that the owners were required to construct "on the front of each lot, a pavilion roofed in slates having arcades and a gallery below with shops opening on to the gallery." Behind, owners were permitted to build as they decided, and the houses' layouts and depths vary markedly. By 1607 Henri was eager to complete the construction, and he gave the entire west range to two men – five lots to Pierre Fougeu d'Escures, who had already built one pavilion on the south side, and four lots to Charles Merchant, the leading speculative builder in Paris. The lots were given free to encourage building on the ambitious lines set down by the king.

It was by now becoming evident that the silk workshops were deterring the building of grand houses on the other sides. In April 1607 orders were given to demolish them and replace them with a row of nine pavilions of houses. Although the deeds prohibited the subdivision of the pavilions, there was a substantial turnover of property and lots were rearranged to

The carriage entrance to No.23 (below), at the back of the arcade, has massive wooden doors inset with studded panels; these are among the oldest surviving doors in the square. Cleaning of the arcade has revealed crisp white stone and red brick. Stone bollards protected the arch from damage by carriage wheels.

The courtyard of 23 Place des Vosges (below right), with a well in the foreground. The tall windows, divided into six parts by a sturdy mullion and two transoms, are the standard pattern for large windows in 17th- and 18th-century France. Although the walls are plain, there is an exceptionally fine carved stone doorway.

form two parcels of two pavilions and six parcels of one and a half pavilions, so the division of the houses does not correspond to the grouping of windows. Also, while the south, east and west sides form one continuous block, the north is a separate range.

Strangely, the architect of the square is not known. Among those suggested are either or both of the royal architects – Louis Métezeau and Jacques II Androuet du Cerceau – or Salomon de Brosse or Claude Chastillon. The last-named published a beautiful engraving of the square recording the festivities of 5–7 April 1612. This shows the arcades of shops and the distinctive pavilion form of the houses.

Although the plots varied slightly in width, from 48 feet to 52 feet (14.5–15.9m), the intended pattern was the same – each pavilion was four bays wide, with two full floors over the arcade. Above there were dormers to the attic, a tall pair of windows in the middle and round "bull's-eyes" to the sides. Chimney-stacks were placed against the party walls, with tall chimneys rising in the deep valleys between the roofs. Chastillon's engraving shows the returns (or rear wings) built onto many of the houses, as well as small gardens with varying walls, balustrades and fences.

The pavilion in the middle of the south side was completed by May 1607. Despite its name, the Pavillon du Roi, or King's Pavilion, Henri never resided there – it was occupied by the court painter Charles de Court – although it was to remain royal property until the Revolution of 1789.

Some houses were taken by the *concessionaires*, but the majority were occupied by aristocrats. The latter chose to abandon the custom of living in distinctive *hôtels particuliers* (or private houses) set back from the street around a courtyard in favour of dwellings with main rooms overlooking the square and identical externally to their neighbours.

The houses were built in brick with stone trim. The main architectural motifs on the exteriors are quoins at the corners and vertical stone "chains" between the windows. The Pavillon du Roi is faced with an "H" crowned with palm fronds, emblems of both the arts and war.

The interiors have been modified and embellished over the centuries. Two *salons*, painted by Charles Le Brun, from No.14, the Hôtel de la Rivière, are now in the Musée Carnavalet, and No.9 has interiors by Jules Hardouin-Mansart.

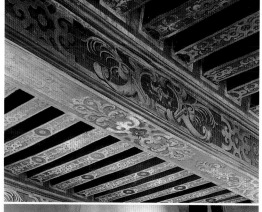

A typical open-beam 17th-century ceiling (top); it has been painted *à la Française* with decorative strapwork and cartouches along the beams and rafters. This example is on the *bel étage*.

The upper section of the house's monumental staircase is constructed in wood, with a massive handrail and square corner posts topped by urns (middle). The lower part of the stair is of stone, with large arches supporting the landing above (bottom).

23 Place des Vosges

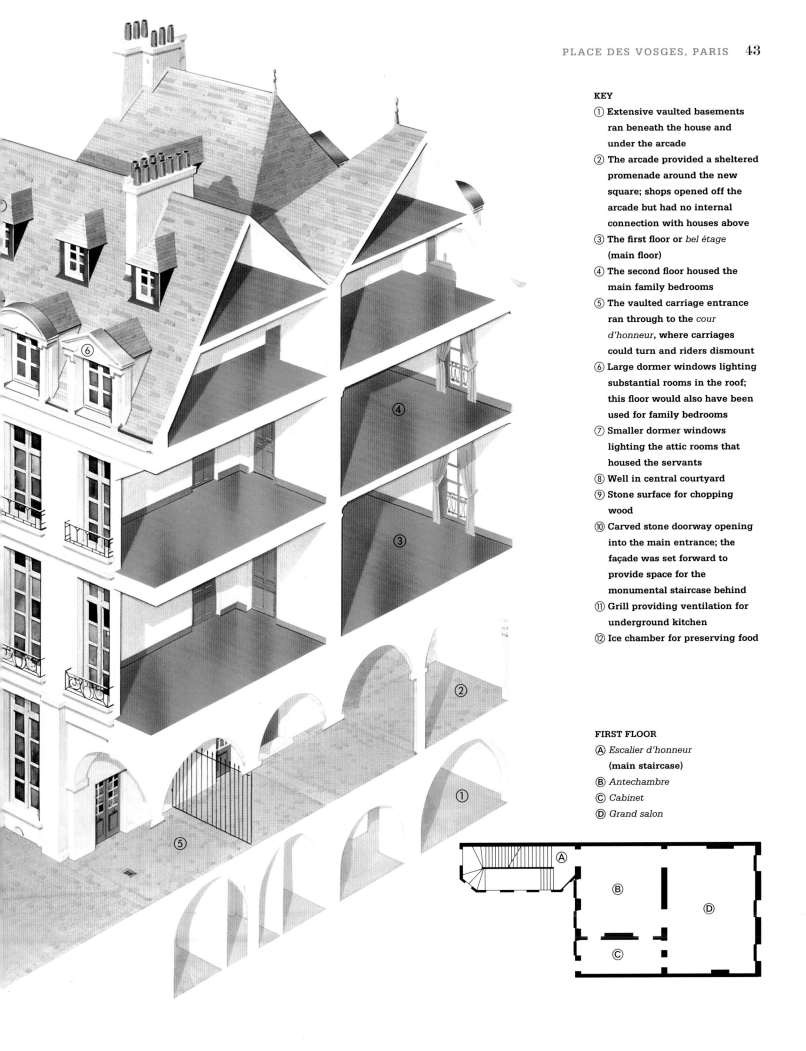

KEY

① Extensive vaulted basements ran beneath the house and under the arcade

② The arcade provided a sheltered promenade around the new square; shops opened off the arcade but had no internal connection with houses above

③ The first floor or *bel étage* (main floor)

④ The second floor housed the main family bedrooms

⑤ The vaulted carriage entrance ran through to the *cour d'honneur*, where carriages could turn and riders dismount

⑥ Large dormer windows lighting substantial rooms in the roof; this floor would also have been used for family bedrooms

⑦ Smaller dormer windows lighting the attic rooms that housed the servants

⑧ Well in central courtyard

⑨ Stone surface for chopping wood

⑩ Carved stone doorway opening into the main entrance; the façade was set forward to provide space for the monumental staircase behind

⑪ Grill providing ventilation for underground kitchen

⑫ Ice chamber for preserving food

FIRST FLOOR

Ⓐ *Escalier d'honneur* (main staircase)

Ⓑ *Antechambre*

Ⓒ *Cabinet*

Ⓓ *Grand salon*

The Paris of today is, to a large extent, the creation of Baron Georges-Eugène Haussmann (1809–91), who reshaped it for Napoleon III, replacing ancient quarters with *grandes boulevardes* and large opulent apartment blocks. Until the 18th century single houses crowded the city's narrow streets, and, although many have gone, we have a remarkable portrait of Parisian houses in the previous century in a pioneering book by Pierre Le Muet (1591–1669). In his *Manière de bien bastir pour toutes sortes de personnes* (1623), a practical guide for builders and patrons seeking to erect a new house, the architect supplies full drawings for 13 sizes of house, in some cases with several variants. He gives a plan of each floor and a drawing of the front to the street and, for larger houses, the main front overlooking the courtyard within.

The smallest house has a street frontage of 12 feet (3.7m) and a depth of 21½ feet (6.6m), while the largest site is 45 feet (13.7m) wide and 100 feet (30m) deep. All the houses are designed to stand in a street with neighbours abutting on both sides. Le Muet's essentials in a house are durability,

The handsome open beam ceiling (below) on the first floor of Place des Vosges 9, a house known as the Hôtel des Chaulnes, is typical of the 17th century. Strapwork decoration is mixed with fruit and flowers, and the interwoven initials "D" and "C" of the Duc de Chaulnes, who owned the house.

Le Muet's seven grades
PARIS

convenience, fine layout and "healthy" apartments. He gave much consideration to comfort and privacy, stating that the principal *salles* (living rooms) and *chambres* (bedrooms) should be accompanied by a *garderobe* (where the owners would be dressed by maids or manservants) and, if possible, a *cabinet* (a small private study used to rest, read or write).

The height of rooms on the first floor should be 13–14 feet (4–4.25m); on the second, 12–13 feet (3.7–4m); and on the third, 11–12 feet (3.4–3.7m). Builders were told to consider the siting of the bed – normally 6 foot (1.9m) square – as well as the space between this and the wall, which should be 4–6 feet (1.2–1.8m). The smallest *garderobe* should measure at least 9–10 feet (2.7–3m), but preferably 15–16 feet (4.6–4.9m). Internal doors should be 2½–3 feet wide (80–90cm), but 4 feet (1.2m) in grand buildings, and 6½–7 feet (2–2.1m) high.

Le Muet's smallest house is of three storeys, with a vaulted cellar below street level and a spacious attic in the steep roof. The floor plans show just one room on each floor. The *salle* is on the ground floor, with a

This house at Rue des Francs Bourgeois 58 *bis* (left and right), in the Marais district of central Paris, is almost certainly the work of Le Muet. The bold design of its early 17th-century dormers, executed in stone to match the façade below, is similar to that of dormers illustrated in the architect's *Manière de bien bastir pour toutes sortes de personnes* (1623).

Le Muet's book illustrated seven grades of house. In the first-grade house (below) each floor had one large room with a sizeable fireplace, and at the back there was a tiny lightwell with outdoor privy. The elevation reveals a shallow oval window or vent just above street level that served the cellar. The fourth-grade house (below right) had a rear courtyard with stables and a gallery at first-floor level leading across the courtyard to a large upper room with its own fireplace. Beds are indicated in outline in the main rooms.

GROUND FLOOR   FIRST FLOOR

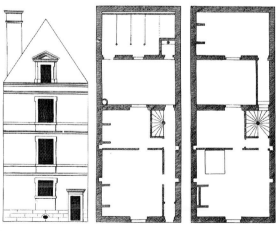

GROUND FLOOR   FIRST FLOOR

large fireplace in the side wall and a well and a privy in a tiny courtyard at the back. A spiral stair leads up to a first-floor bedroom that also has a large fireplace. The second-grade house is slightly deeper, winning just enough space for a tiny *cabinet* at the back of the first and second floors. The third grade, 15–18 feet (4.6–5.5m) wide, has a kitchen on the ground floor beside the front door and a spacious *garderobe*, with its own fireplace, occupying the width of the first-floor frontage. There is a variant plan that swaps all rooms front to back.

The fourth grade has a detached stable block at the back of a small rear courtyard. At first-floor level a gallery runs along the side of the courtyard to a second well-proportioned bedroom, evidently for family use, over the stable. Houses of the first four grades have just one window on each floor at the front. Interestingly, the sill of the ground floor window is always set high, to stop anyone looking in.

The fifth, sixth and seventh grades are all more substantial – three windows wide and with spacious internal courtyards. Intriguingly, the fifth grade has a lower two-storey (with attic) front block, rather like a gate lodge, with a three-storey block behind that has higher ceilings. The *premier étage* – actually the ground floor – of the front block has a kitchen on one side of the central entrance passage into the courtyard, and a *gardemanger* (larder) on the other. The front door into the house opens onto a staircase hall at the side of the courtyard, with a *salle* and a *cabinet* at the back, looking onto a second smaller courtyard or light-well. Above, the main bedroom has a small lobby, a *cabinet* and a *garderobe*. The largest of the "terrace" houses has a central carriage arch that leads to the main court, with a garden beyond. After this, Le Muet's houses become *hôtels particuliers*: individual mansions that are much grander than any terrace or row house.

Although the houses in his book are clearly his own invention, to some extent he was codifying current practice. Around the Rue Dauphine on the left bank, and the Rue St-Martin on the right, are rows of houses conforming to his plates. Closest to some of his largest designs is Rue des Francs Bourgeois 58 *bis*, which has the distinctive prominent dormers with rounded pediments that appear in his designs.

Amsterdam's canal-side merchants' houses were evoked vividly by the 19th-century Dutch author Neel Doff when she wrote of "the 17th- or 18th-century houses with their double-height stoops of blue granite, fenced off with railings and chains of wrought iron, a stately door rich in carvings, dark-green like the murky water of the canals."

The Singel, Herengracht, Keizersgracht and Prinsengracht – the city's four main canals – are lined by some 2,200 houses – 1,550 of which are protected as historic monuments. The Singel, which forms the innermost semicircle, was completed in 1593 and followed by outer rings extending northward from the natural harbour of the Ij. A second phase, which was begun around 1660, continued the concentric rings of canals southward. As Amsterdam prospered, merchants' houses grew to serve as offices and warehouses as well as homes, like many Venetian palaces before them, because transport by canal was the easiest way to deliver and dispatch goods.

Among the most important early surviving canal houses are three by Hendrick de Keyser (1565–1621), who in 1595 became Amsterdam's chief municipal stonemason. They are The Dolphin, at Singel 140–142 (1599–1602); the Bartolotti house, Herengracht 170–172 (1617); and the Huis met de Hoofden (House with the Heads), Keizersgracht 123 (1621–22). These are broad, brick houses with carved-stone detail and highly elaborate stepped gables.

The architect Jacob van Campen (1595–1627) advocated a purer, restrained classicism, which is exemplified by a double house with classical pilasters, Keizersgracht 177, designed in 1625. His assistant

Burghers' houses
AMSTERDAM

Herengracht 504–510 is a group of four gabled houses (opposite), three windows wide, built to a repeating design. One house has lost its rounded gable pediment, but the scrolls, displaying sea creatures, remain, and the houses also retain the projecting hoists that were used to convey goods up from the street.

Herengracht 386 was built in 1663–5 to the designs of the architect Philips Vingboons. A handsome example of restrained classicism, the house has a double order of pilasters, Doric below and Corinthian above, with large windows filling the wall space between them. The substantial pediment, in which a central oval window lighting the attic is set in a scrolled cartouche, allows sufficient room for a dormer window at each end. The windows of the main floor are raised to accommodate windows below them large enough to light the half-sunken basement.

Philips Vingboons (1607–78) built numerous houses for Amsterdam merchants on standard plots 26 or 30 feet (8 or 9m) wide. These narrow houses were built in the traditional way with the gable end to the street, replacing the stepped gable with the "neck" gable, a form of giant dormer window flanked by scrolls concealed the slope of the roof behind. Two early examples by Vingboons are Herengracht 168 (1637) and Keizersgracht 319 (1639). One such house is illustrated in a fire-fighting manual by Jan van der Heyden of 1690 (opposite). The low-ceilinged lower floor is evidently a cellar in use for storage, although these cellars were often rented out. The ground floor, approached by a short flight of out-door steps – a stoop – has a low hall with a mezzanine above. This hall often served as the *comptoir* (the owner's office). At the back, and spectacularly ablaze like every part of the house, is a grand double-height reception room. As was usual in narrow houses, the staircase is a spiral that becomes even narrower toward the top. The bedrooms were on the floor above the salon. Often the upper floor was used for further storage and for drying washing on clothes horses, with trestle-tables for stretching, wringing, ironing and starching linen. The garret under the roof held peat, the fuel used in all the fireplaces.

In broader houses built after 1660, Vingboons placed the more formal reception rooms at the front and the family rooms at the back. The façades of

these 50-foot (15m) wide houses were finished with classical cornices and in some cases pediments. The houses were built on newly purchased adjoining plots with a width of 26 feet (8m) in the second sector of the canals, allocated in 1663. The by-laws of December 7 of that year stipulated that the new stretches of the Herengracht and the Keizersgracht should be elegant residential areas from which trade and industry were barred. Plots could be built on to a maximum depth of 100 feet (30m), in order to conserve room for a

spacious garden behind each house. The fencing around the gardens was not to exceed 9 feet (2.75m) in height, and garden houses, of which the Dutch of this period were very fond, were not to be taller than 12 feet (3.7m) or deeper than 15 feet (4.6m). The stoops here could rise to 7 feet (2.1m), 2 feet (0.6m) more than in other parts of the city, but this was not sufficient for the fashion-conscious burghers, who wanted a *piano nobile*, an impressively elevated ground floor, as in French mansions. Stoops became less common, entrances descended to ground level and grand stairs were built within.

One of the architects working in the new "flat style" was the mathematician and military architect Adriaan Dortsman (1636–82), whose houses are marked by monumental simplicity. A good example is Herengracht 619, which dates from the 1660s and has only three rooms on each floor of a house with a width of 32 feet (9.6m).

A new era of sophistication and comfort opened with the arrival in 1686 of the great French Huguenot designer Daniel Marot (1661–1752), who introduced the latest decorative fashions from France. Among his many widely used engravings are plans for single- and double-fronted houses where symmetry reigns in every room and more spacious stairs are introduced. The plans show houses with the new small-paned vertically sliding sash windows that came into use in both England and the Netherlands during the 1680s, though the Dutch are usually given primacy. These windows superseded casement windows with smaller leaded panes and wooden mullions. Marot's plans are for narrow houses that stretch back for a considerable length, with internal courts to light inner rooms.

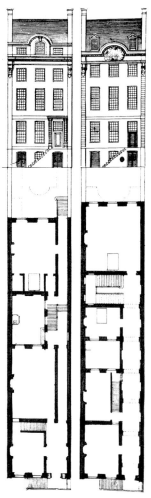

Stingel 36 (left), built in 1754, has an impressive top to its façade. The triglyphs in the crisp Doric frieze resemble those on ancient Greek temples and contrast with the richly carved balustrade and Rococo crest above.

The carved stone doorway on the Herengracht (below left), which dates from 1739, is a fine example of the Baroque love of swagger. The door, ornamental fanlight and first-floor window are united in a rich sculptural composition.

Daniel Marot's ground plans and elevations (below) for two early 18th-century canal houses show characteristic tall sash windows, with 16 panes to each sash, on the main floors.

One house has a *grande salle* on the entrance floor and a bedroom. The other has the *comptoir* and two bedrooms – one large and overlooking the garden, the other small.

The main bedrooms in merchants' houses usually had grand beds, of four-poster or canopied design. Children and servants often slept in built-in beds or on mattresses unrolled on the floor. It was the Dutch custom to equip a maternity room for the birth of a child, and after the event the mother and child would have been cared for by both a nurse and a wet nurse. There would be a cupboard for baby linen and a wicker chair for the nurse to sit in while swaddling the baby or changing it. Privies were found in gardens, inner courtyards and in cupboards or the corners of rooms, while chamber pots were kept in cupboards or under beds.

In the 17th century, tapestries of landscapes and woodland scenes were the most expensive form of wall covering, and the warmest. At first they were attached loosely so that they could be folded back over doors, but from about 1680 they were stretched on frames to harmonize with formal panelling, with the result that many were folded or even cut. Gilded "Spanish" leather was another prized wall covering, resistant to the moist atmosphere and to light. The technique involved using thin sheets of silver leaf which were given a varnish of yellow lacquer to turn them gold. Sometimes the leather was left silver, and in the 18th century more colours were introduced.

The illustration in Jan van der Heyden's fire-fighting manual on page 47 shows open-beam ceilings, but after 1700 stucco ceilings became widespread, allowing walls and ceilings to be treated as part of a single decorative scheme. Contemporary inventories show that floor mats were the most common floor covering; carpets were more often used as table cloths.

One of the most fascinating books on Amsterdam's houses is *The Canals of Amsterdam* (1993), which surveys them individually and reproduces the *Views of Houses and Buildings along the Keizers and Herengrachten* of 1768–70 with matching modern photographs. The book is powerful testimony to how much has survived and how much has been altered, subtly or otherwise. The most common change is to the sash windows, where the original small square panes were often replaced in the 19th century by larger panes. Patterns of nine over nine panes, twelve over twelve and sixteen over sixteen were common, and are still to be found. The other great change was to the gables, many of which were simplified or removed in response to changing tastes or to reduce maintenance costs.

The Rembrandt House, Jodenbreestraat 4–6, was built in 1606 for the merchant Hans van der Voort. Around 1627 the characteristic stepped gable was replaced with a pediment by Jacob van Campen. Rembrandt bought the house in 1639, as he approached the peak of his career, for the enormous sum of 13,000 guilders (£3,850/$6,150). It was here that his son Titus was born and many of his most famous canvases, including *The Night Watch*, were painted. Rembrandt and his wife Saskia lived on the ground floor, and on the floor above them was the studio, where his pupils and assistants worked.

The building was acquired by the Rembrandt House Foundation in 1907 and opened to the public four years later. An inventory of Rembrandt's possessions was made in 1656, when he was declared bankrupt after a steady decline in sales, and provides a detailed picture of the way the house was furnished, complementing the artist's drawings of the interior. In the entrance hall were six fine Spanish chairs and a cupboard containing silver and linen belonging to Rembrandt's mistress, Hendrickje Stoffels. The side room at the front was hung with paintings by Rembrandt, Hercules Seghers, Adriaen Brouwer and Rembrandt's teacher, Pieter Lastman. A large marble cooler held bottles of drinks for visitors, who could

Around 1627 the Rembrandt House (right) was divided into two, so when the artist bought it in 1639 he was able to live, paint and conduct business there. He and Saskia lived on the ground floor, and he taught most of his pupils in the studio above. The upper parts of the windows did not open and so lacked external shutters.

This pair of handsome classical houses (above) on the elegant Keizersgracht bears the date 1671 and the coat of arms of Jeremias van Raey, the rich armaments merchant who built them. The first has the small-paned windows typical of the 17th and 18th century in Holland. The houses (Nos.672 and 674) were recorded by Cornelius Danckerts in a print (right) made around 1700, which shows the tiny attic windows set into the frieze. Apart from the statues at the edge of the roof, a curve in the middle of the parapet balustrade is the sole Baroque flourish.

discuss purchases and commissions sitting on one of seven chairs upholstered in green velvet. The back room was the best room, serving as both sitting room and bedroom, and had a large carved fireplace. Rembrandt's cabinet of curiosities – a common feature in grander Dutch houses – contained shells, fossils and minerals, as well as oriental arms and clothing, "two globes, an East Indian powder box and a head of the Roman Emperor Tiberius."

The Van Loon House, which opened to the public as a museum in 1973, is a beautifully furnished and decorated example of a double-fronted house on Amsterdam's fashionable Keizersgracht. In order to encourage the building of large houses beside the newly completed stretches of canal, the City Fathers stipulated that the purchasers of one lot at auction could acquire the neighbouring lot at the same price. The Van Loon House at No.672 and its neighbour to the left, 674, were built by a rich merchant, Jeremias van Raey, and completed in 1672. Van Raey was a

trustee of the nearby Walloon Orphanage, which was built in 1669–71, and commissioned its architect, Adriaan Dortsman, to design the pair of houses.

Their reserved classical style anticipates that of Parisian houses a century later. The statues along the roof add a Baroque note; these symbolize the goods in which van Raey traded – arms, iron and grain. Mars and Minerva stand as twin deities of war, Vulcan for metalwork and Ceres for agriculture. In the centre of each front the merchant set his arms and the date 1671. He built No.674 for himself but let No.672 to the painter Ferdinand Bol, who had married an heiress and was a friend of Dortsman. In 1752 No.672 was bought by the physician Abraham van Hagen, who had married the daughter of Burgomaster Dirck Trip. On van Hagen's death in 1771 it was recorded that he had been working on the house for 20 years but still had more to do. In the rich brass banister of the new stair he had the names V[an]HAGEN and TRIP worked into the metalwork in ornate capitals. (Additional curlicues were added during the late 19th century by owners concerned that small children might fall through the large holes between the letters.)

Van Hagen's nephews and nieces inherited the house and sold it for 78,000 guilders, plus a further 8,000 for the lavish furniture, which made it impractical to let. The purchaser, Coenraad Hendrik Sander, had made a fortune in Indonesia and continued the redecoration with the same craftsmen. The ceiling of the main bedroom contains a wheel with spokes in the form of his surname's initial "S" and a hook in the centre – not for a chandelier, since it is at the side, but to support a canopy over the bed.

An inventory of 1778 lists "a double width *lit d'ange*" with "carved blue and white silk damask hangings, cords and tassels, six French carved and gilt armchairs with blue and white silk damask backs and seats and gilt nails, with their dust covers, an English blue carpet, an oak dressing table with gilt ornaments, two gilt wall candelabra each for three candles." In 1884 No.672 was bought by the banker Hendrik van Loon for his son Willem, who that year married Thora Egidius, who was to live there until her death in 1945.

The basement contained the kitchens, storerooms and servants' sitting room. The ground floor was entered by a shallow stoop and contained the main living rooms; this floor now appears as it it did when completed in the late 18th century, with Louis XV panelling and plasterwork.

The box-edged formal garden behind the house was laid out when the house was restored in the late 1960s and early 1970s, on the model of gardens that were shown by 17th-century bird's-eye views of the city. The coach-house at the far end faces onto the Kerkstraat, which runs between the Keizersgracht and Prinsengracht canals. Most large houses had such coach-houses, with stables, but few examples survive. Thanks to the fact that Bol, the first tenant, sued his landlord because the promised stables were not ready when he took up residence, we know that the architect was Dortsman. In 1775 a temple front

was added to the coach-house on the garden side, with statues of Silenus, Bacchus and Flora – no doubt attesting to the hospitality of the owners.

A book on the mansion, *The House with Purple Windows* by M N van Loon and I H van Eeghen, describes the Van Loon House as it was in the late 19th century, when the lady of the house moved through it like clockwork as she went about the day's activities. She was dressed by her lady's maid, had her hair done by the hairdresser, breakfasted in the garden room and then moved to the small drawing room, where she discussed the menus with the cook and wrote her letters. Her husband would return for lunch, ringing the bell because he never carried a key to the front door. Tea was at five o'clock, followed by dinner at seven, or, if there were guests, at eight. All dishes were brought up from the basement kitchen on silver dishes under silver covers to keep them hot.

At the end of the attractive formal garden belonging to Keizersgracht 672 (below) stands a temple front concealing a stable block that formerly opened onto the street at the far side. Because the owners of the house did not want the coachman's family to look onto the garden, the stable block's windows are false, with dummy curtains painted on them.

The garden room (right) was panelled in the French Rococo manner in the 1770s. Characteristic of the style are the tall, narrow panels above the chair rail, which protects the decoration, and, over the fireplace, the pier-glass reflecting another mirror. The bust is of Louise Borski, the wife of Hendrik van Loon.

There is not a single obviously modern intruder in Rothenburg ob der Tauber's harmonious combination of Gothic and Renaissance buildings. The town itself stands in a spectacular position nearly 300 feet (90m) above an oxbow bend in the River Tauber, protected by medieval walls with inner and outer perimeters and a covered sentry walk offering superb views over the old town.

For Germans, Rothenburg is a high point on a national pilgrimage along the "Romantische Strasse," the Romantic Road, which winds from Würzburg to Augsburg past some of the country's best-preserved towns, including Bad Mergentheim, Dinkelsbühl and Nördlingen. Rothenburg is famous for the annual re-enactment of the "Meistertrunk" when, in 1631, the mayor persuaded the Catholic General Tilly not to raze the town by winning a challenge to drain the municipal tankard of some ¾ gallon (3.25l) of wine.

The Celts built a small fortress here, and the Franks made the town the capital of the duchy of Franconia. In 1106 Rothenburg passed into the control of the Hohenstaufen emperors, who fortified the town with gates and walls, and in 1274 it gained the status of a Free Imperial City. In 1524, during the Reformation, Rothenburg became Protestant, narrowly escaping destruction for supporting Sweden's King Gustavus Adolphus. Although the Peace of Westphalia in 1648 confirmed Rothenburg's free status, it never fully recovered its prosperity and it is partly because of this that so many Renaissance buildings remain, for in more prosperous times these would undoubtedly have been swept away or modified.

Rothenburg's finest Renaissance house is the Baumeisterhaus, so called because the town's master builder, Leonhard Weidmann (fl 1568–96) designed it. Weidmann, who was also a stonemason, was paid for a plan to build a new Renaissance wing on the

Rothenburg is a remarkably complete historic town, with large red-roofed gabled houses fronting the narrow streets. Medieval timber-framed houses – such as that in the bottom right of the picture below – jostle with houses that date from the 16th and 17th centuries. The Baumeisterhaus is the second house along on the street that is seen to lead out of the square.

Gabled mansions
ROTHENBURG OB DER TAUBER

town hall, on which work began in 1570. It is worth noting that he did not qualify as a master craftsman until 1575, so this commission may indicate early recognition of exceptional talent, for the town hall is one of the finest in Franconia, with its high gabled façade and a spectacular three-storey oriel window. In 1574 Weidmann worked on the reconstruction of the town's hospital, contributing its Renaissance doorway, and on the Jägermeisterhaus in the hospital courtyard. The old Gymnasium, or Grammar School, built between 1589 and 1591, has been attributed to him on stylistic grounds.

The Baumeisterhaus, at Obere Schmiedgasse 3, is graced by a carefully ordered sandstone façade and is clearly the work of an architect seeking to achieve classical regularity and purity, even if the gabled format is still traditional. Each storey of the house, built in 1596 for a town councillor, Michael Hirsching, and now a café-restaurant, is treated individually, and a prominent pediment marks the entrance. The entablature is carried right across the façade in order to create an emphatic division. The first and second floors have long bands of windows richly carved with figures, combining the main elements of the mason's art: architecture and sculpture. The statues on the first floor represent the seven cardinal virtues, those on the second the seven deadly sins. The gable is

and Herrngasse, where the homes of leading citizens of old are equipped with pulleys for lifting goods. Rothenburg's principal hotel, the Eisenhut, occupies four of these patrician houses. In the Market Place a fountain dating from 1608, Georgsbrunnen, stands over the cistern containing the town's 26,400-gallon (100,000l) emergency water supply.

Rothenburg was incorporated into Bavaria in 1802 and its rediscovery by Romantic poets and painters helped it to survive the 19th century unusually unscathed. After a heavy bombing raid in 1945, J J McCloy, the USA's future High Commissioner for Germany, who knew the town well, successfully pleaded for it to be spared further destruction. Today Rothenburg has some of the strictest preservation laws in Germany – even international chain stores must use wrought-iron hanging signs.

A section of the Baumeisterhaus shows the vaulted cellar and the internal columns supporting the wide floor spans. The plans reveal that, despite the size of the rooms, the staircase is a small spiral in one corner.

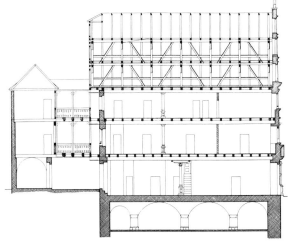

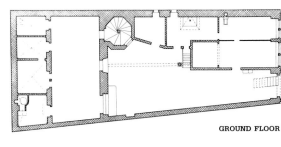

GROUND FLOOR

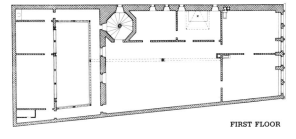

FIRST FLOOR

The Baumeisterhaus, which was built by the master builder and stonemason Leonhard Weidmann in 1596, is not only the finest surviving Renaissance town house in Rothenburg but also one of the best examples to be found in Germany. The sandstone façade is carved with two rows of caryatid figures: the seven cardinal virtues and the seven deadly sins. Ornamental scrolls enrich the stepped gable, inset with doors to take in merchandise from the street.

stepped in five stages and flanked by scrolls that are shaped like old-fashioned clay pipes.

The Baumeisterhaus, which is equally architectural in its layout, may be considered an early example of the open plan. An octagonal stair descends to a cellar with cross vaults supported by a central line of columns. The ground floor is a huge open space that extends the full depth of the building and has a central supporting column. The upper floors have slightly lower ceilings, also supported by columns.

Next door is the Gasthof zum Greifen, once home to Burgomaster Heinrich Toppler, who led Rothenburg to prosperity during the 14th century. No.21, the Roter Hahn (Red Hen), was the home of Burgomaster Nusch, who saved the town from Tilly's wrath during the Thirty Years War (1618–48). Other streets on which fine gabled houses can be found are Burggasse

In 1666 the Great Fire of London destroyed 13,200 homes – practically all of the city, including St Paul's Cathedral. Tragically, those houses that escaped the blaze were torn down when the decision was taken to rebuild London in brick rather than in the flammable timber used in earlier centuries. As a result, practically all physical traces of how Londoners lived before 1666 have vanished.

One valuable exception is Nos.52–55 Newington Green, four houses overlooking a busy square in the former merchant suburb of Newington, about two miles (3km) north of the City. The houses date from 1658, the year of Oliver Cromwell's death (as a cut-brick panel that is embedded in the façade of No.54 records). They were clearly designed as a group and for this reason have been hailed as the earliest surviving example of terrace housing in London.

Terrace houses are usually said to have arrived in Britain with Inigo Jones's Covent Garden Piazza, begun in 1630 (London's counterpart of Paris' Place des Vosges; see pages 40–41), and the speculative houses built by Nicholas Barbon in and around Red Lion Square in 1686–98. The latest research by architectural historians Schofield and Leech links terrace houses with a well-established tradition of "rows," such as survive in Chester (see pages 22–3). Rows are groups of houses built to a common pattern (the word is still used in America). The British term "terrace house" dates from the 18th century and may originate in the Adelphi, a row of palatial houses designed by the Adam brothers in 1768–72, and built on a terrace raised above a bank of the River Thames.

Of the Newington Green houses, Tim Mowl and Brian Earnshaw write in their book on Puritan architecture under Cromwell, *Architecture without Kings*

Gabled Cromwellian houses
NEWINGTON GREEN, LONDON

The stout turned balusters of the staircase in No.53 (below) are typical of the mid-17th century, as are the square newel posts with balls on top to give firm support to the user.

(1995): "It was facades like this ... with their cheerfully inept evocations of a brick republican Rome, that were beginning to give a timbered London of leaning gables and small Gothic church towers some of the gravitas of a Renaissance capital." The houses are united by a giant order of plain Tuscan brick pilasters rising through two storeys. Above are triangular gables; these reflect the medieval tradition of houses with gable ends to the street.

The group of four houses is laid out symmetrically, two on each side of a central passageway. The plans of the two on the left are a mirror image of those on the right, so that both the outer and inner houses form matching pairs.

against the side walls, but here they are placed on the cross walls opposite the windows and backing onto the staircase. The size of these fireplaces and chimney breasts is remarkable by later standards – they are 3 feet 6 inches (1.1m) deep and 7 feet 6 inches (2.3m) wide, narrowing to 6 feet (1.8m) at the top. This is partly because the flues of the lower fireplaces rise behind the fireplaces above, not to the side, as later became the practice. The depth of the chimney breast meant that there was space for a substantial cupboard or closet to contain a privy (or, today, a shower cubicle).

Two of the houses retain the original elm stairs. The inner houses, where the central passageway reduced the space, had tight "winders"; in the outer houses there was enough room for half-landings.

Throughout there is evidence of economy. The fronts are of fine red-clay bricks, but at the back the bricks are more ordinary, while on inside walls they are plainer still. Roger Mears, the architect in charge of recent sensitive restoration, pointed out a leaded window in an oak frame that predated the building and was evidently reused from an earlier house. Salvaged timbers were reused in the basements and to support the stairs. The original internal finishes were very plain – none of the rooms had panelling at the time of building.

According to an early-18th-century source, Thomas Pidcock built 52–55 Newington Green. The houses are first mentioned in documents of 1664, and a full list of occupants from 1731 has been established.

The ground-floor plan of the original houses shows that large fireplaces were set in the cross walls rather than the side walls, as became common in the 18th century. The great depth of the fireplaces allowed space for a closet on one side. No.54 is shown here with its slightly larger 18th-century stair and altered chimney breasts.

The three restored houses (above) are seen here in 1998, after completion of the work. No.54's Georgian upper storey has been retained and sashes repaired or reintroduced.

This reconstruction (left) of the houses as they were built in 1658 shows the original matching gables. The central archway leads into a passage that runs between the houses. When new they had hinged windows, not sashes, and steps up to each front door to allow for basement windows.

After falling into an appalling state, the houses were under threat of demolition. The Greater London Council compulsorily purchased Nos.53–55 in 1985; the following year they were taken over by English Heritage, which carried out essential repairs before reselling them to a new owner who completed the work so that they could be lived in again.

The houses were built with basements and a railed-off front area. Later, probably in the 1870s or 1880s, shops were inserted along the front, but an earlier photograph shows the railings and the steps up to the front door. When the shops were introduced the ground floor was lowered in order to make a level entrance to the street.

Each house has one room front and back on each floor, with the staircase placed across the centre. In 18th-century terrace houses the fireplaces are set

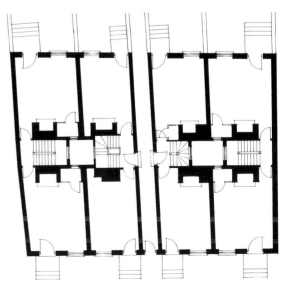

When you approach St Malo by sea, the old town comes gradually into view across the water – bastions, encircling walls and great gateways and, inside, the steep roofs and chimneys of innumerable grand houses packed tightly together. What you see is one of the great success stories of postwar conservation, for its German U-boat pens were to make this Brittany port an obvious and repeated target for Allied bombers; and then, following the D-Day landings, the Germans took refuge in the old town. In the subsequent shelling more than 2,000 dwellings were destroyed – 80 per cent of the buildings – leaving in most places little more than battered walls and perilous chimney-stacks. Only the ramparts and the castle at the northern entrance remained almost intact.

Thanks to plentiful Canadian money, and the determination of General de Gaulle, St Malo was restored from smouldering ruins. The decision was

and Granada. Old photographs taken before the Second World War show sea captains' houses with rich panelled interiors of the kind to be found on Paris' Ile St Louis.

Many of the finest of these houses were built in four great *accroissements* (or enlargements) to the walled town carried out in 1701–42, initially by the great military engineer Vauban (1633–1707) and then by his successor, Garangeau. The story of these houses was carefully researched by the curator of the town museum, Philippe Petout, and told in his *Hôtels et Maisons de Saint-Malo*.

In the opening years of the 18th century the war of the Spanish Succession brought fabulous riches to St Malo when local ships captured Spanish galleons that were returning from the Americas laden with precious metals. In 1703 a cargo worth 7 million livres was captured, followed by another worth 12 million. The shipowners and arms dealers who equipped these expeditions were soon enjoying fabulous wealth, and

Sea captains' houses
ST MALO

Carved wooden doors with a pattern of inlaid wood in the lower panels are among the features of the magnificent house (above) begun in 1711 in the Rue St-Vincent for the St Malo shipowner Guillaume White.

taken to rebuild according to the old street plan, using traditional Brittany granite and slate in order to recreate the town's memorable silhouette as seen from the sea. From outside the walls this reconstruction is scarcely noticeable – the local granite has a timeless quality. Within it becomes more apparent, because only key buildings were reconstructed in every detail; others were simply rebuilt in granite to the same proportions, with the same steep roofs but unmistakably modern windows.

Some who visit St Malo question whether it would not have been better to have rebuilt it in the style of the times. The answer is given effectively by the bland centres of numerous Normandy towns rebuilt in a tame modern style after the devastation that followed the D-Day landings. The glory of St Malo today is that it has not become a museum but is a flourishing community.

This was a corsair town whose sailors led the bombardment of Tunis in 1609, and between 1692 and 1697 captured more than 1,300 enemy vessels. In 1655 Louis XIV declared that his flagships' crews should be exclusively composed of Malouines. The Compagnie des Indes et des Mers de Sud operated from St Malo, and in 1732 Louis XV gave its people the coffee warehouses of Martinique, Guadeloupe

After the completion of a new stretch of ramparts overlooking the bay, this terrace of substantial mansions (right) was built behind them in the Rue d'Orléans in the 1720s.

Strongly defended against attack from land or sea, St Malo grew immensely rich from privateering during the late 17th and early 18th centuries. Immediately within the ramparts stood the imposing mansions built for those who fitted out the ships and provisioned the expeditions. Tall and with steep roofs, these houses are a magnificent sight when approached from the sea.

the colossal fortunes they amassed opened a golden age for St Malo. Among those who profited was the Irishman Guillaume White.

The Hôtel White or Hay stands at No.2 Place Châteaubriand, just inside the main north gateway. White bought lots 1–3, and during September 1711 "several masons were working there erecting a grand *corps-de-logis*." This and the adjoining houses overlooking the square are of princely dimensions, although with a severity and simplicity that speaks of military rather than domestic architecture. The entrance portals are monumental but without the carved detail that would have been found in Paris. Only in the doors and balconies is there a degree of decorative richness.

Typically these houses had stone-vaulted ground floors where the owners, as in Venice, would store merchandise and equipment. Under the courtyards were vast vaulted cisterns for storing water, often with pumps set in niches in the walls. Massive stone

stairs led to the upper floors, which were laid out in the French fashion as apartments. On the landings a door on one side opened directly into the kitchen, and one on the other into a salon or antechamber. Inventories provide details of layouts and show that the rooms had precise functions.

In 1723 Jacques White, Guillaume's brother, planned the first floor of a house to be built at Rue de Toulouse 12, with a *cabinet*, a *salon*, a *chambre d'honneur* (state bedroom), a *salle*, a *chambre-à-coucher*, a *garderobe*, a *chambre d'enfants* and a kitchen. A detailed contract survives for woodwork and panelling. A master carpenter made all the doors on the ground floor, specifying thickness of wood, and all the panelling of rooms on the upper floor. The contract stipulated that the profiles of panels and door-cases must be approved and designs provided for each chimney piece. Photographs taken before the Second World War show Régence carving with exquisite ribbonwork in the style of Jean Berain.

Few small preservation groups can take credit for having saved more fine terrace houses than the Spitalfields Trust. The saga of Spitalfields is of a battle against neglect and greed, which is often the case within the field of architectural conservation.

In this area of the inner East End of London, which is just to the east of the capital's financial centre, stood, until the 1960s, London's largest and most intact group of early-18th-century terrace houses. These had survived largely unaltered simply because their use as cheap lodgings and sweatshops for the garment industry, which continues to dominate the area, generated no funds for improvement. Now, some 250 years old but still handsome despite suffering from neglect, the houses were threatened by the expansion of the City as speculators bought them in groups in order to demolish them and create large sites for new office blocks.

The tide began to turn with the foundation of the Spitalfields Trust in 1977. Since then just two of the formerly endangered houses have been demolished and today nearly 130 survive, 64 of which have passed through the hands of the Trust. Douglas Blain, who has been the Trust's secretary since its formation, recalls that "the trouble with Spitalfields in 1977 was not so much that it was derelict as that it was empty. Elder Street, Folgate Street, Fleur-de-Lis Street were by then a social desert. The merchants' houses in Spital Square were gone. When I stood in Spital Square in 1961 the atmosphere was extraordinary. Staring across the glistening cobbles, all I could

Huguenot weavers' houses
SPITALFIELDS, LONDON

Red-brick window dressings and gently arched window heads, as at 15 Elder Street (below), are characteristic of the early 18th century. Here the sash boxes are set almost flush with the façade because Spitalfields, lying just outside the City of London, was not covered by a fire regulation that required wooden sashes to be set back no less than 9 inches (23cm).

see in any direction was early Georgian domestic architecture. The scene was like an early photograph, taken on a long time exposure and thus bereft of life: the subtle glow of purple- and rose-coloured brick, the glint of crown glass in every window, each house drab but dignified, untouched, virtually, in all its details."

The Spitalfields Trust decided to set out to attract lively single people and couples who would make the revival of the area a priority; these would be enthusiasts for whom a 1720s panelled room would represent more than just somewhere to live. Already Spitalfields was the home of the celebrated artists Gilbert and George. Other residents followed not long after the formation of the Trust, among them the music critic and broadcaster Edward Greenfield; Jocasta Innes, whose transformation of her derelict house prompted her study of historic paints and paintwork; the American Dennis Severs, who has made his house in Folgate Street the focus of the most unusual guided tour in London; and Michael Gillingham, antique dealer and champion of church organs, who is responsible for the restoration of one of the finest houses in the area.

In a transaction that enhanced the standing of the Spitalfield Trust's endeavours and brought prestige to the area, in 1981 the last 18th-century house in Spital Square, No.37, was bought from the Trust by the Society for the Preservation of Ancient Buildings. The Society converted the house, which was built

The whole first floor front of 15 Elder Street (right) is panelled, although the mouldings are very simple. The stone chimney-place, complete with keystone, is typically Baroque. To its right is a door leading into a small closet.

At 19 Princelet Street (above) a row of weavers' lights can still be seen. The Huguenot weavers who settled in this area in the early 18th century sometimes worked in the same houses in which they lived – the weaving was carried out at the top of the houses, where the light was best. Here the windows are old-fashioned metal casements rather than the wooden sashes used on lower floors.

between 1740 and 1750, into a headquarters building for itself and its offshoot the Georgian Group, whose specific aim is to protect Britain's Georgian heritage.

The Spitalfields houses were built in ones and twos by bricklayers and carpenters who took short building leases, usually of two years, from four or five landlords. In some cases they failed to complete their work on time, lost the property and went bankrupt. But those who were successful were able to obtain and sell a long lease. The principal buyers were Huguenots, many of them weavers, fleeing religious persecution in France after the Revocation of the Edict of Nantes in 1685, which meant the end of a climate of tolerance towards French Protestants.

Spital Square was laid out in 1719. Leases in Elder Street were being granted in 1723 and 1724. These were for the relatively short period of 60 years, a fact that is sometimes used to explain why many of the houses were far from substantial in construction. Each house was basically a brick box of four external walls, with an internal crosswall that was most often timber-framed but in a few cases was of brick. Floors

were of timber, supported on timber joists that ran in opposite directions on each floor to provide extra rigidity. All the wood was Baltic pine, imported from northern Germany, Scandinavia and Russia. Roofs were in the shape of an "M" with a central valley gutter – this was the cheapest way of roofing houses with a depth of some 30 feet (9m). Repair work has revealed that the houses were built directly on the ground without foundations, which limited their height to three or four storeys.

Some of the early houses were just one room deep, with only one room on each floor. No.15 Elder Street, which was restored by the architectural historian Dan Cruickshank, began this way. House sizes varied, but most consisted of a basement, a ground floor, first floor and second floor, and sometimes an attic. Basements were set lower than in later houses, without a front area and with just three or four steps up to the front door. Street levels were usually built up at the time of construction, occasionally with vaulted coal cellars built out beneath what is now the pavement. For this reason backyards are often at

60

In the entrance hall of
15 Elder Street the floor,
panelling, doors, door cases
and staircase are of wood.
Although the hall is narrow,
the treatment is strongly
architectural; pilasters, with
bases and capitals, frame
the way through the house
to the stair.

In the staircase of 15 Elder
Street (above) the joiner
showed great ingenuity in
handling the necessarily
rapid decrease in size of
the turned balusters. The
scrolled ends of the stair
treads provide a further
ornamental flourish.

basement or natural ground level. Gardens were rare, although the grander houses in Fournier Street, behind Christ Church, Spitalfields, have spacious gardens that survive today.

The front basement room was usually a kitchen with a stone floor, built-in dressers (many of which are extant) and a big fireplace for cooking. The front door opened into a passage leading to a staircase, usually at the back of the house. At the front was the dining room, and at the back a parlour in which the owner often carried out business. The drawing room was on the first floor, and bedrooms were on the second. Ground- and first-floor rooms were usually panelled, those above rarely so. Fireplaces had blue Delft tiles and built-in cupboards, often fitted with shaped "Baroque" shelves for displaying china.

A number of owners conducted business from their homes and, because money and goods changed hands

there, security became an important consideration. For this reason there were bars on the basement windows as well as internal shutters, and in about half the houses there is evidence of external shutters to the ground-floor windows. Householders were in fear not only of robbery but also of violent protests from the low-paid weavers toiling in sweatshops all over the East End, especially in neighbouring Bethnal Green, where riots periodically broke out.

Behind the houses were some of the first mews to be built in London. The mews buildings, which have all disappeared, included, in addition to coach-houses and stables, smaller houses.

Many of the houses still possess their original sash windows – with six panes in each sash – and sash boxes. One house in Princelet Street still has the old pulleys for festoon curtains. All rooms had fireplaces except the back basement room and the attics, which

No.4 Fournier Street (right) is one of the largest houses in Spitalfields and has a correspondingly spacious hall and staircase. The mahogany stair balustrade turns in a grand sweep at the bottom, where it meets a stone-flagged floor.

Although the overall appearance of the façade of No.27 Fournier Street (below) is reserved, a Baroque note is struck by the keystones above the windows and the hooded doorways. At the top is a well-preserved row of weavers' lights.

would have benefited from warmth rising through the building. The chimney-stacks, set in the side walls, still project substantially into the rooms (although not as far as in the 17th-century terrace houses in Newington Green – see pages 54–5).

Dan Cruickshank points out the subtle hierarchy of detail from room to room at 15 Elder Street. The ground-floor front room has six-panel doors, with a full architrave or frame. The panelling has an ovolo moulding with a course of dentils, although in the room at the back the ovolo was not used. On the first floor there are two-panel doors and on the second floor the back room is only panelled to dado height. An interesting detail here are the peepholes in the shutters, which, even when closed at night, provided a view of the street.

The treatment of the staircase becomes simpler as it ascends, changing at the first half-landing, where the stairs disappear from the sight of guests, who would in most cases penetrate no farther than the ground floor. "The builders of these houses knew the classical language of architecture. It's not naïve, charming and misunderstood. There are proper Doric cornices, correctly detailed," says Dan Cruickshank. An example of such attention to detail is seen in the skilful handling of the cornices, which are unavoidably interrupted by the tops of windows that sit beneath relatively low ceilings.

Privies were in the yards at the back of the houses. One survives behind the Rectory of Christ Church, at 2 Fournier Street, and is attributed to Nicholas Hawksmoor (1661–1736), the great architect of this and other fine churches in London. Upstairs there were small powder closets, which were sometimes squeezed beside a chimney breast, where a box privy containing a bucket could be kept.

Some of the houses have "weavers' windows": long bands of casement windows providing ample light for the attic storey. There is dispute as to whether any are original, but Douglas Blain says that those at 5–7 Elder Street are built into the brick fabric. Others were added later, providing a parallel with weavers' cottages in West Yorkshire, for example at Hebden Bridge (see pages 126–7).

The fortunes of the Spitalfields weavers of the 18th century were dependent on constantly changing government policy on imported fabrics, and it is believed that few of the houses survived in grand single-family use for more than a generation. This is the main reason why so many early features are retained. Serious decline set in with the introduction from France of the Jacquard loom, which was widely in use by 1810, putting out of business all handloom weavers except those who could make a speciality of ties, ribbons and hatbands.

The Czech town of Litomerice stands above the River Elbe halfway between Prague and Dresden, in neighbouring Germany. Litomerice is in the northern part of the former kingdom of Bohemia, which, like Bavaria and Austria, possessed its own extravagant brand of Baroque architecture. The best-known exponents are Christoph and Kilian Ignaz Dientzenhofer, who worked in Prague and central Bohemia. In the north the most prominent architect was Ottavio Broggio, who was responsible for the ravishingly ornate town house (see opposite) built in Litomerice's main square between 1725 and 1730.

Following the devastation of the Thirty Years War (1618–48), many craftsmen migrated to Bohemia from northern Italy to help with the great rebuilding. However, rather than replan ruined town centres, builders of most town houses of the later 17th and 18th centuries used the existing deep medieval plots,

incorporating as much of the old structure as was possible. This made economic sense as the old houses were often massively constructed with stone vaults. Occasionally three or four plots were amalgamated to create a new aristocratic palace. However, for all the wealth of flamboyant Baroque town-house façades in Bohemia, there are very few complete Baroque buildings with a characteristic Baroque plan.

Broggio's father, Giulio, settled in Bohemia in the mid-17th century. The house on the square was long thought to have been built by Ottavio Broggio for himself, to show off his talents, but it now appears to have been built for a local family. It incorporates an earlier Gothic house, and there is a cellar below street level, reached by an internal staircase. The ground floor, set back behind a deep arcade (which formerly ran on through the houses on the left), is a mix of simple medieval cross vaults and more complex Baroque vaults.

Ottavio Broggio's Baroque house, shown in the middle (opposite), was built around 1725–30. The house incorporates the shell of a much earlier building, as do many apparently Baroque and Rococo houses in the area. The painting is as rich and elaborate as that of contemporary churches.

Bohemian Baroque
LITOMERICE

The staircase has flights that rise through a vista of arches, thus providing a good example of the Baroque love of perspective effects. The treatment is strongly architectural, with stone columns, vaults and iron railings.

Typically the ground floor of such a house was a workshop if the house belonged to an artisan, or a shop if it was owned by a merchant. The big change that came with Baroque was the introduction of more monumental staircases. First-floor rooms were for family use, with servants on the second floor or in the attic. Most rooms had open beam ceilings until the reign of the Empress Maria Theresa in the mid-18th century, when a decree necessitated the introduction of plaster ceilings as a fire precaution. These new ceilings were simply inserted below the beams, so that many beautiful painted examples from the Baroque, Renaissance and even earlier periods are still being found above later plaster.

Bohemian houses had casement windows, and toward the end of the 18th century second pairs of windows, outside and level with the façades, began to be introduced to provide better insulation. A debate continues as to whether these additions, which create picturesque, mirror-like reflections, should remain. The deep plan deprived rooms in the middle of the house of windows, but it must be remembered that fresh air was widely regarded as best avoided. During the 18th century skylights became more common.

Decorative effect was concentrated above all on the main façade, and took the form of the abundant delicate ornamental detail that would normally be

The plan (below) shows the original design of the row above. The arcade once continued under all three buildings, and the house in the middle formerly had two shaped gables at the top, while the one on the left had an extra storey, emphasized by arches and pilasters.

reserved for interiors. The architects who designed such façades freely mixed stone and stucco – to the extent that in some cases it is difficult to distinguish between the two – and a thin layer of stucco was sometimes applied over the stone. Façades were also brightly painted, further blurring the distinction between materials. During the 17th century paintwork was often used to simulate strongly coloured stone or even marble. Later in the 18th century pastel colours were introduced.

The Broggio house is like a slice of a grand palace in Prague or Vienna, with giant pilasters rising through the storeys. The architectural and decorative trim is in one colour, the background in another. At the top is a more traditional gable, fronting the end of the roof, although this too had a Baroque swan pediment with a scrolled top and larger scrolls to the side. The delight of this façade is that it exhibits all the first frothy exuberance of Rococo, visible in the "S" and "C" curves and shellwork under the second-floor windows. Flowers and garlands abound, hanging from the capitals of the pilasters and around the gable window.

The first-floor windows, which feature "pinched" pediments, are typical of central Europe, and were derived from engravings of Italian Baroque palaces. Broggio took pleasure in elaborating every detail: the pilaster strips framing the windows, with their own bracket capitals, the bulbous scrolls beneath them, and the aprons below the sills embroidered with lace-like decoration.

During the Communist era private property was expropriated, but now, with the return of democracy, many town properties like this are being "restituted" to their former owners. That so many have survived is a tribute to the heroic work of the official Czech monuments service during the years of Communism.

NEO-CLASSICAL
Elegance

The imposing Circus in Bath, England, was begun in 1754, to the design of the architect John Wood the elder. The design is based on that of the ancient Roman Colosseum, turned inside out and reduced in scale to become the front of 32 town houses. The monumental effect is increased by the pairing of the columns and the elaborately carved Doric frieze over the ground floor.

The 18th century saw the ascendancy of Palladianism in England, at the same time as the fashion for Rococo embellishment swept all of Europe. France led the way in sophistication and comfort, but the English terrace house set the pattern for urban living in North America, from New England to the Deep South. In both Georgian Bath and Regency Brighton streets and squares of terrace houses offer some of the most elegant domestic classical architecture to be found anywhere, while in Potsdam, Germany, Frederick the Great lined the streets with a distinctive form of miniature *palazzo*.

This remarkable house, at Rue de Seine 57 (below), was designed by the architect Pierre-Jean Varin for himself in the 1740s. Above the ground floor the façade is exactly symmetrical, with Rococo iron grilles. Typical of the period are the soft curves of the arches, the richly carved keystones and the characteristically French banded stonework.

The 18th century, like the 17th, was a period of intensive building in Paris. Mercier, in *Le Nouveau Paris* (1797), talks of no fewer than 600 fine houses either newly built or renovated with interiors that "seemed to be the work of fairies." The architect Pierre Patte (1723–1814) had no regrets for the passing of a time when the grand French house was like a shell, with everything within sacrificed to "a magnificent exterior." Of the interiors he writes: "The drawing-rooms were two storeys high, the saloons vast, the ballrooms immense, the galleries so long that they ran out of sight, and the staircases gigantic ..." Houses were used solely for the purpose of entertaining guests, he says, so Parisians knew nothing of living in comfort and privacy.

Patte continues: "All the convenient arrangements which one admires in our modern houses, in which one room is so artfully separated from another, the staircases so cunningly hidden ... none of these were invented till our day." These innovations he dates to the Palais Bourbon in 1722: "As regards interior decoration this change led to the substitution of delicate and light carving, at once tasteful and capable of a thousand variations, in the place of ornaments with which rooms had hitherto been overloaded." Beams

Refinement and comfort
PARIS

were abolished or concealed by ceilings and rich cornices. Paintings and enormous bas-reliefs were removed from their traditional place above the mantelpiece, and mirrors began to appear on the walls. With their play of reflections these gave rooms "an air of gaiety and grandeur."

Throughout the 17th century many of the most fashionable houses had been built in the Marais, just to the east of the centre, and, from the 1650s, on the nearby Ile-St-Louis. During the reign of Louis XV (1715–74) the nobility moved to the district of the Faubourg St Germain, on the Left Bank, while the financiers settled in the Rue de Richelieu and the neighbourhood of the Palais Royal and the Tuileries, on the Right Bank. The hub of Paris continued to be the Pont Neuf, which links the Ile de la Cité with both banks of the River Seine.

Mercier provides a vivid description of a typical day in the heart of late-18th-century Paris: "At seven all the gardeners appear with their empty baskets, on their way to their gardens, astride their worn-out hacks. There are no coaches about and one only meets clerks, already dressed and curled, at this early hour." At nine came the wigmakers and then the confectioners' boys carrying coffee and syrups to furnished apartments. At ten came a black host of minions of the Law, followed at noon by stockbrokers and jobbers crowding to the Bourse. At two o'clock appeared those who were dining in town, walking on their toes for fear of soiling their white stockings. At three the streets were deserted while everyone was at dinner, but at a quarter past five the streets were packed again as people hurried to entertainments or

The façade of the Maison Dumet (above), completed ten years before Varin's house in the Rue de Seine, displays the same precise symmetry. At the same time the architect, Martin Goupy, emphasizes the central portion of the façade by providing variations in the design of the windows.

Rue Montorgueil 19 (right), built in 1776 by the little-known architect Treffeuille, lacks the curved ornament found on Rococo houses. The bold treatment of the first-floor windows echoes that of the central window of the neighbouring house, Goupy's Maison Dumet, dating from almost half a century earlier (see above).

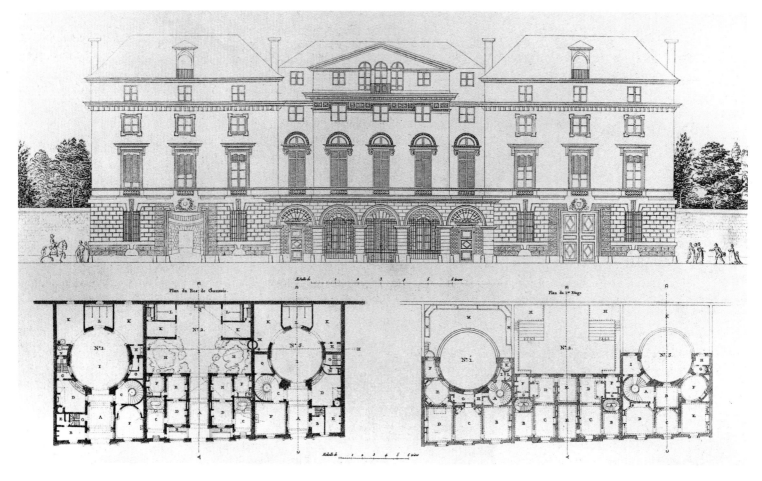

Plan du Rez de Chaussée.

Plan du 1er Étage.

These houses in the Rue St Georges (above) were built in 1788 by the architect François-Joseph Bélanger (1744–1818). The façades and roofs suggest that there are three houses, but the doors and the plans reveal that the central portion was two matching houses, one each side of a carriage arch. Architects in 18th-century France strove to meet clients' demands for a large number of rooms with specific purposes. The plans of the house on the left of the pair show that the ground floor had a vestibule, porter's lodge, kitchen, office, small dining room and lavatory. On the first floor was an antechamber, drawing room, bed chamber, lady's closet, cabinet, dressing room, *garderobe* and lavatories.

entrance leading through to a courtyard. Above the shop there might be an entresol. Above this was the *noble étage*, which contained the main apartment; this housed the owner or principal tenant, who sublet the other floors.

In Paris the 18th century was a period of transition to apartment-house living, when larger houses were let as single-floor, self-contained apartments, serving every class of inhabitant. By contrast, in London it was usual to rent a single room in a town house, or perhaps to have a bedroom upstairs and the use of the drawing room at certain times of day.

As you climb the stairs in the tall houses of Paris, the ceilings become progressively lower, an arrangement that was much criticized during the Revolution, but which ensured a healthy mixed community. The writer Arthur Young, in *Travels in France* 1787–89, remarked that the French lived much more often as families than did his fellow Britons, with married sons and daughters living at home in an apartment of their own, "which makes a joyous number at every table … nothing but good humour can render such a jumble of families agreeable or even tolerable." On some narrow plots there would be two or three *corps de logis* – in effect, separate households – with courtyards between them linked by archways.

Plans for the layout of 18th-century town houses are provided for us by the architect Tiercelet in his *Architecture* and also by Jacques-François Blondel in his nine-volume *Cours d'Architecture* (1771–77). French houses of this period stand out from their counterparts in Britain and North America, first for their much more elaborate floor plans and second for their greater emphasis on symmetry, even in houses no more than three windows wide.

The extent to which architects pursued symmetry in floor plans is evinced by J-Ch Krafft's *Plans, coupes, élévations des plus belles maisons à Paris et dans les environs*. Plate 17 shows three houses that were built by "Bellanger [Bélanger], Architecte, in the rue St Georges." There are floor plans for four houses; the larger central house being, in fact, a pair.

An interesting group of 18th-century houses is to be found in the Rue Montorgueil, which runs between the 1st and 2nd *arrondissements*, on the right bank of the Seine. No.15 is a remarkable house constructed by Martin Goupy in 1729. No.17, the Maison Dumet (or Chenot), was built in 1729–30 for the grocer Nicholas Dumet, which shows just how much a fashionable tradesman could prosper. This is a symmetrical front, five windows wide and with subtle emphasis on the central bay, which alone has

Place des Vosges 9 was acquired in 1701 by the Nicolaï family and is an eloquent example of Neo-classical decoration. Aymard-Charles Nicolaï redecorated, in Louis XVI style, a series of rooms, including this *salon* (right). The marbled walls give way to a beautifully coved ceiling, and the octagonal panels diminish in size to exaggerate the perspective effect. The central part of the ceiling is painted as open sky, suggesting a weariness with the gods and cherubs so beloved of the preceding Baroque age.

This exquisite Louis XVI decoration in Place des Vosges 9 (right) uses the pale-grey paint fashionable in the late 18th century; it is matched by a grey marble fireplace. The plasterwork panels of the walls are decorated with a succession of motifs: swirls of acanthus at the bottom, surmounted by birds, candelabra, foliage and fruit – and the cornice is richer still.

ornamental carving above and below the windows. Next door, in perfect contrast to the soft Rococo lines of the first two houses, is the severely Neo-classical Maison Gobin, built in 1776 by Treffeuille, an otherwise unknown architect. This is "stripped down" classicism so severe that it might almost date from the 1920s. Most of the windows are without moulded surrounds, the openings are starkly rectangular, and there are none of the garlands or swags often found in Louis XVI. The only architectural features are a pair of bold, symmetrically placed window heads and a prominent, very blockish cornice repeated at intervals up the front.

At Rue de Seine 57, in the Latin Quarter (7th *arrondissement*), is a house constructed by the architect Pierre-Jean Varin for himself. This is a delightfully elegant and restrained example of Louis XV. The Rococo detail is confined to the "S" and "C" scrollwork of the window grilles and the rich stone carving over the double-height entrance portal, which has a shellwork cartouche over the top of the arch, flanked by scrolled brackets that have the soft, almost molten look of much Rococo detail. Although the house is only three windows wide, it has double doors leading into a carriage entrance and a very substantial entresol. The main reception rooms, marked by the tallest windows, are at second-floor level. Also characteristic of Rococo are the gently arched "segmental" window heads.

Thanks largely to one organization – The Building of Bath Museum – which is perhaps the best of its kind anywhere, a wealth of documentation on the city's houses is available to the public. Bath, situated on the River Avon in south-west England, epitomizes classical harmony and order, so it is all the more surprising that it is not the creation of some enlightened but despotic grand duke, as would be the case in central Europe, but of a series of individual developers and speculators.

The presiding genii in the creation of the city were the two John Woods, father and son. John Wood the elder (1704–54) was the son of a local builder, and a visionary with a rare practical bent for getting things done on a grand scale. In London he struck up an acquaintance with the surgeon John Gay, who had inherited extensive lands to the north and west of Bath. Gay agreed to lease a large plot for 99 years, on which Wood was to build Queen Square (1729–39), where, for the first time in Britain, terraces of houses were designed to look like grand palace fronts. In the year of his death Wood the elder began the Circus,

The Royal Crescent (right) was built in 1767–75 to the designs of John Wood the younger. Constructed in the form of a large half-ellipse facing down a grassy slope, it was the first, as well as the largest and grandest, of its kind in Britain. The completely plain ground floor is surmounted by giant Ionic columns.

Classical perfection
BATH

The houses stepping down the hill are in Chatham Row and date from 1755. Each house had a pair of vaulted cellars built out under the street. At the top left the Paragon, built in 1768, is shown in section, revealing the huge task of terracing that was required to achieve a level site.

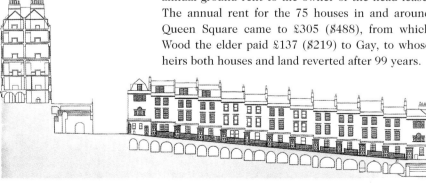

which was completed in 1767 by his son, who went on to build the Royal Crescent (1767–74), the first crescent in Britain.

The Woods and other entrepreneurs would sub-lease the building plots to developers, many of whom were in the building trades. These tenants would sign an agreement to build a house within a set period, usually two years, paying only a token rent. When the shell was complete the developers would advertise for a buyer, who paid a lump sum for both the shell and the lease of the plot, as well as an annual ground rent to the owner of the head lease. The annual rent for the 75 houses in and around Queen Square came to £305 ($488), from which Wood the elder paid £137 ($219) to Gay, to whose heirs both houses and land reverted after 99 years.

Bath's high land values led to the building of tall houses with narrow frontages. The developers were responsible for setting out the plots and preparing the land. The first step was to lay the "Grand Common Sewer" under the middle of the future street: an arched stone channel, about 5 feet (1.5m) high, that would carry away rainwater. The elder Wood had hoped to build on the level plain between Bath Abbey and the River Avon, but Gay's estate was on the other side of the city, and after the success of Queen Square the city rose on higher ground to the north. The stepped land required that many houses were built on a man-made platform known as a "terrass," from the French word for such a feature.

Each developer had to construct his house to an agreed design, and it was customary for a drawing of the façade to be made on the back of the lease. While 18th-century London was largely of brick, Bath is predominantly of stone. From 1726 a local landowner, Ralph Allen, who had made a fortune reorganizing the country's postal services, began to buy up quarries and bring blocks of local stone to Bath on a specially built railway. These were

The formal adoption of street names was in Bath, as elsewhere, a sign of growing orderliness. The handsome Roman letters were either painted straight onto a wall or carved into the stone facing (right) and then painted.

"dressed" into shape in open shelters called lodges, and sawn smooth at the front to create "ashlar." The ashlar blocks were used for the front of the house and laid with barely visible hairline mortar joints. Then the façade was combed down with a mason's drag to smooth out any blemishes so that it looked almost like a single piece of stone. Rougher "rubble" stone was used for the inside faces and for the rear.

The characteristic English sash windows had sash boxes set almost out of sight in a slit in the stone. Unusually, in Bath the lower sash descends straight onto the stone sill. The tops of windows, known as lintels, were usually a single block of stone, although sometimes the ground-floor lintel might be a long timber beam. This "bressumer" absorbed settlement in the wall and allowed the ground floor to be left open during construction so that builders could bring in heavy materials with ease.

The typical Bath terrace house has a sunken basement, to which access is gained by steps leading down to a large front area. Here, under the street, there is a row of vaults for coal, ashes, wood and weak beer. The basement contained the original kitchen and the servants' hall. On the ground floor were the dining room and the parlour, and on the first floor was the drawing room. The second floor contained the main bedrooms, while the children and servants slept above in the attic. Thanks to the abundance of springs, Bath had a reliable water supply. Hollowed elm trunks, laid beneath the road, delivered water into a large cistern in the kitchen. Most houses had a privy in the backyard, with a cesspit beneath it that was emptied in the early hours of the morning by "night soil" men.

These houses in Sydney Place have beautiful round-arched windows and doors. The ornamental ironwork contains a lampholder, and pretty drum-shaped balconies embellish the first-floor windows.

During the Second World War bombs devastated many German cities, but Potsdam fared better than most. Although no trace remains of the Royal Castle of the Prussian kings in the centre, Frederick the Great's (1740–86) legendary summer palace and gardens of Sanssouci survive immediately to the west of the town. Perhaps more surprisingly, street after street of well-preserved late-18th-century town houses still stand, as well as a fine Dutch quarter of the same period.

In 1739 Baron von Bielfeld wrote of Potsdam: "This town, very much smaller than the capital, serves as the ordinary residence of the king [and] his regiment." The *Imperial Gazetteer* of 1876 described it as "one of the handsomest and most regularly built towns in Germany ... laid out in straight, spacious, well-paved streets, or large and elegant public squares."

Another vivid picture is provided by John Moore in *View of Society and Manners in France, Germany and Switzerland* (1774): "The houses are built of a

These gabled houses (right), to be found at the western end of Charlottenstrasse in Potsdam's well-preserved 18th-century Dutch quarter, front the street – a common practice in the Netherlands. Their frontages are of brick, whereas the other houses in the town are faced in stucco.

Courtiers' houses
POTSDAM

fine white freestone, almost all of them new and nearly all of the same height. The streets are regular and well paved, and there are some very magnificent public buildings." The king, he continues, desired to see the town increase and "several monied people built houses, partly to pay their court to his Majesty, and partly because, by letting them, they found they would receive very good interest for their money." However, the town did not grow as fast as Frederick wished, so "his Majesty ordered several streets to be built at once, at his own expense. This immediately sunk the value of the houses, and the first builders found they had disposed of their money very injudiciously."

Moore was surprised to "see buff-belts, breeches, and waistcoats, hanging out to dry from the genteelest looking houses till I was informed, that each housekeeper has two or more soldiers quartered in his house, and their apartments are, for the most part, on the first floor, with windows to the street." It was Frederick the Great himself who chose to quarter his troops with citizens rather than in barracks.

The Potsdam houses are distinctive. Most terrace houses are tall and narrow in proportion; these are low and wide. Typically they are just two storeys over

a virtually submerged basement, with three or four steps up to the front door. In style they are soberly classical, like Louis XVI architecture in France. Some are monumental, miniature palaces with giant pilasters and statues and urns on the parapet. Strong horizontal lines dominate – a cornice and shallow parapet at the top and pronounced bands or string courses between the ground and first floors. Windows are emphatically treated, with crisp surrounds, and many have pediments and panels above or below.

That they are houses is evident from the regularly spaced front doors. Inside, the closely spaced windows dictated the positions of internal walls, and rooms with just one window were in some cases very narrow. Houses were two rooms deep, with staircases set at the back. Moore had a poor opinion of the finishing, furniture and conveniences within the houses, where, interestingly, the details of the staircases are still almost Baroque.

Most of the houses are by known architects, notably A L Krueger, J R H Richter and G C Unger. Good runs are found in streets running east from Sanssouci: Charlottenstrasse, Brandenburgerstrasse and Kaiser-Wilhelmstrasse. Numerous Neo-classical houses survive, most with rusticated stonework on

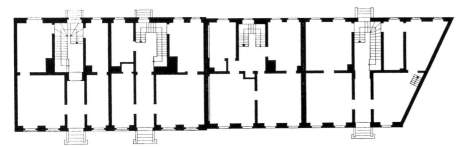

GROUND FLOORS AND ONE FIRST FLOOR

the ground floor and distinctive repeating window treatment on the first floor. The "pinched" or arched pediments are typical. In some cases the windows are set in recessed panels to give a clean geometric look. In the communist era many of these houses were left unpainted, so the stucco was a bare drab grey. Today some are picked out in pastel pinks, blues and yellows, very often in two tones – pale for the background and stronger for the architectural trim.

The houses in the Dutch quarter form four harmonious blocks. The houses, which are faced in brick rather than stone, are mostly three windows wide and of two storeys topped by powerful shaped gables that rise almost as high again. Bielfeld approved of the "quarter built absolutely in the manner of towns of north Holland, where the inhabitants, most of them Dutch, ensure cleanliness reigns." This was a district where craftsmen and merchants lived side by side with soldiers and officials. After the long, drab years of communism it is now being revived as a Bohemian quarter that is home to artists and craftsmen.

An elevation and plan of four Neo-classical houses at Charlottenstrasse 16–19 (above) that were built in the reign of Frederick the Great of Prussia and still stand. They are designed like a series of small palaces, but the number of front doors indicates that they are more like terrace houses – in this case conceived as matching pairs. The plan of the third house from the left shows the layout of the upper floor.

After years of decay, many of the houses, including this one in Kiezstrasse (right), are now being painted in pastel colours. The treatment of the windows, whether arched or square-headed, is always elaborate, with ornamental panels both above and below.

Nos.3–6 Grafton Street, Mayfair (right), are part of a group of 14 houses built from 1768 onward. Their plain brick exteriors give no hint of the opulence within. The architect, Sir Robert Taylor (1714–88), was surveyor to several substantial London estates, including those of the Duke of Grafton and the lawyers of Lincoln's Inn.

No.4 (below), built for Lord Villiers, was completed in 1775. With its stone paving, columns and cross vault, the hall is strongly architectural in treatment. The stone stair beyond it is cantilevered out from the wall.

The typical Georgian terrace house in London is four, five or six storeys high and the first question many visitors ask is: "How do you manage all those stairs?" One answer was provided in 1817 by a Frenchman, Louis Simond, who wrote that "the agility, the ease, the quickness with which the individuals of the family run up and down and perch on the different storeys give the idea of a cage with its sticks and birds." Each family, he says, "occupies a whole house, unless very poor," with one storey "for eating, one for sleeping, a third for company, a fourth underground for the kitchen, and perhaps a fifth at the top for the servants."

While fashionable Parisian streets were lined with aristocrats' mansions set back in large courtyards, in London a large part of the nobility owned terrace houses that were indistinguishable from those of their neighbours. The peculiar uniformity of London houses sprang from the system of leases granted by ground landlords as fashionable London spread west

The four grades of house
LONDON

during the 18th century, from Soho to Piccadilly and Mayfair, and then to Chelsea and Paddington, as well as northward through Fitzrovia and Bloomsbury.

After the Great Fire of London of 1666, a series of building acts established a growing body of regulations governing the design of London houses. These were aimed first at eliminating fire risks. From 1709, sash boxes and sash windows had to be set back at least 9 inches (23cm) behind the façade. Timber eaves and cornices were banned, as fire could spread along buildings from one house to another.

These various acts were codified and elaborated in the Great London Building Act of 1774. According to tradition, this was drafted by two of London's leading architects, Sir Robert Taylor and George Dance the Younger. The Victorians later dubbed it the "Black Act," because of the uniformity it introduced, and Gower Street, which is one of the longest runs of Georgian houses in London, was the subject of a famous tirade by John Ruskin, the English art critic and social reformer.

Today many are unaware that these houses were once of a warm, even golden-yellow, stock brick, which two centuries of coal fires and industrial soot have darkened to charcoal. Yet when cleaned, as

These plans illustrate the layout of the basement and ground floor of a "first rate" house, as defined by the London Building Act of 1774. The basement contains the front kitchen (A), wine cellar (B), back kitchen (C), servants' hall (D), butler's pantry (E) and water-closet (F). On the ground floor was the dining room (G), library (H), water-closet (I), bathroom (J) and stable (K).

The view up the staircase of No.4 (below) reveals the stairhall and the second-floor gallery bathed in light by the large oval dome above. The slender elegance of the decorative plasterwork and ironwork matches the graceful curve of the stair.

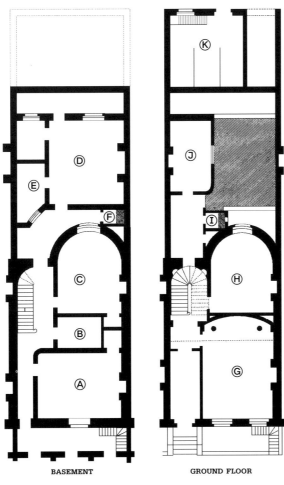

BASEMENT   GROUND FLOOR

Robust columns in No.4's first-floor ballroom (right), contrast with the shallow relief of the Wedgwood-like medallion and trailing garlands. The ornament of the white marble fireplace matches the plasterwork of the walls.

balcony above. Inside, the ground floor consists of a dining room and library behind, with a water-closet and ample bathroom beyond. The third-rate house is simply a slightly scaled-down version of the second-rate, with one window on the ground floor rather than two. Nicholson's drawing shows how the flues run up the sides of the house to a long bank of chimneys at the top; those on the second floor snake dramatically to avoid the fireplaces immediately above. The fourth-rate house is of three storeys over a basement entirely below ground, and has the benefit of arch-headed windows with especially elegant glazing bars.

First-rate houses were often occupied by wealthy, fashionable families, whose needs were typically attended to by a butler, up to three footmen, a groom, a coachman, a nursery maid, a cook and two or three housemaids, a housekeeper and a governess. Second- and third-rate houses were usually the homes of professional men and merchants, and fourth-rate houses those of artisans. There was a strong correlation between a house's location and the social class of its occupants. A person of any class was likely to be able to afford a larger house in a less fashionable or outlying district. Individual rooms, or whole floors,

many examples have been south of the Thames, especially in the borough of Lambeth, they appear startlingly colourful on a sunny day.

The 1774 Act defined four "rates," or grades, of house in London; these are beautifully illustrated in a pattern book of 1823, Peter Nicholson's *New and Improved Practical Builder*. The first-rate house is of four storeys above a sunken basement. It has bands of "rusticated" stone on the ground floor and pairs of pilasters above. The first floor has the tallest windows, descending almost to floor level; above, the windows reduce in size from sashes of six over six panes to four over four. The sections show grand rooms on both ground and first floors – there are double folding doors leading into the back on the first floor. The staircase, ascending in a gracious curve, is what Americans call a "winder." An extra flourish was provided by giving unusual shapes to the rooms – an alcove in the ground-floor dining room (suitable for an Adamesque sideboard) and a bowed library behind. Nicholson's plans show water-closets in the basement and on the ground floor, and at the back is a bathroom, an innovation at this date. Beyond this there is a small stable block with stalls for three horses, and a coach-house next door.

The second grade of house, far from being "second-rate," would today sell for a sum in the region of £1 million ($1,600,000) in a good location. The only ornament is provided by columns and a fanlight framing the front door, and the elegant Grecian iron

The first floor of this elegant Georgian house in George Street, in the West End, has a drawing room with long sash windows opening onto a continuous balcony. Under the 1774 London Building Act, the house was classified as "second-rate."

This plan of the ground floor of a second-rate house appears in Nicholson's *New and Improved Practical Builder* of 1823. The room at the front with rounded corners is the dining room; behind is the library. The wing at the back contains a water-closet and a bathroom.

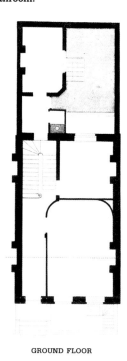

GROUND FLOOR

were regularly let to visitors when families grew up, or simply in order to supplement the family income. Benjamin Franklin lodged with a widow in Duke Street, Mayfair, who had a daughter, a servant, a shop boy and a 70-year-old lady living in the garret. In poorer houses there could be as many families as rooms – the usual practice was for the master of the house and his family to live on the ground floor, although the back room might also be let.

One purpose of the 1774 Act was to set construction standards for party walls between houses, which frequently caused disputes. Nicholson explains that "to combine strength and stability in an edifice, the walls, as they rise, should diminish in thickness." It was usual, he said, to diminish the walls on the inside faces, with the setbacks immediately under the ceilings, providing a secure support to the floor beams above. The floors "will tie the walls firmly together, and prevent them from spreading or approaching towards each other."

Nicholson also had advice on roofs: "Roofs that are high-pitched discharge rain and snow more quickly than those that are lower; they are less liable to be stripped of their covering by the wind, and the rain is less easily blown through their joists; but they are more expensive than low roofs as they require longer

timbers, and a greater quantity of covering. But though low roofs possess the advantage in point of economy, they require larger slates and greater care in the execution."

A classic group of first-rate houses was built in Grafton Street, Mayfair, to the designs of Sir Robert Taylor. Originally there were 14, but today only Nos.3–6 remain. No.4 was built for Lord Villiers, and appears in the rate books of 1775 at the substantial annual sum of £210 ($336). The house, which was built for entertaining, is now a company headquarters, and has a spacious stone-flagged vaulted entrance hall opening onto a elegant stone stair, cantilevered out from the walls. Hanging staircases are a virtuoso feature of the grander London town house. Each step is an individual slab of stone that is set no more than 6 inches (15cm) into the wall, yet the weight of brick pressing upon it is such that it remains perfectly firm. Taylor and his contemporaries heightened the sense of daring by sharply undercutting the individual treads, so much so that later owners felt compelled to put in columns to support them. The stair in the Grafton Street House leads only to the first floor, although there is a gallery at second-floor level. Access to the upper floors and basement is by means of a much narrower back stair immediately behind.

Stucco rustication (right) emphasizes the ground floor of this second-rate house in Blandford Street, Marylebone. As defined in the 1774 Act, second- and third-rate houses were similar externally, but the former had more floor space.

No.3 St Peter's Square, Hammersmith, a third-rate house built in the 1830s, consists of a basement with three storeys above. The first-floor drawing room (below) has the full-length sash windows typical for this date; these open onto a cantilevered balcony that overlooks the central garden. The room retains its original white-marble fireplace with the arched opening typical of late-Georgian houses.

On the ground floor two main rooms are set end to end; that at the back is the grandest in the house, with three-quarter-height columns carrying full entablatures, which, in turn, support arches. Below there is not only the usual sunken basement, lit from a front area, but also, below that, another complete storey of vaulted cellars, which had the great advantage of keeping the basement dry.

An idea of how these houses were used is provided by a sale catalogue of 1812 for No.9 Grafton Street, also by Taylor. On the ground floor were an entrance hall with a vaulted roof, a "capital dining parlour," "a library communicating," and a porter's room. On the first floor was a "a handsome lofty drawing room in front," with a marble chimney-piece and papered walls, communicating with a "breakfast parlour correspondingly finished." Above were "three excellent bedchambers, with closets," and above them "four very commodious servants' rooms." In the basement were a "housekeeper's room, fitted up with closets, etc, and a chamber adjoining," a water-closet, butler's pantry and "a very commodious and lofty kitchen, fitted up with dressers, shelves etc." In addition there were "a scullery with water laid on, coal holes, laundry, servants' hall, and cellars for wine, beer etc."

The internal layout of an 18th-century London house was very simple in comparison with those to be found in contemporary Paris, which featured, in addition to the principal rooms, a multitude of small rooms used for bathing, storing clothes or simply sitting cosily in private – all of which were planned with the greatest geometric intricacy.

Taylor's own house in Spring Gardens, Westminster, now long demolished, was, according to his obituary, a "great curiosity for the economy of space, fanciful shapes and multiplied accommodations." Nicholson also writes: "All rooms beside square and rectangular are denominated fanciful, or fancy rooms, which may be made very beautiful." Another means of creating variety during this period was to introduce coved rather than flat ceilings.

A description of "common houses in London" can be found in *A Complete Body of Architecture* (1756) by the architect Isaac Ware. Here he describes the layout of a small house "for the reception of a family of two or three people, with three or four servants." The front room below was the kitchen. On the ground floor the fore-parlour was the best room (reserved for visitors and special occasions), with a back parlour behind for everyday use. On the first floor there was a dining room at the front, a bed-chamber at the back and a closet in a small back extension. Ware continues: "In houses something better than the common kind, the back room should be a drawing-room, or a dressing room, for the lady"

These three-storey houses in Harrowby Street, Marylebone, conform to the 1774 Act's fourth rate. The ground floors have stucco to imitate stonework but there are no first-floor balconies.

into animal fat. A rush light of the typical length of 2 feet 4 inches (70cm) would burn for just under an hour. Of better quality were the tallow candles used by artisans and the middle classes. Made of rendered animal fat, these tended to smell and to require constant snuffing and trimming to stop the tallow melting too quickly. Best, but much more expensive, was the beeswax candle, which burnt more slowly, gave more light and smelt less.

London houses were heated by coal fire and had a fireplace in almost every room, as the number of chimney-pots on the chimney-stacks between houses indicates. Foreign visitors always remarked on the smog that hung over London; Benjamin Franklin wrote in 1758: "The whole town is one great smoaky House, and every street a chimney, the air full of floating sea coal soot and you never get a sweet breath of what is pure, without riding some miles for it in the country." London houses consumed huge quantities of coal, for cooking as well as heating, and this was stored in cellars beneath the street.

The London Building Act of 1724 required the fronts of houses to carry rainwater pipes, which in many cases fed a butt or tank in the front area; many houses also had wells. Water was also available from water carriers, but 18th-century London was also served by several private water companies, which provided a supply through wooden pipes made of elm trunks buried beneath the streets. Connections to individual householders who paid the required fee were made through small pipes, or "quills." Water was supplied for a set number of hours a day or week. In the 1760s Soho was "charged" for seven hours on three days a week; Oxford Street for 15 hours a week. Water was stored in handsome lead cisterns, often embossed with the date and initials of the owner, which stood in either the front area, the vaults under

to receive guests, "for it is better not to have any bed on this floor." The two rooms on the second floor were for bedrooms, and there was a third bedroom if the back extension continued up. Over these were garrets, "which may be divided up into a larger number than the floors below, for the reception of beds for servants." However, the need to separate the sexes meant that sometimes "a bed for one man, or two maid-servants is contrived to let down in the kitchen." In this case, Ware advised, the floor should be of boards not stone, out of "the necessary care of those peoples health."

A wealth of fascinating detail about 18th-century terrace houses is provided in *Life in the Georgian City* by Dan Cruickshank and Neil Burton. In England little use was made of the oil lights popular on the European mainland. Poorer houses would be lit by rush lights, made by dipping common rushes

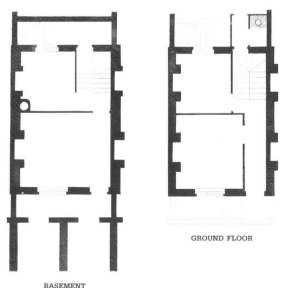

GROUND FLOOR

BASEMENT

the streets, the backyard or the kitchen itself. Water-closets on floors above were sometimes served by water pumped through lead pipes set in the walls. From 1816, according to William Chadwell Mylne, Surveyor to the New River Company, iron pipes were introduced in place of wood, so the "Company could serve the top floor of any house in the district, and the pipes are always full."

In the great majority of 18th-century houses the drains discharged into a cesspool. These were periodically emptied by nightmen, who gained this name because they were compelled to operate between the hours of midnight and five o'clock in the morning. This made Georgian London a noisy place at night. According to the poet Robert Southey, "the clatter of the nightmen has scarcely ceased before that of the morning carts begins."

Today many London terrace houses have thriving well-tended back gardens, but during the mid-18th century these were a rarity. "Some attempt to make flower-gardens of these little spots," Ware wrote, "but … plants require a purer air than animals."

This West End house (right), in Molyneux Street, is equivalent to fourth-rate under the 1774 definitions. Although simple in design, houses such as this are an ideal size for family living today. The long first-floor windows are those of the drawing room. Slight differences between houses indicate the work of different builders, who nonetheless all worked to a plan stipulated by the ground landlord.

The plans (left) show the basement of a fourth-rate house in St Peter's Square, Hammersmith, with two large coal cellars under the street, a kitchen at the front and a washroom at the back. On the ground floor there is a dining room at the front, a back parlour behind it and a water-closet beyond the stairs.

Wide stone steps, flanked by iron railings, lead up to the front door of 46 Fitzwilliam Square (right). The door is a replacement dating from the 19th century, but the fanlight above it is Georgian in style.

This fine matching pair of front doors in Merrion Square (below) has, in addition to the fanlights, narrow windows at each side of the door to increase the amount of light entering the hall. The arch within an arch is in the style of Robert Adam (1728–92). Particularly characteristic are the garlands above the fanlight and the unusual capitals to the columns, which support a frieze without an architrave below.

Dublin is one of the most delightful of all Georgian cities. Here is a wealth of well-preserved domestic architecture, covering the whole Georgian period, Baroque and Rococo, Palladian and Neo-classical. The beauty – and the surprise – of Dublin's terrace houses lies in a wealth of often exquisite and always lively plasterwork; not just the rich cornices found in standard London houses, although these are to be seen too, but also the rich ornament flowing across ceilings, walls and staircases.

Many of those who visited Georgian Dublin were struck by the proximity in equal measure of beauty and poverty. John Barrow in his *Tour round Ireland*, published in 1836, observed that "Of all the cities which I have seen, not St Petersburg even excepted, Dublin displays every species of patchwork in its buildings and its inhabitants, more in extreme and more in juxtaposition, than any other I believe in the world." Other visitors simply admired Dublin's wide streets. Anne Plumptre, in her *Residence in Ireland* (1817), described Portland Place in London's West End, Sackville Street in Dublin and the Canebière in Marseilles as being "the three widest streets I have anywhere seen."

Streets and squares
DUBLIN

Apart from an agreement governing the alignment of the fronts of the buildings (and in St Stephen's Green, in the heart of the city, there is not even that), there is no repeating plan or elevation in Dublin. Some houses have ground floors of rusticated granite, but most are brick. Whereas both Georgian Bath and Edinburgh are built of stone, Georgian Dublin is almost entirely of soft pink brick. An individual house may be of three, four or five windows in width, and some are of just two, squeezed in between larger neighbours. The parapets or eaves step up and down from one house to the next. Local blacksmiths responded with robust Baroque, swirling Rococo and slender Regency designs. Their early 19th-century black verandahs display a lace-like intricacy.

Fitzwilliam Square, smaller and more intimate than St Stephen's Green or Merrion Square, retains a marvellous sense of tranquillity. Its history has been explored in fascinating detail by Mary Bryan, conservation officer of the Irish Georgian Society. The first leases were granted by Viscount Fitzwilliam in 1791

Dublin houses, among them these in Fitzwilliam Square, are of brick rather than stone or stucco, with little architectural trim and rarely even a cornice at the top. Their appeal lies in the pure elegance of proportion, the handsome doorways and the iron balconies of widely varying pattern.

and 1792 for plots on the north, west and east sides of the square. These stipulated that the houses should fill the width of the plots, with fronts of red stock brick and slate roofs, and should be not less than three and a half storeys high above the cellars, with a front area 8 feet (2.4m) wide, enclosed with a stone kerb and iron palisades, with "flags," or stone paving, in front to form a continuous pavement.

The leases carried with them a covenant stipulating that building should take place within four years, but the Napoleonic Wars of 1800–1814 brought

recession to Dublin, and Mary Bryan quotes one leaseholder as writing to Lord Fitzwilliam: "Eject me if you will, I will be glad to get rid of my bargain." As in London, the early leases were taken by builders who erected one, two or occasionally more houses at a time, hoping to sell them quickly. Initially a peppercorn rent was charged. When a house was completed, a lease of 150 years was offered.

The building of Fitzwilliam Square began in 1797 and took 30 years to complete. Four houses are shown on a map of 1798. In all there were 69 houses, compared with 72 in Mountjoy Square and 84 in Merrion Square. The width of plot varied between 25 feet (7.6m) and 27 feet (8.2m) and the usual length was 200 feet (61m) from front to back. The typical layout consisted of a main block two rooms deep, and a narrower wing (a "return") at the back, then a garden. Backing on to this was a coach-house overlooking a yard that opened into the stable lane.

Seven of the houses are three bays wide – that is, with three windows within their full width – and the rest have two bays. A number have granite rustication on the ground floor. The red brick was brought from Bristol, Chester and Liverpool; it was considered superior to the local yellowish Dolphin's Barn brick which was used for chimney-stacks, inside walls and to build the "rere" – the rear in British and North American English. Parapets, usually with granite coping stones, hide the shallow-pitch roofs behind. As built, all the houses have four full storeys above the basement, but the parapet line varies just a little from house to house, in typical Dublin fashion.

Windows in Georgian Dublin were always sashes, tall on the first floor and square at the top. As in London, the ground-floor window was sometimes out of line with those above, reflecting a preference for internal symmetry over external. Mary Bryan notes that 35 houses retain original guards to the second- and third-floor windows, and that all but 17 of the houses have original basement windows, complete with window bars. However, wooden sashes have been removed from houses and replaced by a mixture of plate glass and small-pane casements.

Fitzwilliam Square has some fine front doors. The typical door-case has Doric or Ionic columns or pilasters, with a fanlight above. A delightful feature is the bootscrapers on the top step, some with an acanthus or anthemion motif, others with griffons.

Houses are described as left- or right-handed, according to the position of the front door. This leads into a front hall with a large front room leading off it. A distinctively Irish feature is a brass rail just inside the front door – possibly a stand for umbrellas. The back hall, which contains the staircase, is separated from the front hall by one or sometimes two arches, occasionally with an inner door and fanlight above. Staircases are of wood with turned wooden balusters. Mahogany handrails are beautifully shaped, with discreet oblique joins.

Although it is of handsome proportion, this drawing room in a recently restored house in Fitzwilliam Square has only the simplest of cornices. This restraint is an excellent foil to the strongly coloured walls and curtains and the polychrome chimneypiece.

The crisp Neo-classical detail in the interior of this house in Fitzwilliam Square is Greek rather than Roman in style. A necking is used beneath the exquisite scrolls of the Ionic columns, and anthemion motifs appear in the frieze above.

Dublin's Georgian terraces were not built as palace compositions, as they often were in London and Edinburgh. The cliff-like effect of identical façades is attractively softened by expanses of Virginia creeper – here, in Fitzwilliam Square West, turning an autumnal red – and the bright white paint of the window reveals.

A half-landing leads to the return at the back of the house. Mary Bryan explains that "in many of the houses the entrance to the return is framed by twin columns set in what is really a very ornate vestibule or anteroom. Where the return goes no higher they are often lit by a semicircular headed window. They're a mystery – no one knows what they were for." Beyond lies a large room filling the entire return, with an end window overlooking the garden. Perhaps this feature is to be explained by the Irish love of parties, cards and other forms of gaming. The first floor is a *piano nobile*, with the best rooms in the house, the front and back, interconnected by double doors. Windows here descend to the floors, as in Regency houses in London, with panelled shutters that fold neatly into the reveals. The back rooms, by contrast, have one window, a tall, wide, three-light "Wyatt" window named after the English architect James Wyatt (1746–1813), who was fond of this feature.

The main staircase sometimes rises only to the second floor. In such cases, it is continued by a smaller dogleg stair at right angles leading to the third floor, which often had four small bedrooms, each with only one window.

As in earlier Dublin houses, the great glory of the interiors of Fitzwilliam Square is the plasterwork. Many of the later houses have coved ceilings, rising arch or cushion fashion from the cornice. Six entrance halls have eagles as centrepieces.

From the ground floor three or four steps descend to the return, from where the stair continues down to the basement. At the back many gardens have been taken over for car parking, but, remarkably, 26 mews houses are extant.

The Act of Union with Great Britain in 1800 spelt dramatic change for Dublin. The aristocracy moved to London, and Dublin lost its Parliament, but a new professional class, mostly doctors and lawyers, carried on with the building of grand, elegant town houses.

A fine example of the unadorned beauty of simple town-house architecture is seen in Mahón, capital of Minorca, one of the Balearic Islands off eastern Spain. Mahón's superb deep-water harbour, where even today's large cruise ships can anchor, attracted the interest of Britain's Royal Navy. Having been devastated during the Turkish assault on the island in 1553, this little town grew rapidly under the British, who occupied Minorca for three periods in the 18th century. Their legacy is the English-style sash window, which survives everywhere (these are known in Minorcan dialect as "window," while bow windows are "boinder" and cobbles "coddles").

The town's identity is established by a harmonious core of white-fronted houses, given character by dark-green shutters and doors, and cornices that step up and down from one house to the next. These are single-family houses that were built side by side along narrow streets, many of them in the 18th and early 19th centuries. They are found not only within the old walls but also spreading out along the roads beyond the west and east gates.

Josep Martorell, architect and the author of *Guia d'Arquitectura de Menorca*, explains: "The typical house is five metres [16ft] wide, corresponding to the normal span of wooden beams available. Larger houses are formed of a double span." Typically the front door opens onto a straight flight of stairs, leading to the first floor. Here the staircase often continues at right angles, ascending dogleg fashion between the front and back rooms to the upper floor. In some cases the rooms at the back are at a different level from those at the front, opening off half-landings.

White-washed houses
MAHÓN, MINORCA

Shutters and doors throughout Mahón are painted in one of two shades of green. These crisply painted houses (right) line the Carrer Isabel II, the town's most fashionable street. The heart of the house, away from the street, is often the coolest place during the hot Minorcan summers. The upper windows of internal rooms in Carrer Isabel II 9 (opposite above), one of the largest houses in the town, borrow light from the airy, spacious staircase hall.
The island was occupied by Britain in the 18th century, and English features such as these sash windows survive in many houses.

Minorcan summers are often very hot and winters rarely cold, so houses are designed to be cool and airy. They are built of the local limestone, sometimes cut from the rock below the plot on which the house stands. Houses usually have submerged cellars, lit and aired only by slits at pavement level (which may also serve as hatches for goods taken down for storage). These cellars, and sometimes the ground-floor rooms, are vaulted in stone, to keep them cool. All floors are paved in stone or terra-cotta tiles and so are cool underfoot.

Under the roof there is often a *porxos*, which is a loft with a paved floor and small openings at back and front that introduce a continuous flow of air – this prevents the baking heat on the roof from penetrating to the rooms below. Often the *porxos* is marked out from the street by a pair of oval openings just below the cornice. All houses have shutters that sit tight against the wall when closed, thus accentuating the façades' distinctive flatness. The earlier shutters, which are often still in place, are solid panels; later ones are louvred (and called, evocatively, *persiana*). Some houses also have internal shutters to provide a totally dark interior.

All houses, grand and modest, stand on the edge of the narrow pavements, without front gardens or terraces, creating an intimate relationship with the life of the street. This is most evident during the numerous summer fiestas, when families lean out of

---

Whether of plaster or stone, white walls, like those of this vaulted entrance and staircase at Carrer Isabel II 9 (right), keep the houses cool. Floors are often paved in stone or terra-cotta, and the ground-floor rooms vaulted in stone, to prevent the interior from succumbing to the heat of Minorcan summers.

upper windows in order to enjoy a grandstand view of the procession below. At the back there is peace and privacy, with small, shaded gardens and often terraces at several levels opening off the back rooms.

On an island where it may not rain for months, water storage was critical before a modern supply system was installed. In winter, water was collected from the roof and terraces and channelled down to a *cisterna*, a water tank holding 700–1,400 cubic feet (20–40m³), through a pipe built into the thickness of the walls. This pipe was formed of earthenware sections one foot (30cm) long, wide at one end and narrow at the other. During the hot and dusty summer months, a tennis ball-sized stone would be used in order to block the mouth of the pipe, and the first winter rain would be run through to wash them clean. The locals maintain that the limestone walls of the *cisterna* purify the water naturally.

Mahón's finest houses line the Carrer Isabel II, on which stands the large handsome residence of the military governor. One of the grandest has been converted into apartments. Another house, in nearby Placa des Monestir, is just two windows wide on the street yet is a large property of 7,500 square feet (700m²), built for a Minorcan family in the early 19th century. Like many of its neighbours, the house is laid out on a narrow, deep plan, with a view over the harbour at the back.

When I visited the house in 1997 its decorative condition was poor; tiles were missing from the walls, and doors had been removed. This was reflected in the sale price of 29 million Spanish *pesetas*, which my guide calculated to be just £113,000 ($180,800).

The front door opened into a broad pillared and vaulted hall of impressive length. Behind the front room on the left were two internal sitting rooms, without outside windows, the first enjoying borrowed light through double doors inset with stained glass. Then came a beautiful stone cantilevered stair rising two floors and lit by an oval dome. Beyond lay an inner hall with the remains of 19th-century Rococo tiles on the lower walls, an internal kitchen on the left (with doors at either end to help ventilation), and a dining room with startling Art Nouveau tiles at the end. A small stair nearby led down to a sunny room opening onto a terrace, from where further steps descended to a small garden. Many of the main rooms still had attractive painted decoration, but, as often proves the case with terrace houses, there was no hint of this from the street.

Not to be missed is the early 19th-century Casa Oliver in the Carrer de la Infanta. This is more a small palace than a terrace house and so perhaps beyond the scope of this book, but its spectacularly frescoed staircase ascending in twin flights compares with the most adventurous examples in Naples.

Philadelphia is one of the best preserved of all Georgian cities. This should not be surprising – until the 1770s it was the third largest city in the English-speaking world, after London and Bristol. Although Philadelphia has few of the crescents or squares of the typical Georgian city, it has a character all of its own, thanks to the rigorous grid plan that was laid out in 1682 by William Penn, the founder of the city and of the state of Pennsylvania. Philadelphia is a red-brick city with a charm that derives largely from the homeliness of its scale; narrower streets and lower buildings than those of Dublin or Edinburgh give it the intimacy of London's Chelsea.

The standard lot for a Philadelphia town house was merely 12–16 feet (3.7–4.9m) wide but 100–150 feet (30–46m) deep; some were built on double plots, but in mid-Georgian times these were rare. Typical houses were three storeys over a sunken basement,

back extension, where the ceilings were lower. The staircase was usually of unpainted pine, with a mahogany or walnut handrail, but in grand houses the whole staircase would be of mahogany. On the first floor was a master chamber at the front and a second one behind. Inventories show such rooms furnished with a fully curtained bed, as well as a tea table and chairs, for it was not unusual to entertain close friends in the bedroom.

In the garrets there was ample sleeping room for servants. There were probably between three and five of these per household, most of whom, in the early 19th century, would have been Irish.

The local construction trade was controlled by the master builders of the Carpenters Company, who had a monopoly on the measuring that determined the cost of construction. Until the Revolution of 1775 almost any house of pretension would be built by one of the Company's masters. Their clients were rich

Red-brick terraces
PHILADELPHIA

with an attic at the top: five levels in all. Houses were three windows wide – these were packed close together in the narrow frontages – and built of local brick. The first brickyards were documented within a year of the founding of the city, firmly disproving the story, common in Philadelphia as elsewhere, that bricks were brought over from England as ballast. Roofs were of wooden shingles; there were no slates or tiles until the 19th century. During its earliest days the city stood surrounded by hardwood forest, so the use of massive roof timbers measuring 20 by 20 inches (50 by 50cm) was not uncommon.

Houses were built right on the street without front gardens or basement areas. The entrance floor was raised just enough to accommodate, under the two ground-floor windows, two small barred windows to light the kitchen below. To the side of the narrow entrance hall was a double parlour, and beyond this a back extension, which in many cases grew in length and filled two-thirds of the width of the plot, leaving space for just one window in the corner of the back parlour. These extensions could stretch back almost half a block and include a carriage house at the end, in which case they had their own staircase.

The stair in the house itself rose at the back of the hall in a space known locally as the "piazza." On the half-landing a door opened into the upper floor of the

This sash window of a Philadelphia house (right) is flanked by panelled external shutters, and a hatch opens into the basement. The brickwork is laid in Flemish bond, with alternating "headers" and "stretchers."

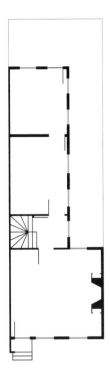

This ground-floor plan of No.403 Marshall's Court shows that that the main part of the building is only one room deep. Behind this main room is a long, narrow wing that contains the staircase and kitchen.

Like these in Society Hill (right), most of Philadelphia's Georgian houses are built of locally made red brick. The larger row houses are three windows wide, but, unlike many 18th-century houses in London, they lack basement areas. Door cases and steps vary from house to house.

merchants, justices and public figures, as well as landowning families who wanted houses in town. Smaller houses were built in groups on a well-documented pattern, with several craftsmen, a bricklayer, a carpenter and a plasterer, buying a patch of land and together building four or five houses, each taking one house to sell or let at the end.

By the 1720s there were joiners as well as master carpenters who could follow standard designs from any English architectural pattern book. By the 1760s they were producing the sophisticated carving and plasterwork illustrated in books by Abraham Swan.

The first study of Philadelphia's row houses was undertaken by Bill Murtagh and published by the American Society of Architectural Historians in its journal in 1957. William Penn had dreamed of a city of single houses that were set in spacious gardens, in complete contrast to the housing found in London. The rapid growth of Philadelphia was to ensure that the large blocks interspersed with green areas, which were envisaged by Penn's surveyor Thomas Holme, were built up with row houses. Murtagh identified four distinct house types: the Bandbox, the London, the City and the Town.

has just three steps up to the front door, with the basement barely visible below. However, at the rear the basement was lit by a light-well similar to those that could be found at the front of many British terrace houses of the same date.

The City and the Town are both variations on the London, but with long, narrow extensions at the back. The City, like the Bandbox, has a single room at the front, with stair, dining room and kitchen in the extension.

The best example of the Town pattern is the Powel House, which is to be found on South 3rd Street. The house features a splendid stone-columned door case, approached by a broad flight of four stone steps with iron railings. Only the tops of the basement windows rise above the level of the street, although a removable wooden bulkhead allowed in extra light and provided direct access to the cellar. Solid external shutters were provided to all windows – evidence of a need for security. (Elsewhere in the city louvred shutters, which admitted cool air during the heat of the day, were widely used above the ground floor from the late 18th century onward.)

The sash windows (although these are inevitably replacements) are what Americans term "12 over 12s" – that is to say, each sash has 12 panes of glass – on the lower two storeys, and smaller "8 over 8s" on the upper storey. Best of all are the beautiful dormers at the top, with arched windows set snugly beneath pediments and interlacing "Gothic" glazing bars in the upper sash.

The Powel House is built of brick with a stone trim. The stone was used for the keystones above the windows and the string courses between storeys. Above the bold dentil cornice is a pair of handsome dormers with arch-headed windows capped by pediments.

The mahogany stair handrail in the Powel House (right) is embellished with a twist at its end, while carved scrolls decorate the ends of the treads. An archway, with the cornice broken forward over the keystone, divides the staircase hall in two.

The Bandbox house was in fact a mews cottage in a narrow alley or "court," at the back of town-house plots on the space reserved for stables. Bell Court, between 3rd and 4th Streets, is a good example. Houses of this pattern were two or three storeys high, with only one room on each floor and a staircase at the back. There were no windows at the back, thus preventing the occupants from looking over into the gardens of the grander houses behind. In Bell Court the privies or "necessaries" were placed in pairs at the end of the alley.

The plan of the London house follows the example of early-18th-century houses in that city, such as those in Queen Anne's Gate or Spitalfields (see pages 58–61), with the stair placed across the middle of the house. This ran from cellar to attic and was either a dogleg with straight flights, or a more elegant "winder" with steps fanning out as it turned. The London was particularly popular with the speculative builders who were building substantial runs of row houses in the 19th century. An example is a group of 22 brick houses built by Thomas Carstairs in 1800–01 on the south side of Sansom Street. A group at 403–411 Marshall's Court, which dates from 1810,

In the front downstairs room, which measures about 20 feet (6m) square, a double-decker fireplace rises to the full height of the projecting chimney breast. Features such as the fireplace and chimney breast were often taken from English pattern books. The moulding that surrounds the windows sits on a panelled dado rather than continuing around the bottom.

This ground-floor plan of the Powel House shows that the main block is two rooms deep and has a very long extension at the back, with fireplaces set in the corners. The fireplaces in the main rooms do not sit fully back to back, reflecting the fact that the rooms are of slightly different widths.

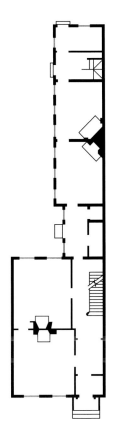

The house retains its splendid original mahogany stair, positioned at the back of a spacious hall. The panelling in the hall was taken to the Philadelphia Museum of Art in order to prevent its loss, only to be returned when the house was acquired by the city's Landmarks Society. The staircase, "broad enough for even the most amply gowned figure," in William Tatum's evocative phrase, has fluted Doric columns as newel posts and ends with a characteristic flourish in a single "twist." Another notable feature is the pediments over the doors.

Contemporary descriptions suggest that the ground-floor front room was the parlour in most 18th-century Philadelphia houses, and thus the most richly decorated. Surveys of the Powel House in 1769 and 1785 mention only that the ground-floor rooms were wainscotted to the chair-rail "pedestal high." As in the best houses, the chair-rail panels on the wall exactly follow the swooping line of the stair's handrail. The back room, which has a buffet or cupboard where china was stored and displayed, was probably where the owners took their meals. (In an age when servants were plentiful, meals were often served in various rooms.)

When first built, the house was equipped with "lead spouts" to discharge the rainwater. These, however, were melted down to serve the needs of the British Army in 1777, although Powel would later receive the substantial sum of £44 19s ($72) in compensation.

Today parts of Philadelphia contain block after block of Georgian houses. However, the historic heart of the city – 2nd, 3rd and 4th Streets, crossed by Pine, Spruce, Walnut and Chestnut – became the commercial area, and many Georgian houses deteriorated or became "Mom and Pop" stores, flophouses, brothels and bars. Revival came after the Second World War. During the 1960s a typical three-storey Georgian house, with its fireplaces, would sell for $12–14,000 (£7,500–9,000) and need $50–100,000 (£30–60,000) still to be spent on it. Today these same houses sell for between $500,000 and $1 million (£300,000–625,000). The number of firmly dated pre-Revolution houses is not more than 200, and there are a further 200 of the Federal period of 1780–1810. The number of late-Georgian (1810–50) houses runs to thousands. Most remarkable is the sheer number of them that are open to visitors.

In 1795 five prominent citizens acquired 18.5 acres (7.5ha) of three hills – known as the Trimountain – behind the overcrowded port of Boston. As the Mount Vernon Proprietors, they bought the land for $18,000 (£11,250) from the fashionable painter John Singleton Copley, who had settled in England in 1774. Copley, believing his Boston agent had let him down, sent his son to challenge the deal, only to find it was legally binding.

Copley may have had a point – on 4 July 1795 the foundation stone was laid for a new State House, to accommodate town and state governments and the State Supreme Court. The chosen site was on Beacon Hill. The statesman Harrison Gray Otis, who led the committee that bought the land and commissioned plans from the architect Charles Bulfinch – both were Mount Vernon Proprietors – realized that there would soon be a demand for new houses nearby.

Plans were quickly drawn up for a grid of streets around building plots intended to appeal to Boston citizens prospering from the city's booming trade

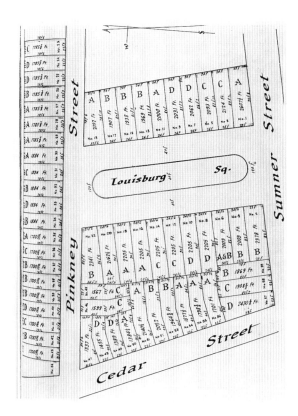

This extract (right) from an early plan of the Beacon Hill development shows the lots allocated to individual houses. Louisburg Square is generally considered to be the heart of this gracious quarter, which represents the embodiment of classical American architecture.

Beacon Hill
BOSTON

Beacon Hill houses are built of plum-coloured brick. Among the finest examples is this row of swell-front houses in Louisburg Square, made more distinctive by the contrast between the warm brick and the dark louvred shutters. The front doors here are set at the top of a short flight of steps, allowing light into the basement.

Many of the front doors of Beacon Hill houses are set back in arches, providing shelter for the occupier while searching for the key or, as was more common in the past, waiting for a member of the household staff to answer the door.

with China, a market that had been taken over from Britain after the Revolution. In the summer of 1799 Mount Vernon, the western peak, was shorn of 50–60 feet (15–18m) to create a level summit.

The original purchase covered the area between Beacon Street, from Charles to Walnut, and Pinckney Street. Later Beacon Hill extended to Bowdoin on the east side and Cambridge on the north. Over a century, stylistic developments can be traced from Federal, a version of English Georgian spanning from 1800 to the late 1820s, through Greek Revival, characterized by columned porches, running from the 1830s to the mid-century, to the larger-scale and more opulent Victorian, continuing into the 1890s.

Architects were involved in some house designs from the beginning, including Bulfinch himself, but the vast majority were designed by "housewrights." These carpenter-craftsmen based their designs on the illustrations found in pattern books such as Asher Benjamin's popular *American Builder's Companion* (1806). The American writer Henry James wryly deemed Mount Vernon Street the most proper,

Beacon Street as grand, Chestnut beautiful, West Cedar intimate, with Mount Vernon having the "long view" that a Bostonian likes to take as well as see.

No two lots are quite the same size, and usually no more than two or three houses were erected at a time. The houses are built of warm, brownish-red bricks from the claypits in Cambridge just across the river, and have stayed clean in Boston's sea air. Stone was more difficult to obtain, although basements may be of white granite. Cornices are mostly in wood. Roofs slope down to the cornices to throw off the snow (in London or Dublin parapets would screen the attic storeys). They have a 45-degree pitch and are covered in slates, and most have one or more dormers. The most distinctive houses have swell fronts: gently rounded bays that rise the full height of the street elevation. A distinctive feature is the entrance doorway, which is recessed in an elliptical arch in order to shelter the top step.

The typical house is a five-storey "walk-up" built for a single family with children, with servants' rooms in the upper two storeys. Basements, where

This drawing room of a house in West Cedar Street, built in 1831, has been refurnished in the style of that time. Richly draped (fashionably asymmetric) valences fill the tops of the windows, but there are no matching curtains to pull – instead, folding shutters, here shown with only the lower panels closed, ensure privacy.

they exist, are either sunk into the ground or at street level, with, accordingly, a short or long flight of steps up to the front door; they contained the kitchen and servants' hall. On the main floor were front and back parlours, sometimes connected by sliding "pocket" doors that disappeared into the partition wall. Here the family ate; it is not clear exactly when dining rooms or "eating parlours" came into use. Typically, above the parlour were two ample bedrooms, front and back. Staircases usually rose in one run from the main floor. Often there was a separate servants' stair immediately behind. If the stair was set in the centre of the house without a window, it circled up around an open well with daylight streaming in from the top. Staircases were built of wood, the painted pine of the earlier houses giving way to Honduras mahogany. Windows were initially sashes, six over six panes, or three over three in the nursery at the top. Later in the century many had attractive louvred shutters, most of which survive.

Today several of the most important houses can be visited. Among these are the handsome twin houses at 39–40 Beacon Street, the Appleton-Parker House, now owned by the Women's City Club of Boston. The houses, designed by Alexander Parris as a matching pair and built in 1819, retain a few panes of purple glass that, all over Beacon Hill, dates houses to 1818–25 (when glass exported from Europe contained manganese oxide, which took on a purple tint when exposed to sunlight). Interesting features are the oval front room behind the bow, with curved mahogany doors, and a beautiful spiral staircase with a so-called "peace button," installed in the end of the handrail when the mortgage had been paid.

No.55 Beacon Street, the Prescott House, which is currently the headquarters of the Colonial Dames of America, is open at times by appointment. This formed a pair with 54 and was built in 1807–8 for James Smith Colburn, a rich entrepreneur who lived here till 1819. Later it became the home of the historian William Hickling Prescott. Just beyond, another pair, 63–64, were built by Ephraim Marsh in 1824. Further on, in Brimmer Street, there are still stables and coach houses to be seen.

Many original houses survive in Chestnut Street. These include a series of eight built for Mrs Hepzibah Swan. The only woman admitted to the ranks of the Mount Vernon Proprietors, she bought into the syndicate a decade after it was formed. Mrs Swan built 12–18 to the designs of Cornelius Coolidge, and lived in 16. Nos.13–17, which Bulfinch built for her in 1816–18, she gave to three of her daughters. No.48 was built for her in or around 1822 by the housewright Ephraim Marsh.

At No.55 Walnut Street is the Nichols House Museum, named after Rose Standish Nichols (1872–1960). Miss Nichols was America's first woman landscape architect and a skilled woodcarver, furniture-maker and embroider. In her will she bequeathed her house as a museum, and it remains exactly as it was at the time of her death. William Pear, curator of the Nichols House, explains: "In the 19th century houses often had wooden sheds at the back, containing summer kitchens – as in New Orleans. These continued until families started to go off to their summer places in the 1840s, taking their servants with them. If father stayed behind he would go and live in the club. Few house had gardens as

These plans for a medium-sized town house were published in the *American Builder's Companion*, by Asher Benjamin, who lived and worked on Beacon Hill. This house, on four floors, measured 25 feet (7.6m) in width by 37 feet (11.3m) in depth. The ground floor had an entrance, a breakfast or counting room at the front and a kitchen at the back. On the next floor was a front parlour with double doors leading into a dining room. The small room at the front was a library; that at the back a china closet. Above were three bedchambers and a smaller dressing room. There were two staircases, for the family and the servants, but only the back staircase continued to the top two floors.

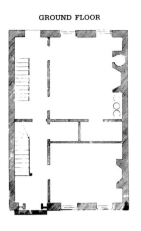
GROUND FLOOR

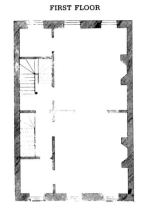
FIRST FLOOR

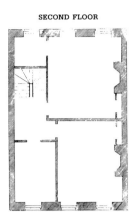
SECOND FLOOR

such – Boston Common was open to all for free. Equally, only grander houses had stables or coach houses behind – Bostonians tended to go on foot."

No.59 Mount Vernon Street, with a fine Greek Revival portico, was designed by Edward Shaw, the author of the widely used *Civil Architecture and Rural Architecture*.

The climax of a walk round Beacon Hill comes in the form of Louisburg Square, named after the great French fortress in Nova Scotia, Canada, taken in 1745 after a siege led by the Massachusetts Militia. In his original plan Bulfinch had envisaged a large square, but the present square was not laid out until 1826, by Mather Withington, and the first house lot was not sold until 1834, the last in 1847. Finest are the row of swell fronts at Nos.8–24, built in 1835–6. These are three storeys, not four, with the tallest windows on the first floor. The large basement areas provided well-lit front rooms, which in some cases served as the family dining room.

Finally, it is worth noting the north slope of Beacon Hill, which developed much more modestly than the fashionable south slope; many of these houses are of special interest because they were owned and rented by free blacks. No.66 Phillips Street, which was built in 1833, was for 40 years the home of Louis Hayden, a former slave who was to become one of the leaders of the abolition movement.

The detailing of this dining room of an 1837 house in Mount Vernon Street is typical of the period of the Greek Revival. Guests entered the room through a central doorway, so a handsomely laid dining table would be seen to best effect. The china cabinets, displaying flat, reeded mouldings typical of the Greek Revival, are placed with pleasing symmetry on each side of the door.

In Brighton and neighbouring Hove, on the south coast of England, fine Regency terrace houses survive in their hundreds. By the 1970s, however, almost every one had been subdivided into flats, and behind their cream or white façades few remain intact. In 1984 Nick Tyson and friends set out to reassemble a complete 1829 terrace house in Brunswick Square. Beginning with a basement flat in No.13, he bought up all the remaining flats as other tenants left before finally obtaining the headlease. He plans, with the Regency Town House's Trust, to restore the house authentically in every detail, open it to the public and use it as a showcase of period craftsmanship.

In the early 18th century Brighton was a fishing town with 2,000 inhabitants. Its rapid rise to being one of England's most fashionable resorts stemmed from a belief in the curative powers of sea water. The Duke of Cumberland visited in 1771, the Prince of Wales came in 1783, and Royal Crescent, the first grandiose composition of terrace houses (and the first to face the sea) was built between 1798 and 1807.

Brunswick Town was a collaboration between the Reverend Thomas Scutt, a landowning clergyman, and the architect C A Busby (1786–1834). Busby designed the new development as a long range of grand terraced housing set along the seafront, with a large central square stretching back from the sea. These houses were all designated "first-class;" behind were smaller second-class houses, a hotel, chapel and public baths. Construction began in early 1824, and the first houses were finished by September 1826.

Brunswick Town is Busby's memorial, a composition as grand as John Nash's palatial terraces around London's Regent's Park. His original drawings include complete sets of floor plans for some of the houses, indicating uses of rooms, including every closet and cellar in the basement. Tyson and his trustees have supplemented this fascinating insight into the life of a Regency house by taking over, at No.10, the last intact basement in the square.

Steps descend from the street to a spacious stone-flagged front basement area. Under the pavement is a large coal cellar providing the coal for fires upstairs,

Regency elegance
BRIGHTON

The grand stair ascends not just to the first floor, as in many London houses, but to the top of the house, with a fine iron balustrade rising its full length. These balustrades were a feature of Regency homes, particularly those in Brighton, which was a great producer of cast iron.

and beside it a beer cellar. Inside, on the right, is the housekeeper's room, with "pull-up and open out" cupboards to save space. The next door leads to the wine cellar. Behind this door is a second, iron-lined as a precaution against thirsty servants.

Beyond is a sizeable servants' hall – such houses had 8–12 servants – overlooking a small courtyard. The kitchen lies on the other side of the small court, with a generous toplight, its layout influenced by the Prince Regent's famous kitchen at Brighton Pavilion. The cooking range stood on the far wall, and beside it survives the trace of a hood over a secondary oven. To the right stood a copper for boiling water. The original fitted dressers are to be replaced with wood-work salvaged from other houses. At the back of the kitchen are three vaulted cellars: two that would have held coal with which to stoke the cookers, and a third to hold cheese and cream.

At No.13 the front entrance leads to a grand stair, ascending not just to the first floor, as in some London houses, but continuing to the top, with a fine iron balustrade rising its full length. The ground floor has a dining room at the front, and behind this there is a parlour (which often served as an office or a library).

The exteriors of Brunswick Square were originally faced with stucco of a biscuit-brown colour. Busby decided on an oak effect for the doors and had the railings painted green, so that the buildings would blend harmoniously with the countryside that surrounded the town.

Elaborate stiff-leaf cornicing in the dining room (above). Such decoration was only built into rooms that would be seen by visitors; rooms for the family's use alone were very simple in comparison. Oil-based paint was used in these grander rooms, and water-based paints made from earth pigments in the servants' quarters.

Above the rear cellars the stable block provides security by housing the rear coal holes through which intruders could otherwise have entered.

Both main rooms on the first floor, connected by double doors, were used as drawing rooms. Sash windows descend to the floor, providing views over the gardens in the square, which were maintained by a garden rate paid by the residents. Most houses have four extra channels outside the sash windows for external "descending" shutters. They were housed in boxes that obscured the tops of the windows, which explains why some surviving pairs of internal shutters in the Square do not rise the full height of the windows. These were evidently storm shutters. The Crown glass used in the early sashes was very fragile and vulnerable to stones swept up from the unsurfaced roads, whereas the large sheets of plate glass that were substituted in the mid-century were stronger and made storm shutters obsolete. The shutter boxes would have lowered the level of natural light below today's norms, but were necessary to prevent the organic dyes used in fabrics from fading.

The two principal bedrooms and dressing rooms (probably for husband and wife) were on the second floor, with other family bedrooms and servants' rooms on the third floor.

At the entrance to the kitchen of No.10 is a remarkable survival: a meat safe with its original tight iron grill (left). Its bars are set so closely that not even a fly could venture through.

13 Brunswick Square

The inside of the door to the wine cellar of No.10 (middle) is iron-lined, and around the lock are the remains of sealing wax. Inside the brick-vaulted and -floored cellar is space for 3,000 bottles. Its original stone shelves are still intact.

The kitchens in No.10 (left) and No.13 are in separate but linked buildings behind the main houses, to prevent food smells from reaching the other rooms. The ample toplight provides natural light, and originally held vents to allow heat and smoke to escape.

KEY

① The façade was originally a biscuit-brown stucco, a colour that would have blended in with the landscape

② Storm shutters to protect the fragile Crown glass from material blown up from the unsurfaced roads

③ Front cellars held coal for the main house and beer; rear cellars held coal for the kitchen, and a cheese and cream larder

④ Housekeeper's room

⑤ Butler's pantry

⑥ Rear stairs

⑦ A rear yard allows light and air to enter at each floor

⑧ The kitchen; its pitched roof holds a toplight and originally had vents

⑨ The ground floor houses the dining room at the front and an adjacent parlour

⑩ The decker's room, used for laying out food before it was carried into the dining room

⑪ The stables and coach-house with, above, the coachman's lodgings

⑫ Waiting room for visitors

⑬ Both main rooms on the first floor were used as drawing rooms, the front one having a view onto the central square of gardens

⑭ The two principal bedrooms with adjacent dressing rooms

⑮ Servants' rooms; those at the front may have been used as bedrooms for the family

BASEMENT

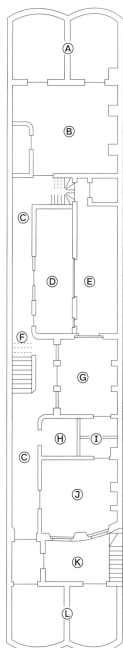

Ⓐ Coal cellar and larder

Ⓑ Kitchen and scullery

Ⓒ Passageway

Ⓓ Butler's pantry

Ⓔ Rear yard with fish larder

Ⓕ Stairs to ground floor

Ⓖ Servants' hall

Ⓗ Wine cellar

Ⓘ Anterooms

Ⓙ Housekeeper's room

Ⓚ Front area with steps to street

Ⓛ Beer and coal cellars

Preservation battles rarely receive such an evocative write-up as the one conducted in Savannah does in John Berendt's widely praised book *Midnight in the Garden of Good and Evil*. Here Berendt goes on a tour of the city's historic downtown with Lee Adler, who pioneered the use of "revolving funds" in urban renovation – that is, buying derelict historic houses and repairing and reselling them.

Savannah's prosperity before the Civil War grew from its importance as a port. The city had been founded in 1733 by General Oglethorpe and laid out on a grid plan with a distinctive pattern of tree-lined streets and squares. Almost from the beginning a series of exceptionally talented architects was employed there. The city escaped the dreadful trail of destruction wrought by General William Sherman as he marched victoriously but vindictively to the sea in 1864–5, burning Atlanta, the state capital of Georgia, and numerous other towns. The long years of depression that followed left Savannah essentially intact until the 1920s; according to Adler, however, by the mid-1950s a third of the old city had gone.

A classic piece of direct action came when Adler read in the local newspaper that a handsome row of four 1855 houses on East Oglethorpe Avenue, known as Mary Marshall Row, had been sold to a wrecker, who was proposing to sell the materials brick by brick. Adler promptly offered to buy the houses, along with the land on which they stood, for $54,000 (£33,750). He set about raising the funds through an appeal to the members of the Historic Savannah Foundation.

The lacy ironwork of the deep porch and verandah (below) is painted black, as are the railings of the stair and those enclosing the front garden. This heightens the dramatic impact of these houses in Bull Street, built by Charles Rogers in 1858.

The classical revival
SAVANNAH

Savannah was built on marshy land, and basements could not easily be set below street level as in Britain and some northern states of America. The streets were dry and dusty, but placing living rooms on the second floor protected them to some extent from the dust thrown up by the wheels of passing carriages. Internally, the usual arrangement in the city's row houses was a kitchen and servants' hall at street level, a dining room on the entrance floor, living rooms on the second floor and bedrooms above. Entrance halls in Savannah row houses, as in those in Dublin, were generous in width and received daylight through a band of glass beside and above the front door. The stairs were set back in line with the entrance. Despite the long, hot summers and usually clement winters of the South, all the main rooms had a handsome fireplace as a central feature. Typically, the first floor formed a *piano nobile* and accordingly had taller windows.

The distinctive feature of the ante-bellum (in other words, before the Civil War) town houses in Mary Marshall Row is that the front door is on the first floor, raised up over a full basement in an arrangement that requires an unusually long flight of steps, as is the case with many examples of 19th-century New York brownstone (see pages 106–11). Some of these steps are almost ballroom staircases, either impressively straight or sweepingly curved, allowing Southern Belles in their crinolines to make an arresting descent.

A handsome marble fireplace graces the Schley house in East Oglethorpe Avenue. In grand American houses, as in those of Europe, a fireplace was the focal point of the main living room.

These houses (above) in Mary Marshall Row, at 230–244 East Oglethorpe Avenue, have front doors raised up above the street to reduce the amount of dust (thrown up by carriages and horses) entering the main rooms. At the top of the houses a continuous cornice and parapet hide the roofs, giving the whole row a dignified classical air.

Mary Marshall Row consists of two pairs of houses with their main entrances placed to one side rather than centrally. The flights of steps leading up to the doors form matching pairs, with those in the middle looking like a double stair in front of a grand country house or public building. Below the steps, service doors open directly into the basements.

The exterior of the row, softened by large trees that provide abundant shade, shows how good proportions and attractive brickwork can by themselves provide handsome architecture. The houses have almost no ornamental features – no surrounds to the windows, and no porches or balconies – and the railings are of the simplest design. Shutters provide rhythm and contrast, and the façades have the

slightest of brick cornices, topped by plain parapets. At the time these houses were built, regulations in most cities in England demanded that the sashes should be set back inside the window reveals to reduce the risk of fire. Here they sit in line with the windows, in an arrangement that combines the warmth of the English William and Mary style with the elegance of the Regency.

Other comparable groups of Savannah row houses are William Remshart Row, which has balconies built out at the back, West Jones Street (1854), and Gordon Row (1854), an impressive run of 15 houses on a repeating pattern, with outdoor steps that descend in a graceful curve.

Two earlier terrace houses are the Thomas Clark houses at 107–9 East Oglethorpe Avenue (1821–2). These have broad front doors set in shallow arches and flanked by fluted Ionic columns (such as were also being built in Dublin during this period). The arches and windows have distinctive incised lintels, and the ironwork railing of the steps has Gothic newel posts as well as a central lamp-holder that serves both houses.

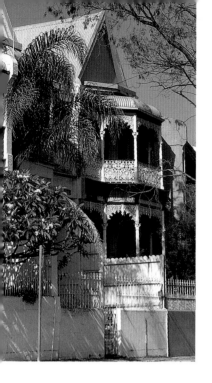

Like Beacon Hill in Boston (see pages 90–3), Sydney's Paddington quarter is largely built on a sunny slope looking down to a great harbour. The first grant of land in the area was made in 1804, to Thomas West, who built his house, Barcom Glen, on the slopes above Rushcutters Bay. Then, in 1817, Messrs Underwood, Forbes and Cooper were given a joint grant of 100 acres (40ha) on the sunny side of Paddington. They built a gin distillery next to one of the streams that ran into the marshy ground at the harbour's edge, and the track that they used to take supplies in and out – known in time as Glenmore Road – became the defining artery of Paddington.

Once the parcels of granted land fronting Glenmore Road had been built on, street blocks developed in response to their boundaries. When the three men argued, Underwood bought out his partners' shares.

His land – which was bounded by Underwood Street, Jersey Road, Sutherland Street and the crooked line of Cascade and William Streets – was subdivided in an orderly fashion. The rest of the land is a maze, but there are some beautiful terraces lining short streets and cul-de-sacs. Paddington burgeoned in response to the building of the magnificent Victoria Barracks (1841–7). Housing was first constructed for some of the free settlers who came in order to oversee the convicts building the barracks, then more followed for the soldiers and their families.

The typical cast-iron-balconied houses that spread over the hillside first appeared in the 1860s but date mainly from the last three decades of the century. The houses are usually of two storeys – occasionally three – with short "wing" walls that project forward between them to give privacy to the ground-floor verandahs and first-floor balconies. Although features

Verandahed houses
SYDNEY

The hot summers of New South Wales produced a local variant on the bay window: a double height verandah with sloping sides. This handsome example on Glenmore Road (above) has almost Moorish notched arches and a roof of corrugated iron (a roofing material commonly used in British colonies).

"Wing" walls project between these three-storey verandahed houses in Elizabeth Bay (right), giving privacy to users of adjoining balconies and verandahs. Although not deep, the walls provide welcome shade from the high summer sun.

such as these seem designed to provide shade from the hot antipodean sun, they are to be found on façades facing both north – to the sun – and south.

Clive Lucas, a leading Sydney architect who has worked on many houses of this kind, says: "Typically these Paddington terraces are short by English or American standards, often consisting of a row of just four, five or six houses – ten would be the exception." Most were speculatively built by local builders rather than by notable local architects.

The houses are the simplest brick boxes, and in almost all cases the brick is rendered and marked to suggest blocks of masonry. Roofs were of slate or corrugated iron; the latter was always used for balcony roofs. What gives these houses their charm is their lacy, often floral, ironwork. From the gold rush of the mid-century, cast iron was made in both Sydney and Melbourne by manufacturers such as Bubb & Rees, G & S Fletcher and the Victoria and Waverley Foundries. The main feature is the railing to the first-floor balcony, which is formed of a dense filigree pattern. The ornamental effect is increased by the iron valance that acts as a decorative fringe in front of both ground- and first-floor windows. Shutters were usually confined to the former, at the front only.

Very few Paddington houses have basements. In the majority of examples the front door opens into a rectangular hall with an archway leading through

The ironwork of these Paddington balconies is as intricately worked as table lace, while, at the top, iron valances fan out at the corners and cast decorative shadows on the walls. White paint, almost blinding in the bright sun, is attractively offset by the lush foliage of the front gardens.

to the staircase, where the hall widens to form a passageway to the back. The ground-floor rooms usually interconnect and have ornamental cornices and ceiling roses. Here fireplaces were of marble; elsewhere they were of wood. When new, the houses mostly had four-panel internal doors.

The joinery was of pine, and interiors were usually painted or grained. Staircases were most commonly of local cedar, beautifully polished or varnished and resembling mahogany. Unexpectedly, stairs tended to be tighter and less imposing as the Victorian period progressed. The half-landing opened onto the upper floor of the wing, where servants would usually sleep. The two main bedrooms were on the first floor. Some houses had a second floor (without a balcony)

but the rear, domestic, wings were seldom of more than two storeys. In a house of three storeys the interconnecting living rooms were on the first floor.

At the back of the house an outdoor lobby led into a wing containing the kitchen and, beyond this, a scullery and sometimes a laundry. Most houses had paved backyards; rear gardens were rare. Mains water and gas were supplied, and "night soil" was collected regularly.

Whereas Bondi Beach was spoiled in the 1930s by high-rise flats, Paddington remained largely untouched, thanks partly to a freeze imposed by the Landlord and Tenant Act, which preserved the status quo. Revival began as protected tenants were able to buy freeholds in the 1960s.

19TH AND EARLY 20TH CENTURY
Eclecticism

In the 19th century Baltimore was one of the USA's most populous cities. The majority of the strikingly uniform houses, built in neat rows on spacious streets mostly laid out to a grid plan, were of red brick, with granite basements. During the 1960s and 1970s major developments threatened a large number of these row houses, and an extensive campaign was mounted to save them. Many have now been renovated, restoring to Baltimore's downtown area a vitality that other American cities have lost.

Prosperity caused town houses to become larger and grander, while, as gas lighting was introduced, ceilings became still higher. Increasing attention was paid to providing improved housing for urban workers. Amerian cities developed their own forms of row houses, such as New York's brownstones and the redwood "Painted Ladies" of San Francisco. In London, model streets of cottage housing were laid out for artisans. Around the end of the 19th century, above all in Brussels, architects sought to design houses that stood out from their neighbours, reviving older styles and inventing new ones.

Although this house (right) in Holzdamm, in Hamburg's St Georg quarter, may have served as apartments from the time it was erected, its handsome frontage was designed to look like that of a grand town house. Completed soon after the savage fire of 1842, it was fashionably Italianate but a little more severe than its counterparts in London or New York. In Hamburg houses stood directly on the street and did not have front basement areas.

For three days between May 5 and 8, 1842, a ferocious fire devastated the north German port of Hamburg. More than 60,000 people, almost a third of the population, were forced to flee their homes, and 20,000 were left homeless. The city fathers acted swiftly, on May 9 commissioning the English engineer William Lindley (1808–1900) to work on a plan to rebuild the city. Lindley had been living in Hamburg for several years while acting as engineer in charge of the new railway line to Berlin. He completed his first proposal on May 12, and a week later a commission of architects and engineers, with Lindley as its chairman, was appointed to plan the reconstruction. Lindley soon had a rival in the Dresden architect Gottfried Semper (1803–79), who attacked his proposals to impose a rigid grid of streets on the old heart of the city, and began an alternative plan linking its principal monuments.

Merchants' houses
HAMBURG

This drawing shows a proposal for the rebuilding of houses along Allerwall after the fire of 1842. The designs for the reconstruction proposed distinctive rows of houses in which each house was different from its neighbour but all shared a nearly uniform cornice line.

Criticism of Lindley led to his replacement by Alexis de Châteauneuf (1799–1853), an architect with a strong interest in domestic architecture. The son of a French nobleman who had fled France at the Revolution, Châteauneuf had been born in Hamburg, studied in Paris and spent time in Rome and England, becoming a member of the Royal Institute of British Architects. In 1839 his *Architectura Domestica* was published in London. He designed numerous houses in Hamburg, most of which do not survive. These included a house for Senator Hudtwalker in ABC-Strasse, two nearby houses for himself, and others on Jungfernstieg, Neuen Wall and Theaterstrasse. Finest of all was the Neo-classical town house he designed for Dr Abendroth at Neuen Jungfernstieg 6 (1832–8), which had some of the finest Greek Revival interiors in Europe, sadly long vanished. Still existing is his Haus Kuhnhardt, Ferdinandstrasse 63.

A series of exemplars for rebuilding the city after the great fire was published, showing groups of façades along actual individual streets. The charm of these is their domestic scale. The buildings proposed have the character of single-family houses rather than the apartment blocks that were the most common form of accommodation in German cities during the 19th century. Houses are mostly four or five storeys above a virtually sunken basement. While in Britain most terraces at this date were uniform in design, here every house is different from its neighbour. This was German eclecticism at its most delightful, with styles ranging from Italian Renaissance to Gothic and Louis XVI. Floor levels and parapets varied from house to house, as did window shapes and building materials.

During the Second World War Hamburg suffered severely from Allied bombing raids that destroyed much of its 19th-century post-fire architecture. However, a good row survives at Holzdamm 39–51, near the main railway station. These four-storey houses,

This well-preserved row of houses in Holzdamm, dating from the 1850s, survived the heavy bombing of the Second World War. The Gothic houses on the right rub shoulders with classical ones, but the houses were all part of a carefully conceived eclectic composition incorporating a variety of styles. This diversity contrasts sharply with the uniform look of contemporary terraces in England and North America.

dating from the late 1850s, are three windows wide, with front doors in the middle or to one side. Hooded Gothic arches jostle for attention with classical pediments. As in London after the Great Fire of 1666, roofs are set back behind solid parapets. The houses are well looked after, although some now have extra storeys. They are the very meat of Hamburg's urban history, and yet no mention of them is made in the major guides to the city's buildings.

Among the best of the new houses was a pharmacy with accommodation above at Grosse Bäckerstrasse 22–24 (1843–5), which Semper designed for his brother. It took the form of a pair of town houses each three windows wide, although this was something of an illusion as Semper's brother lived on the first floor, across the full width of the two houses, and there were rented apartments above. Semper had the masonry of the ground-floor façade cut and finished in Dresden and shipped down the River Elbe by barge. For the upper floors he chose *sgraffito* ornament

emulating 16th-century Florentine palaces. In the middle was a statue of St George, the patron saint of health, and on the balconies were a griffin and a sphinx, protectors of Nature's secrets. Baskets of fruit and plants portray the sources of medicine, while in the frieze children play with retorts, mortars, bellows and other laboratory equipment. The pharmacy was demolished in 1896 but is recorded in illustrations in the *Allgemeine Bauzeitung* of 1848. Noteworthy survivors are Schwanenwik 38, by the architect Jean David Jollassa, in Rundbogenstil, "round-arched style," and a house at Deichstrasse 19, built after the fire, with a remarkable staircase and a trio of arched windows that are pure Venetian Gothic.

Row houses are rare in Hamburg, but another interesting group, the Falkenried-Terrassen, survives in Falkenried and Löwenstrasse in the Hoheluft-Ost district. These three-storey houses, laid out in long rows, were built in 1890–1903 for the workers of the Falkenried tram company.

On this row of almost perfectly matching brownstones on West 88th Street, only the heavy cornices differ in decoration from one house to another. Builders strove to make the masonry joints almost invisible, so that the houses looked as if they were carved from solid stone. In egalitarian New York submerged basements were rare and the servants enjoyed full-height windows.

The brownstone houses of New York are almost as famous as Manhattan's skyscrapers. In a city where buildings often overwhelm, they give a sense of human scale and domesticity. In essence they are row houses, built for single families of means. Although erected in small groups they have a strong consistency, with a single pattern repeating throughout the length of a street. Thousands have been lost, including some of the best, such as London Terrace of 1845 and Rhinelander Gardens of 1854, but thousands survive, particularly on the streets off Central Park on the Upper East and West Sides. Good examples can be found in Greenwich Village, Murray Hill, Gramercy Park, Harlem and, in Brooklyn, on Park Slope and Brooklyn Heights. Above all, brownstones are contemporary with the great wave of speculative building that from the 1840s carried Manhattan uptown from Washington Square.

The brownstone most commonly used came from a 20-mile (32km) line of quarries centred on Portland, Connecticut (a town named after Portland, England, which produced much of London's best building stone). Brownstone is a soft sandstone which, when first cut, is pink but soon weathers to a rich brown. In *A Backward Glance* Edith Wharton, who was born in a brownstone in 1862, denounced "this little low-studded rectangular New York, cursed with its universal chocolate coloured coating of the most hideous stone ever quarried." In the 19th century these houses were known as brownstone-fronts because they are, in fact, built of brick, with the

Brownstones
NEW YORK

stone used as a facing 6–18 inches (15–46cm) deep. Improved cutting machinery made brownstone economic for a wide variety of new houses. Builders liked to use large slabs set so close that the joints were barely visible.

The term "brownstone" came to refer to the entire category of 19th-century row houses, whether faced in brick or in stone. As they fell from favour during the 20th century and were subdivided into often shabby apartments, they became a symbol of inner-city decay. Today, however, preservationists have restored an impressive number as single-family homes.

The design and layout of a typical brownstone followed the pattern of the Federal or Greek Revival row houses of the early 19th century. At first these were built in generous lots measuring 25 feet by 100 feet (7.6 by 30m) but, as the city prospered and land became more expensive, plots narrowed to 23, 22 and even 18 feet (7, 6.7 and 5.5m).

Brownstone houses, therefore, were for the most part narrower and taller than their predecessors, a trend encouraged by the desire for higher ceilings that developed with gas lighting. The dominant style of the 1850s and 1860s was Italianate, as in London. Each builder maintained the cornice line and string course fixed by earlier houses in the street, as well as the pattern of windows. Rarely did a street form an Italian palace-style composition with raised centre and ends, but sheer repetition often gave a striking monumentality, as illustrated in Charles Lockwood's

Most brownstones were built in small groups, but even within a group the houses may show slight but noticeable differences in design, height and, occasionally, width. Some examples, such as those on the right of this row, retain chunky Victorian iron railings; others lost them long ago.

This bird's-eye view of New York in 1849 looks south from Union Square and shows both the East and the Hudson rivers. By 1850, Manhattan as far north as 14th Street, just south of the square, was built up with row houses and commercial premises.

Bricks and Brownstones and by the photographs in *Lost New York*. These include a memorable run of 28 identical houses at 322–350 West 46th Street. Many brownstones were designed by their builders, but one of the best groups is at 20 West 71st Street, designed by the architect Albert A Schellenger.

Little is known about the builders and speculators, mostly small-scale operators, who built the brownstones. Architectural historian Professor Mosette Broderick believes that many of them came from

England, often escaping a shady past. Usual practice was to rent rather than sell, requiring continuous refinancing about which information remains sparse. Even in the case of major builders, says Professor Broderick, there is not an iota of documentation.

With very few exceptions, brownstones have an imposing straight run of steps up to the front door. These steps are called the stoop, a reflection of New York's Dutch origins and the fact that in flood-prone Holland the principal floor was usually raised. Stoops are most often of stone, with balustrades of cast iron. Beneath the stoop was a doorway providing separate access to the kitchen by way of the basement hallway. Whereas 19th-century London terrace houses usually have a sunken basement looking onto a below-street front area, the sills of the windows in brownstone basements may be at street level. London's grander Italianate houses commonly have boldly projecting porches resting on columns, but these are rare in New York, where the imposing hooded door cases frame deep-set doors. External shutters also appear to have been scarce, and by the middle of the century many windows were glazed with ever-larger panes of the new plate glass, one sheet often filling an entire sash.

The internal staircase was often a straight run rather than a dogleg, so the front and back parlours could be of almost identical size, connected by sliding or folding "pocket" doors. An Englishman, Joseph J Gurney, wrote that "the private houses … are

In 1919, when Theodore Roosevelt died, the Women's Roosevelt Memorial Association was formed to honour the President's memory and decided to rebuild his birthplace as a museum. Roosevelt's parents had moved into the house in 1854, when it stood in a fashionable tree-lined street. The house had been torn down in 1916, and the Association hired the architect Theodate Pope Riddle, who began her design for the reconstruction by taking measurements from the identical house next door and by consulting Roosevelt's two sisters, who remembered the house as it used to be. With Roosevelt's second wife, the members chose wallpapers and returned some of the family furniture.

Lavish decoration (opposite, above) was popular among the owners of brownstones during the 19th century and the early part of the 20th century. This florid Victorian wallpaper is complemented by crisply modelled swirls of acanthus in the cornice.

Sliding, or "pocket," doors (opposite, below), here inset with coloured and patterned glass, allowed two or even three of the main rooms to be opened up when the family entertained.

generally of neat red brick-work, four stories high, beside the basement. This last in New York generally contains the dining-room; so that we descend to dinner … the drawing room … usually occupies the whole of the first story, being divided in two by large folding doors. These apartments are often very spacious." The rooms that they served had elaborate chimneypieces and cornices to impress guests, who did not go further upstairs.

Room use inevitably varied to some extent; in some instances the basement front room held the nursery, although more often it was over the stoop or entrance hall. At the back many houses had "tea rooms" some 10 feet (3m) deep, overlooking the yard or garden. By the 1850s these became, in bigger houses, large dining rooms 15–20 feet (4.6–6m) deep.

Two handsome Manhattan row houses that can be visited are the Theodore Roosevelt House at 28 East 20th Street, rebuilt to the original plans, and the Old Merchant's House at 29 East 4th Street. Below the parlour floor, the front room on the street was typically the original family dining room, explains Mimi Sherman, the curator of the Old Merchant's House. "If you doubt me, look at the marble mantelpiece – that certainly wasn't for the servants," she says, "the family usually entered under the stoop." The kitchen here, as elsewhere, was set behind. Water would have been collected from the roof and stored in a large cistern in the back yard; by 1850 the house had been connected to the city's water supply. At the back of the yard was the privy.

In many houses the main bedroom floor had a distinctive layout that took advantage of the deep plan, allowing walk-in wardrobes in the middle. The bedrooms, two at the front and two at the back, were connected by a passage, often lined with cupboards.

Parlours were the most elaborately decorated rooms, but often kept in darkness during the day so that the sun would not fade the furnishing fabrics. Theodore Roosevelt remembered his family's parlour as "a room of much splendor … open for general use only on Sunday evening or on rare occasions when there were parties."

Brownstones continued to be erected through the 1890s and until about 1905, when rising land prices forced a shift to apartment buildings. They continued to represent old money and even in the 1920s children who lived in brownstones were forbidden to play with apartment-dwelling children.

During its days of deepest decline in the 1950s, at a time when many were predicting the death of the American city, the brownstone remained a symbol of New York. Osbert Lancaster wrote in his classic work on architectural styles, *Here, of all Places* (1959), "as every keen student of American detective fiction knows, there is hardly one of these mansions in all

New York that has not witnessed the rubbing-out of an eccentric dowager, or heard the unseasonable death rattle of a miserly millionaire."

As houses were divided into apartments, upkeep declined. The thinnest brownstone facing, 6–8 inches (15–20cm), began to spawl. In winter water can turn to ice in an evening, and as it expands it breaks off layers of stone. Today social diktats have helped set a reverse trend in motion. The social tests set by some cooperative apartment blocks are so strict that some of the new super-rich have begun to move into brownstones. Today about 1,500 survive as single houses. As ever, poverty is the best preserver – some of the least altered brownstones are found in Harlem and in Brownsville and Bedford Stuyvessant in Brooklyn, where, because of fears of gentrification, they are not even designated as Landmarks.

Looking through the first-floor closet to the front bedroom (top). The Roosevelt House was built before the age of the en suite bathroom, but the first-floor bedrooms had the luxury of a handbasin with running water.

Window shutters fold back snugly into the window cheeks (middle). Here there are solid panel shutters below and louvred shutters above, which allow the breeze to enter but not the sun.

The first-floor front bedroom has a marble fireplace (bottom). When the house was rebuilt in the 1920s, Roosevelt's family helped to choose wallpapers similar to those they had known as children, in the 19th century.

Theodore Roosevelt Birthplace

KEY

① The façade is faced with brownstone, a soft sandstone that is pink when first cut, but weathers to a soft, rich brown

② The front door does not have a portico, but is set back enough to provide some protection from the rain

③ Stone steps, known as the "stoop," with a cast-iron balustrade, lead up to the main entrance

④ The half-sunken front basement area, protected by railings, with steps leading down to a separate entrance

⑤ Tall windows indicate that the main reception rooms are at this level, where full-height windows open onto a balcony

⑥ The main cornice follows a common line, with slight variations, along most rows of Brownstones

⑦ Dormer windows light the attic. The depth of the house means that a flat roof offered cosiderable savings

⑧ Cellar

⑨ The basement contained the kitchen at the rear, which held a dumb waiter that rose to the dining room above, and a sitting room at the front

⑩ The raised ground floor houses the dining room at the rear

⑪ The library is in the middle of the ground floor

⑫ The parlour faces the street; all three rooms are connected by sliding "pocket" doors

⑬ Master bedroom with closet

⑭ The nursery, in the middle of the first floor, gives access to the children's porch at the rear

⑮ Further bedrooms for the family, with adjacent closets, and servants' rooms are on the second and third floors

GROUND FLOOR

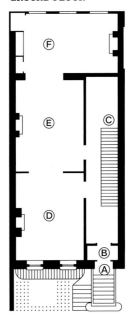

FIRST FLOOR

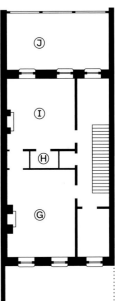

Ⓐ The stoop, or front steps
Ⓑ Entrance lobby
Ⓒ Staircase hall
Ⓓ Parlour
Ⓔ Library
Ⓕ Dining room
Ⓖ Master bedroom
Ⓗ Closets
Ⓘ Nursery
Ⓙ Children's porch

A rare group of single-family terrace houses on the Rue de Pomereu (right), dating from the late 19th century and in the Beaux Arts style. Faced in golden stone, they have stylized Gothic detail, which includes hood moulds over the windows.

This terrace of Beaux Arts houses (below) stands in the Rue de l'Elysée. Built within a single year, in 1861, they emulate grand London houses such as those in Kensington.

During the Second Empire (from 1852 to 1870) Paris, under the auspices of Napoleon III and his indefatigable town planner Baron Haussmann, became a city of *immeubles*, large, comfortable apartment blocks. The very rich still built *hôtels particuliers*, private mansions often set back behind courtyards, and many such houses had large gardens behind them. Terrace houses of the 19th century on the English or American model, in which the house fronts the street and abuts on its neighbours, are rare in central Paris. However, a few fascinating examples survive, built during the Second Empire and until the First World War in the richly decorative style promoted by the Ecole des Beaux Arts.

A remarkably complete specimen is the Maison Opéra at Rue du Docteur Lancereaux 5, in the fashionable 8th *arrondissement*. No.5, originally known

Beaux Arts homes
PARIS

as the Hôtel Bourbon de Rouvre after its first owner, a wealthy government official, is built of stone in Renaissance style and is just three windows wide, but the height of the storeys proclaims grand rooms within. Double doors open not into an entrance hall but into a stone-paved carriageway, complete with narrow sidewalks, that formerly led to a carriage house behind. Because this is still "outdoors" the walls are faced in stone, punctuated by ornate "waist-banded" columns and inset with coats of arms. This was the era when large sheets of plate glass first became available, as illustrated by the doors opening on the right into the entrance hall.

The style throughout most of the house is an opulent Louis XIII, reviving the Renaissance style of the first half of the 17th century when the initial simplicity of the Renaissance had been succeeded by a love of ever greater richness and complexity. This was a time when classical motifs would be deployed to fill a whole wall, and painted decoration and gilding were used in profusion.

The delight of the Maison Opéra is that it is a house so evidently designed for entertaining, in which the main rooms form a continuous circuit so that you are never trapped in a cul-de-sac. Typical of the Second Empire style is the fact that each room is strikingly different in colour and treatment from the previous one, so that the whole design is like a magnificent meal to refresh and revive the palate constantly. The French love of symmetry and placing things in line is everywhere apparent. Everything seems even larger and grander than it actually is because each vista is cleverly framed by a magnificent door case.

While most staircases of the late 18th and early 19th century were light and slender, the one in this house is a substantial construction of dark polished wood, with turned balusters solid enough to suggest stone, and square newel posts at the corners. The staircase arrives on a spacious first-floor landing. Ahead are double doors into the Blue Salon; to the left, double doors lead into the Red Salon, and there is a smaller single door that leads into the more intimate library. On the right, further doors open into a semicircular conservatory, the winter garden. To the guest arriving at a soirée the house deliberately offers an embarrassment of choice. The panelling on the

landing is dark and rich, and the size of the space is cleverly multiplied by large built-in mirrors.

The Red Salon is a surpassing example of the way in which French architects trained in the Beaux Arts tradition were masters of the art of interior decoration, bringing together all the decorative arts to create a single magnificently orchestrated effect. The almost overwhelming richness is held in check by the harmony of the green, pink and gold colour scheme. The green serves as the base colour for the doors and lower walls, the pink for the ceiling, upper walls and inset panels, although the frames of the panels, like those of the doors, are green and gold. The cornice is punctuated by pairs of almost luminous gilt brackets with painted garlands and three-dimensional fruit. The painted decoration of the panels evokes the most delicate Aubusson carpets, with large vases of flowers overhung with tasselled valances. The flamboyance is completed by a scrolled-gilt chandelier rich enough for the Opéra itself.

The winter garden has built-in jardinières, painted in imitation of blue and yellow tiles. To heat the room there is a huge radiator, rising to eye level and neatly concealed behind a black trellis.

In 1906 the Maison Opéra was acquired by Doctor Dupeyroux, to whose family it still belongs. The doctor was also a pharmacist and had made a fortune from pills for tuberculosis, which he manufactured in the basement. Once every week, to the outrage of other doctors, he would hold a free clinic in the Red Salon – old photographs show patients sitting round the sumptuous room waiting their turn to be examined. The doctor's daughter, Madame Toussaint du Wast, held regular soirées to which she invited guests from the world of the arts, including senior architects responsible for the care of historic monuments.

Madame Toussaint du Wast's children have been able to keep the house in the family by creating a recording studio in the basement and letting the main rooms for parties, receptions and operatic recitals. Movie director Franco Zeffirelli was so impressed by the grand salon that he recreated it for his screen version of Verdi's opera *La Traviata*.

Paris boasts one remarkable row of terrace houses in the Rue de l'Elysée, which runs south from the fashionable Rue du Faubourg St Honoré along the east flank of the Elysée Palace, the residence of the President. Details are in the dossier accompanying the inclusion of Rue de l'Elysée 2 on the supplementary list of protected historic monuments in 1994.

On February 15, 1861, the city of Paris sold a large part of the land along the new street to the banker Pereire for 173,788 francs. The contract stipulated that Pereire was to complete the houses within a year. At each end there was to be a large house: "*une grande maison à usage d'habitation* (a large house

The imposing Maison Opéra, built in 1867–8, is a fine example of the French Renaissance Revival style. This private house is not set behind a courtyard, as was the custom with earlier aristocratic residences in Paris, but stands on the street, neatly aligned with its neighbour. The central carriage entrance led through to a rear courtyard.

This view from the Red Salon leads the eye through double doors to the impressive black and gold library. Here each moulding of each panel was picked out in different colours, and gold leaf was used lavishly to create highlights.

Hardly an inch of plain wall is to be seen in the Red Salon. Jean-Louis-Charles Garnier (1825–98), who is believed to have been the architect, sought here, as in his Paris Opéra, to create an effect of dazzling richness by reviving a lavish 17th-century style. It is strange to think that only a few years after the room was completed it was filled with patients suffering from TB, although today it is once again available for grand soirées.

for residential use)," which indicates that the house was intended to be lived in and not simply appropriated for use by courtiers or palace staff. Between were to be three "*maisons dites maisons anglaises*," signifying that they were to be built on the model of London terrace houses. In the middle there were to be three "*hôtels*," that is larger *hôtels particuliers* or town mansions, and then three further *maisons anglaises*. The decision to construct a series of houses in a regular terrace came from the Emperor himself and was inspired by architecture "*à la mode*" in England. The nine houses were completed, with impressive speed, by June 1861. The architect was Alexandre Azemar.

The plot at the corner of the Avenue Gabriel was sold to the Empress Eugénie, who commissioned the architect Lefuel to build a house for her mother, the Comtesse de Montijo. Here the architect Lesoufaché installed in the dining room some superb *boiseries* (panelling) acquired from the Château de Bercy, just east of Paris, which was demolished at this time.

Faced in stone, with large, columned porches, they might be in London's wealthy Kensington district. However, two main features distinguish these Beaux Arts houses from their English contemporaries: their wealth of ironwork, all painted in black, as on houses in New Orleans, and the ornamental detail, derived from the Rococo of Louis XV, that dominates the French Second Empire.

Another even more unexpected group of English-style terrace houses is to be found in the Rue du Pomereu, among the apartment blocks of the prestigious 16th *arrondissement*. In this private road is a series of handsome terrace houses faced in a warm golden stone, each three windows wide and three storeys high. English as they appear, they are, in fact, more like contemporary houses in Brussels than in London since they lack front basement areas. Instead, short flights of steps, beginning outside but continuing inside the front doors, raise the ground-floor rooms enough to allow reasonably sized half-windows to light the basements. The windows do not have balconies but instead shallow ornamental iron grilles that may contain window boxes.

Although these houses are built in the same stone as a group, the style varies from one to another. One has flame-headed ogee window heads like those of Gothic houses in Venice, while others are classical.

The Maison Opéra's opulent
suite of first-floor rooms,
including the Blue Salon,
was consciously designed
for entertaining. Each room
opened into the next, so that
guests were never trapped
in a room with only one way
out. The light of the candles
in the huge gilt chandeliers
and ornate candelabra on the
mantelpieces was reflected
in the mirrors to create a
dazzling display.

Just south of the River Thames, little more than a mile (1.6km) from busy, fashionable Chelsea on the other side, there exists a secluded enclave known to few Londoners. The Shaftesbury Estate consists of 1,135 houses, all built in a distinctive cottage-Gothic style between 1872 and 1877 by the Artisans', Labourers' and General Dwellings Company Limited.

This housing association was formed in 1867 to rehouse people driven from their homes in the City of London by large-scale rebuilding. It was one of the largest and most successful of a series of housing associations and cooperatives that met the demand for new homes during the last four decades of the 19th century. The founder was William Austin, who, having started his working life scaring birds at a penny a day, moved to London and worked as a labourer until he pledged himself to total abstinence from alcohol and began to prosper.

This cottage in Elsley Road (right), with a Gothic gable over twin porches, is typical of the estate. The shield of the housing association responsible for it is inset over the doors. Upstairs, the window-sill retains its original cast-iron window-box holder.

Artisan dwellings
BATTERSEA, LONDON

This plan of the estate shows long and short rows of cottages, originally built for people of modest means. The streets remain an oasis of calm, almost free of traffic passing through, thanks largely to the main railway line to Victoria Station that borders the north side.

Enlisting the support of Lord Shaftesbury, Austin and his colleagues bought 42 acres (17ha) of open fields known as Poupart's market garden. Their prospectus of 1872 proposed to erect 1,200 houses suited variously for clerks, artisans and labourers, plus a lecture hall, cooperative store, schoolrooms, baths and washhouses.

Soon after the visit in 1874 of the Prime Minister, Benjamin Disraeli, who praised the estate, financial irregularities were uncovered and the founders had to resign. Lord Shaftesbury's son, the MP Evelyn Ashley, became chairman, rents were raised twice in a year, and proposed pleasure grounds were sacrificed to further housing to redress a financial shortfall.

Henry Simmonds, in his book *All About Battersea* (1879), wrote: "Work People's Town [Simmonds's term] ... has 1,100 houses and 8,000 inhabitants ... the houses are artistically constructed having small gardens front and back." The houses, he explained, were built in four classes, containing five, six, seven and eight rooms (the latter including a bathroom). Weekly rents were 6s 6d (32.5p/50 cents), 7s 6d (37.5p/60 cents), and 8s (40p/65 cents), with the best houses available at between £26 and £30 ($42–48) a year. Houses were also offered for sale on 99-year leases at prices between £170 and £360 ($272–576). The architect was Robert Austin (not, it should be noted, related to William), the association's architect and surveyor from 1872 until 1877.

John William Stevens, a local historian, notes from the census returns for 1881 that residents of the estate included "a clerk to the Admiralty, a stone carver, domestic servant, lodging house keeper, solicitor, plumber, gas fitter, paper stainer, general porter, clerk to the Royal Artillery, butcher, cab driver, school teacher, railway worker ..."

The typical internal layout was "two-up, two-down," although today many of the two ground-floor rooms have been turned into a single living room. Many houses had back extensions, built as pairs with a gable on the garden end, with a kitchen below and

This photograph, which was taken during the 1870s, shows the promoters of the Shaftesbury Estate (wearing top hats) with some of the builders standing in front of a group of newly completed houses. Many of the houses have polychrome brickwork that emphasizes the arches of the windows.

doors, in many cases in a boldly striped red and black brick that occurs over the windows also. Bands of red brick enliven the yellow London brick – now mostly dull with age – and are also used in the cornices. On many houses the original cast-iron ram's-head door knockers can be seen, as well as cast-iron holders for window-boxes. Most distinctive of all are the stones that are emblazoned with the interwoven initials of the housing association.

The Battersea houses were copied at the Mount, an estate built by the biscuit manufacturers Huntley & Palmer at Reading in Berkshire. This company clearly wasted no time, for the Reading houses are recorded in a local directory dating from 1876. Unusually, these retain the original iron railings and gates, whereas elsewhere these were stripped out at the beginning of the Second World War. Other close copies may be seen in the Caird Street area of Queen's Park, north London.

The Shaftesbury Estate retains its character largely because many of the houses continue to be rented inexpensively by local people. However, the Peabody Trust, which now manages much of the estate, recently began to take advantage of rising prices to sell houses, and offered money to long-term tenants to help them buy homes elsewhere. The estate is now popular with young professionals, and, thanks to its designation in 1976 as a conservation area, the houses still possess their cottage-like charm.

a third bedroom, today more usually a bathroom, above. An imaginative feature was a system of ventilation in each room by valves connected to air shafts in the external walls, where the grilles are still to be seen. A sense of airiness and light is provided by the generous width of the streets.

The delight of these houses lies in the detail, notably the church-like Gothic double porches on some examples. Others have arched hoods over the

These cottages in Elsley Road have two storeys with roofs that are, luckily, too shallow to allow disfiguring attic extensions. Much of the appeal of the estate lies in the fact that most of the houses have hardly been altered since construction, and much of the ornamental detail survives.

The Vollmer house (right) at 1735–37 Webster Street in the Western Addition was designed in 1885 by Samuel and Joseph Cather Newsom. This is the most elaborate surviving example of the Stick-Eastlake style, typical features of which are the rectangular bay windows and the abundant architectural motifs. These motifs create an overwhelming sense of richness because they leave a minimal amount of bare wall. There are large and small columns, emphatic keystones topped by brackets, and strangely shaped pediments over doors and windows.

Exuberant, ornate and brightly painted, these houses are some of the great exotics of street architecture. In some ways they stretch the definition of row houses; they can be detached houses, standing just feet from their neighbours, and often within one porch you can find two front doors opening into separate houses or apartments, one above the other. However, they also draw upon archetypal street architecture – they are built in matching rows, with all the "features" concentrated on the front.

The beginning of modern San Francisco can be dated precisely to March 1, 1847, when the United States military governor abolished the communal landholding system that persisted under Mexican law, thus opening an era of land speculation. Then the famous California Gold Rush of 1849 precipitated a huge building boom.

Many of these houses were built by tract builders, or developers, who would construct an identical row of eight or so houses. The biggest was William Hollis's The Real Estate Association (TREA), which built more than 1,000 homes in the 1870s. For its numerous row houses TREA used standard plans, not

The Painted Ladies
SAN FRANCISCO

Among a block of row houses built between 1875 and 1885 was this Italianate house at 1919 Pierce. It has the slant-sided bay windows characteristic of the time, with a bold bracket cornice.

individual designs by architects. Good examples are on the 2,600 block of Clay Street, facing Alta Plaza. Most of these houses were sold on an instalment plan, with a fifth to a half of the purchase price as a down payment, and the balance paid in monthly instalments over one to twelve years.

Unfortunately, very few houses built before 1870 survive. The early buildings were constructed mainly of stone and suffered badly in the 1868 earthquake. Wood buildings fared better. Architectural historian Anne Bloomfield explains: "Usually the worst that happens with wood is that the house slips off its foundation and with luck it can be put back again." The lesson was learnt, and her researches show a sharp drop in masonry construction after 1868.

Wood had the advantage of being both cheap and plentiful; California redwood in particular is durable. In addition, the new iron steam presses and gang and scroll jigsaws made it possible to bend, curve, shape and stamp wood into exotic shapes. One classic study, *Painted Ladies* by Morley Baer, Elizabeth Pomada and Michael Larsen, records that some

48,000 wooden houses were built in San Francisco in the 65 years between the Gold Rush and the Panama Pacific exhibition of 1915. Many were destroyed in the earthquake and fire of 1906, but numerous smaller houses survived to the south and west of the devastated downtown.

In broad terms, San Francisco's Painted Ladies can be said to follow four main styles: Italianate (1860–1880), Stick-Eastlake (1880–90), Queen Anne (1890–1900) and Edwardian (1900–15). The best concentrations of surviving examples are to be found on Pacific Heights – which covers 130 blocks from Van Ness Avenue in the east to Presidio Avenue in the west, and from California Street in the south to Union Street in the north – and also in the Western Addition, which also lies west of Van Ness Avenue. (There is a wealth of detail about these houses to be found in Randolph Delehanty's *In the Victorian Style* (1991).)

Italianate houses, typically, have bold, bracketed cornices and bay windows with slanting sides. When they were built they were often called "London Roman" after the Italianate gentlemen's clubs in London's Pall Mall. Whereas the earlier Greek Revival houses often had projecting porches, Italianate houses more usually had simple doorheads with

bracketed cornices. Many details are similar to those found on Victorian stucco houses, and at first many Italianates were painted to look like stone.

In the 1880s ornament became increasingly elaborate; right-angled three-sided bay windows were fashionable, and the windows often had small triangular pediments built over them. The term "Stick style" refers to the plainer houses of the period, although they exhibit a preponderance of turned, notched and studded detail. Stick-Eastlake is a still richer version, festooned with ornament, which takes its name from Charles Eastlake, apostle of the Greek Revival, whose *Hints on Household Taste* (1868) was very much in vogue in North America. In the words of the *Painted Ladies* authors, San Franciscans piled "gingerbread on top of treacle, flowery forms on top of fruit salad."

Queen Anne refers not to the English Queen Anne (1702–14) and the early 18th-century domestic style that was named after her, but to the Queen Anne Revival style pioneered by the English architect Richard Norman Shaw in the 1870s. This is a "free-style" that forsook symmetry for a homely, vernacular look, creating picturesque compositions of pointed gables, rounded turrets, tall chimneys and arched windows. Typical San Francisco Queen Anne houses have front doors set beneath broad arches,

These houses on the 1400 block of Golden Gate Avenue in the Western Addition were designed in 1884 by John P Gaynor for the banker William Sharon. They step up the hill in matching pairs, each half of which consists of two maisonettes. At the top of the hill there is a single, two-maisonette house.

Original wallpaper, ceiling paper and paint on the ceiling medallion survive in this front parlour of an Italianate house dating from 1883. The house, which stands in the Mission District, was built by the architect Joseph Gosling for Frank G Edwards, an importer of English carpets and wallpapers.

large gables fronting the street and often round turrets with conical roofs. Two-unit houses, with twin front doors opening into top and bottom apartments, were rare in the 1880s but more common in the 1890s.

Edwardian marked a return to a more sober style, with a minimum of ornament, regular bands of identical windows and an emphasis on simple, classical proportion. The main feature is the bay window, with its plate-glass windows in double hung sashes designed to catch the sunlight. The proliferation of these was such that in 1886 a city fire ordinance was issued – it stated that no bay or oriel window was to be built projecting more than 3 feet (0.9m) over a street, or more than 9 feet (2.7m) in width.

Plots for each style were mostly long and narrow. The standard city block measured 412 feet (126m) from east to west and 275 feet (84m) from north to south. House lots were usually 25 feet (8m) wide and 100 feet (30m) or more deep. Although it is not immediately apparent from the street, the houses are deep, with long gardens behind.

Few of the houses had basements, and most were constructed on brick footings covered in cement. They were of wood-frame construction, using a combination of California redwood and Oregon pine. Redwood siding was applied directly to the frame. The rainwater gutters were of wood, often shaped from a single shaft of redwood.

Inside, much use was made of wood, with redwood staircases, and, in fancier houses, abundant use of graining, "faux" mahogany and bird's-eye maple.

The properties followed a typical layout, with a long, narrow hall and the staircase rising in line with the front door. To the side were three interconnected rooms: a front parlour, with bay window, for formal occasions; a second, family parlour; and a dining room. These three rooms were connected by 10-foot (3m) high sliding doors. The kitchen and pantry were located at the rear of the house. As San Francisco houses often stood free of one another, with a narrow alley no more than 3 feet (1m) wide between, it was possible to insert windows in the flanks, and to introduce lightwells, by means of jigs, or insets in the side walls, to light those rooms without windows at the front or back.

Above, the main bedroom was usually at the front, with the children's bedrooms behind and servants' rooms at the rear or in the attic. The bathroom was over the kitchen to concentrate plumbing in one place. Many houses had running water from the 1870s, and the original brick sewers are only now having to be considered for replacement.

A volume of *Picturesque California Homes* of 1885 describes rich colour schemes for these houses: "body, maroon; trimmings, seal, brown; sash, ash yellow; roof, dark brown; base, dark Indian red" and "base, Pompeii red; body, olive green; trimmings on body, bronze green; underneath cornice, terra cotta; roof, Venetian red and black." The exuberant colours of the 19th century gave way later to battleship grey, due, it is said, to a surplus of Navy paint rather than a taste for "functional modern." However, it is these colours that were picked up in the great revival of the 1960s, led by artists such as Butch Kardum and colour consultants such as Tony Canaletch (who travelled around with a hundred quarts of paint and mixed them by hand), by Foster Meagher of Color Control and Jazon Wonders of Blissful Painting.

In addition, a massive home-grown spare parts industry has developed, with the result that today there is no feature or ornament in these properties that cannot be replaced. Indeed, the revival and painstaking restoration of the Painted Ladies represents one of urban preservation's greatest success stories, and a recognition of the unique contribution made by these houses to the city's character.

The Keller House (above) on the 1300 block of Waller Street in the Haight-Ashbury District was built by the developer J A Whelan in 1896. It is one of a group of the fanciest Queen Anne style houses in the city. Typical features are the large gable pediment, the broad enclosing arch over the door, and the rich ornament in the friezes and gable. Set on a steep embankment it stands unusually high, allowing for the insertion of a garage.

The dining room in the Keller House has a patterned ceiling and a steep coved cornice that is ornamented with William Morris-style flowers and foliage and threaded through with an inscription. The room houses a handsome collection of Gothic Revival furniture.

Harrington Gardens and neighbouring Collingham Gardens, in Kensington, can rightfully be numbered among the most individualistic streets ever built in London. They were built between 1880 and 1888, and are the creation of the five Peto brothers, whose firm, as one of the capital's most enterprising building concerns, flourished between 1872 and 1891. The fifth brother, Harold Peto, had become, aged only 21, a partner of Ernest George (1839–1922), an architect then winning a reputation for imaginative domestic architecture.

From an early age George had accompanied his father on his travels in Europe, sketching in cities, where his eye was caught by the gabled town houses of merchants in the Netherlands and Germany. This

The back of No.39 Harrington Gardens (right) overlooks a shared garden. The rich detail includes octagonal lead glazing, tile hanging and scrolled "aprons" below the upper windows.

Arts and Crafts house
KENSINGTON, LONDON

No.39 (below) was built in 1882–3, as one of a pair with No.41, by the architects Ernest George and Harold Peto. Elaborate stepped and scrolled gables, flanked by tall chimneys, face the street.

influence provides a clue to the design of the London houses, which evoke Dutch Renaissance architecture and the medieval houses of Hanseatic city states.

Nos.35–45 Harrington Gardens are built on shallow plots and overlook a communal garden behind. Turning these shallow plots to advantage, the houses were built with unusually broad frontages, some 60 feet (18m) wide, with backs that are as stylish as the façades. As a result this is a row of just six opulent houses, four being designed as two pairs.

The most striking is No.39, which carries a blue plaque announcing that it was the home of William Schwenck Gilbert (1836–1911). By tradition it was the success of Gilbert and Sullivan's *Patience*, produced in 1881–2, that led Gilbert to commission so large and lavish a house, costing a reported £19,000 ($30,400). He moved into the house during October 1883. Crowning the great stepped gable (stepped in no fewer than 19 stages) is a galleon, alluding to the descent Gilbert claimed from the Elizabethan seafarer Sir Humphrey Gilbert (the founder of the first English colony in North America) and not, as some suggested, to his work *HMS Pinafore*. "Sir, I do not put my trademark on my house," was Gilbert's retort.

The house is built in red brick with stone trim, but the virtuoso feature is the leadwork of the windows, which varies from floor to floor and sometimes from window to window. Instead of simple diamond panes there are interlocking squares and octagons, circle and cross patterns, and diamonds and octagons – patterns redolent of de Hooch and Vermeer paintings. Further enrichment comes from the ornamental iron ties placed at regular intervals up the façade, and the heraldic beasts on the crow-stepped gable. This is a giant among row houses, with six storeys, visibly diminishing in height towards the top. Slender, soaring chimneys and steep roofs add to the height.

The windows of No.39 (below) sharply diminish in size toward the top, and the design varies from storey to storey. Above the projecting porch are smaller rooms opening off the half-landings on the stairs. The sculptural details are in terra-cotta, and the intricate iron ties echo those used to strengthen 17th-century Dutch houses.

The front door opens into a lobby with a small waiting area to one side, where visitors could sit without intruding on the routine of the house. Any feeling that the visitor has been consigned to a mere waiting room is dispelled by the oak panelling and the elaborate black and gold wave-pattern mosaic floor. The double-height hall, as in so many large late-Victorian houses, is the fulcrum of all activity. Henry James conveys the atmosphere of such a space in his novel *The Other House*: "bright, large and high, richly decorated and freely used, full of 'corners' and communications, it evidently played equally the part of a place of reunion and a place of transit."

The lobby also possesses homely details that are taken from English vernacular architecture: a large inglenook fireplace, oak panelling up to the top of the doors, and an oak staircase that rises in one corner, screened off by arches made from the same wood. A small bay window looks down from a cosy mezzanine room over the entrance, and is inset with rich Renaissance-style coloured glass. There is more painted glass in the large main window that lights the hall from the side.

It was Hermann Muthesius, in his classic work *The English House*, which was published at the turn of the 20th century, who noted the increasing popularity of the inglenook during the previous 30 years. Such fireplaces, he explains, were just high enough for a person to stand upright, with seats at the sides that had to receive direct light so that people could sit and read. Inglenooks, as in Gilbert's house, had therefore to be in outside walls.

Gilbert loved to entertain – at children's parties he would appear in the bay window above the entrance and scatter sweets – and above all he relished the company of attractive women (at Grim's Dyke, in Harrow Weald, where he moved in 1890, he even had a room he called "The Flirtorium"). After dinner the men were never permitted to linger over the port before rejoining the ladies; at Harrington Gardens, notably, the drawing room and the dining room are both on the ground floor. Both have inscriptions above the door that today seem slightly ponderous; to take one example: "And those things do best

please me, that befall preposterously." By contrast, the shapely brass door handles might almost be the work of a modern designer such as Philippe Starck.

The drawing room, measuring 40 by 18 feet (12 by 5m), opens onto the garden. The walls are panelled with solid rosewood, and at one end there is a superb alabaster fireplace with an elaborately carved marble overmantel worthy of a Renaissance *palazzo*. The ceiling is a very rich and beautifully crisp version of late Elizabethan or Jacobean plasterwork, with a complex geometric pattern that is enlivened by trailing vines and grotesque figures.

The unusual door handles (above) are specially shaped to suit the human hand. Their sinuous quality complements the carved panels of Renaissance-style scrollwork that are set into the doors.

A richly carved stone chimney-piece (right), inset with blue and white Dutch tiles, stands in the hall. It is large enough to sit in and is provided with a window.

The 17th-century-style painted glass in the hall (right) was executed by Lavers & Westlake and bears the date 1883 and the letter "G" for (WS) Gilbert, the operatic librettist, for whom the house was built.

The oak staircase rises in short flights, in the manner of English 16th-century versions. The steps are made of single oak blocks, while the balusters are voluptuous "S"-shaped scrolls, some with grotesque heads and tails, others inset with the tops of Ionic pillars. On the half landing is the little room with the bay window that overlooks the hall. It was intended as an intimate space, and has shelves and recesses for the display of china.

The first floor contains Gilbert's capacious study, with a bedroom next door, which allowed him to slip into bed after a performance without disturbing the household. His desk stood in a deep bay window overlooking the tranquil garden, and, so that no sound could destroy his concentration, the leaded windows have one of the earliest examples of double glazing. A deep frieze at the top of the wall-panelling is hung with what appear to be panels of gilded Spanish leather. Picked out in burnished gold, they seem to date from the 17th century but are in fact stamped anaglypta. No less virtuoso are the radiator grilles by Starkie Gardner: brass repoussé panels of swirling acanthus leaves. On this floor, too, was another male preserve: the billiard room.

On the second floor Lady Gilbert's suite repeated the layout of her husband's. Above were two further floors of nurseries and servants' rooms, utilizing every possible space beneath the eaves. Although the ceilings are lower, these upper rooms are still light and airy. Beatrix Potter, the children's writer, noted in December 1883 that there were "twenty-six bed-rooms with a bath-room to each (fancy twenty-six burst water pipes!)." This was certainly an exaggeration, and Gilbert was unlikely to suffer from burst water pipes, having installed, among other modern conveniences, central heating and electric lights.

In this first-floor room (right), which overlooks the garden, the deep frieze appears to be gilt leather that has been embossed with a pattern of flowers and fruit; in fact it is anaglypta wallpaper.

In total, 77 Swan lamps were supplied, 53 for flexible pendants and 24 for brackets (with an additional 23 because early filaments broke more frequently than they do today). Gilbert was also the owner of one of the very first telephones.

From the upstairs windows the sheer quality of the building work is apparent, for example the zig-zag lead flashing (used for waterproofing) behind the gable, complete with neat scroll details. *The Building News* of 13 July 1883, which illustrated a series of houses in the street, praised the way each varied in appearance "like a casual bit of some ancient city," and lamented the fact that this style of building had not arrived "until most of the available space in London had been covered with the dull monotonous terrace." In the same year, however, *The Builder* put forward a somewhat different view: "Old streets do occasionally assume this kind of appearance of … different manners all muddled together and they have a picturesque suggestiveness then, but to go about to make this kind of thing deliberately is child's play."

Today Gilbert's house is sympathetically looked after by a firm of architects and design consultants; it would be ideal if the property could be acquired by a British heritage organization and opened to the public when the opportunity next arises.

The town of Hebden Bridge, high in the north of England's Pennine Hills, is home to several rows of terrace houses like no others, where one house (and sometimes two) is set on top of another. From the front they seem to be stone-built, two-storey dwellings, two windows wide. But at the back, where the land falls away, rises a towering cliff of what look like four-storey tenements. The explanation is that these two-storey houses have another terrace house below, entered from the street behind. It all came about because of a shortage of building land in a fast-growing textile town set in steep-sided valleys. The two sides are so different that it is hard to believe one is looking at the front and back of the same building. Yet the game can be given away where owners have cleaned their stonework – two storeys will be clean and two still memorably blackened by soot.

Preservation history was made during the 1980s when the local civic trust won the battle for Nutclough Terrace, a typical row of such houses. The terrace

Machpelah (below), built in 1805, is characteristic of the "over-and-under" terraces of Hebden Bridge. The two long rows of small windows in the gable lit the corduroy makers' workshops. Below these windows are two-storey dwellings; the top windows at the front in fact belong to separate dwellings entered from an outdoor staircase at the back of the terrace.

One house over another
HEBDEN BRIDGE, YORKSHIRE

was not listed for protection by the Department of the Environment, but the trust secured a court ruling that it shared protection with adjoining Nutclough Mill. Indeed, most of the town's "over-and-under" houses were unprotected until 1984, when a new list of its historic buildings was published. "It took the number of listed buildings from 35 to 350," says Peter Thornborrow, the local historian who did much of the research.

The earliest of the terraces is the Biblical-sounding Machpelah, built by the Reverend Richard Fawcett. Its most striking feature is the broad gable end, into which are set two long rows of mullioned windows, providing light for the fustian cutters who made cotton corduroy in the lofts at the top of the house.

During the 19th century the town became Britain's leading area for the manufacture of corduroy. Textiles produced on the Yorkshire side of the Pennines were usually woollen, with weavers working at home until machinery was introduced, but Hebden Bridge became an outpost of neighbouring Lancashire's cotton industry. However, it preserved its small scale because minimal equipment was needed to produce corduroy, and both fustian cutting and weaving could be done at home or in small loft workshops.

Original windows (left) light
the top storey at the back
of Machpelah. These are
small, old-fashioned mullion
windows, whereas those on
all the floors at the front have
Victorian plate-glass sashes.

Machpelah is a terrace of eight two-storey houses, dating from 1905. Toward the middle an archway leads to the back, where stone steps are built into the hillside, joining up with balconies that give access to the doors of the third-floor dwelling. The windows on the street side are, interestingly, of sash construction, but those at the back are the more traditional mullion windows, small and narrow. The whole row was due to be demolished but was saved by emergency "spotlisting." The rising slope behind the houses is

divided into a series of what look like small garden terraces. On these "tenter banks" the cloth was stretched out and left for several weeks to shrink.

Another early group is Nos.71–87 Bridge Lanes. These houses, which have two storeys facing the road and four or five at the rear, were also about to be demolished, but again spotlisting preserved them. During restoration the under- and over-dwellings were converted into single tall terrace houses. Thornborrow says: "They originally had stone stair-cases cantilevered out from the walls, but these had been so worn away by clogs the decision was taken to build new wooden stairs."

Several well-preserved streets of over-and-under houses open off steeply rising Birchcliffe Road. At the end of each pair of streets is a larger villa at right angles to the two terraces – one "over" and one "under" – behind it. One villa is named "Eiffel Tower 1893," a tribute to the structure finished four years earlier. To the rear are two terraces, Eiffel Buildings and Eiffel Street. As you walk up the hill you pass four storeys on one side of the block, then two on the other. At the lower level, the under-dwellings, built of the gritstone found in the Pennines, are plain, two-storey cottages set into the hill, with windows only on the entrance side. Above, and seemingly part of the same house, are the over-dwellings.

The end buildings on the next two terraces up the hill are dated 1898 and 1899, showing that the whole remarkable group was built in little over a decade.

At the front, these "over-dwellings" in Bridge Lanes (above) appear to be simple two-storey cottages built of the local gritstone. However, at the back (right) they rise four storeys and enjoy a view over a valley. The "under-dwellings" at the rear open onto Calder Place, a lane at a lower level that is still paved with the original stone setts. The long bands of mullion windows, giving good light, suggest that weavers worked within.

The Hôtel Ciamberlani, at Rue Defacqz 48 (right), was built by the architect Paul Hankar for the mother of Albert Ciamberlani, a painter. The twin tunnel-shaped windows retain their unusual glazing, and the elaborate *sgraffito* paintings revive a technique practised in 16th-century Florence.

The extravagant house at Square Ambiorix 11 (below), completed in 1903, has a narrow façade almost entirely of glass; its windows and balconies are a riot of interlacing curves.

Before the advent of the autoroutes, one of the strangest sights to be observed while driving through Belgium was the occasional single terrace house standing beside a main road between cities. Although they stood in open country, these houses had windows only at the front and back; the side walls were faced in quilted slates to give protection as well as insulation.

In Belgium a house is said to have two, three or four façades, which indicates whether it is a terrace house, semi-detached or free-standing. The tax payable on houses has long been calculated according to the number and width of the façades; a town house with a wide frontage proclaims wealth, while house width shrinks dramatically in poorer districts.

Parisians began living in large blocks of apartments, *immeubles,* the 18th century, and terrace houses were a rarity in the Paris of the following century.

Eclectic houses of 1900
BRUSSELS

By contrast, the Belgians continued to build houses in rows – not only in Brussels but also in Antwerp, Liège and, for that matter, all the country's major towns – well into the 20th century. Although apartment buildings were constructed in Brussels between the two World Wars, they did not become widespread until as late as the 1960s.

The main difference between many Belgian town houses and those in Britain and North America is that those in Belgium are rarely built to a repeating design, but instead vary sharply in style and materials. Belgians are attached to individuality in their houses, and there is an expression, *"avoir un brique dans l'estomac,"* which might be translated as "having bricks and mortar in your veins." In addition, strict copyright laws made Belgian architects wary of repeating designs; each house is different, even when part of a row is designed by one architect.

International attention has normally focused on Brussels' striking Art Nouveau houses. Outstanding among these are the Maison Tassel and the Hôtel Solvay, both built in the 1890s by Victor Horta (1861–1947), and the work of his contemporaries such as Paul Hankar. However, Belgian magazines of the turn of the century are filled with no less opulent and exotic terrace houses in revivalist styles; a fine example is the Renaissance-style Hôtel Goblet

d'Alviella at Rue Faider 10, built in 1882 by Octave Van Rysselberghe. The best of these magazines was *L'Emulation*, a folio-size production with photography of the highest quality. Here are plans and elevations of new houses supplied by the architects. Many architects undertook development themselves and streets are named after them, such as the Rue Henri Jacob and the Avenue Carsole.

In another practice of the time, a proprietor would build a group of three houses, one for himself and the others for members of his family. Alternatively, the second and third houses were built to be let, and many retired people sought to secure a regular income in this way. Among such groups of houses it is usual for one, the *maison de maître*, to be more opulent than the rest, with fine ironwork, stained glass and decorative effects such as *sgraffito*.

The typical plot is 16½–19½ feet (5–6m) wide and 82 feet (25m) deep, although some plots are as deep as 164 or 197 feet (50–60m). Sunken basements were a standard feature of Brussels houses, but, unlike in England and Scotland, they had no front area to provide air and light. Depending on the whim of the owner and the architect, the basement might be almost completely submerged, with a dungeon-like window to light the kitchen. In some cases the main floor was accessed by between five and ten steps.

Ernst Blérot's group of houses at Rue Vandercshrick 13–21 has the banded stonework popular in Brussels around 1900. The architect enlivened and gave individuality to the flat façades by incorporating curves and projections, arches over the windows and protruding bay windows.

The front door at Rue de Vanderschrick 7 (above) belongs to one of a series of houses in the street designed by the architect Ernest Blérot. Each house is stylistically distinct; this is a geometric design in which the wild curves of Art Nouveau give way to symmetry and angularity.

This allowed a substantial basement window, with the sill at the level of the pavement. Where a house had a shop on the ground floor, as in the cluster of Art Nouveau houses in the Rue St Boniface, the ground floor would be no more than a step above the street. Here a sunken slit allows a shaft of light in the basement, which nevertheless was used as the kitchen, complete with a vaulted ceiling built in the then new fireproof brick.

In grander residential areas – for example, along the Avenue Palmerston and around the Square Marie Louise, where opulent houses have front gardens – the basement is only half submerged. Narrow street fronts indicate deep plans, and many Brussels town houses have three rooms in a line on the main floor, the middle one with no direct light. One of Horta's significant innovations was the light-well, bringing daylight to the heart of his houses.

Frescoes by Paul-Albert
Baudoin adorn the staircase
hall of the Hôtel Hannon.
The metal stair rail, without
a single vertical strut, is
an extreme but successful
example of curvilinearity.
This motif of constantly
curving forms is taken
up on the mosaic floor.

The Hôtel Hannon (above),
at Rue de la Jonction 1, was
designed in 1903 by Jules
Brunfaut. This corner house
is richly sculptural in design,
with curving shapes that
suggest natural forms. Both
the tops and the bottoms of
the windows are rounded.

The architect Ernest von Humbeck designed this house (below) in the Rue du Monastère, a photograph of which was published in the Belgian magazine *L'Emulation* in 1905. The accompanying plans, showing seven floors and two half-landings, illustrate the complexity of the layout of this fairly narrow house.

Each of the houses on the Rue St Boniface, like those in the well-preserved districts on the other side of the Avenue Louise, has a bootscraper set into the wall next to the front door. In some Art Nouveau houses this survives as a miniature *pièce de résistance* showing the touch of an individual architect. Art Nouveau letter-boxes, again stylishly individual, are a frequent survival, although, being small, these are under threat from the postal authorities.

Brussels town houses are remarkable for their wealth of decorative motifs, varied and adventurous combinations of materials and bold use of colour. From the 1880s striking use was made of the Italian technique of *sgraffito*, a form of incised ornament used in Renaissance Italy (see pages 36–39). A fine example is Ernest Acker's 1892 façade at Chaussée de Charleroi 229. The whole façade is covered in bands of *sgraffito*, which architects like Hankar employed for inset decorative panels and friezes – for example, in the Hôtel Ciamberlani, at Rue Defacqz 48, dating from 1897. Frequent use was made of polychrome brick; bands of coloured brick run across façades, and window heads are picked out in colourful patterns. The architect Gustave Strauven made inspired use of striped pink and white brick at Rue St Quentin 30–32 in 1899, and went on to design, for the painter G de Saint-Cyr, the most exotic of all Art Nouveau houses, at Square Ambiorix 11 (1900–03). Here the wild shapes suggest a sinuous underwater world. This riot of ironwork also illustrates the hierarchy of balconies found on many Brussels town houses. In such cases the first-floor balcony is large enough for a table and chairs, that on the second-floor is large enough to stand on, and there is a recessed balcony at the top. In some cases the top balcony was simply a *garde-corps*, a grille serving as a safety measure when French windows were opened.

Art Nouveau went out of fashion almost as quickly as it came in. *"Végétal"* Art Nouveau, sometimes known as the "noodle style," was disappearing in 1907, to be succeeded by "geometric" Art Nouveau, a version of the Viennese Sezession style. A superb example may be seen at Rue des Francs 5, the house and studio that Paul Cachie built for himself in 1905, which have recently been beautifully restored.

A new burst of eclecticism followed, immediately before and after the First World War. The city had grown in concentric rings around the original pentagon formed by the city walls. First came an inner ring of residential development between 1865 and 1910, the Première Couronne, or first crown, followed by an outer ring, the Deuxième Couronne, built up from the 1920s to the 1960s.

The town houses along the boulevards forming the Deuxième Couronne survive in gratifyingly long runs. Red and brown brick came into vogue with a revival of the classical 18th-century town house – the style called neo-Georgian in Britain and Colonial Revival in America. More exotic still are the neo-Baroque houses in a delicious pink brick, with windows and doors as exaggerated in shape as the most riotous 18th-century Portuguese Baroque.

Today many Brussels town houses are under threat from development. The city has just 700 protected buildings, whereas in Amsterdam, which is of similar size, there are some 7,000. Worse still, in Brussels there is no effective legislation to protect neighbourhoods or create conservation areas. The battle to save and protect them has in recent years been led by a vigorous new group, Pétitions-Patrimoine.

Repeatedly, developers take up the cry of the *"dent creuse,"* the "hollow tooth." Where two, three or more older terrace houses are left standing between taller, more recent apartment blocks, the developers wring their hands at the ugly gap-toothed look (a cry repeated parrot fashion in the local media) when the real issue is the possibility that eight storeys will spring up where there were just three. Nowhere in Europe are outstanding architect-designed terrace houses under such great threat. At the same time, nowhere does such a wealth of varied town-house architecture still survive.

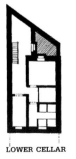
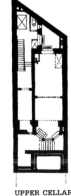

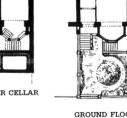
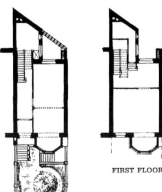
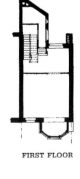

LOWER CELLAR

UPPER CELLAR

GROUND FLOOR

FIRST FLOOR

LANDING BETWEEN GROUND AND FIRST FLOORS

LANDING BETWEEN FIRST AND SECOND FLOORS

SECOND FLOOR

THIRD FLOOR

FOURTH FLOOR

The balcony (right) on the *bel étage*, or first floor, of Horta's house, built between 1898 and 1901, is illustrative of the architect's fondness for exposing structural iron and steel. Particularly noteworthy here are the lintels above the windows. Before Horta these would seldom have been revealed in combination with stone, regarded by architects as a "noble" material not to be debased in this way.

ictor Horta created the Art Nouveau style when he designed the Maison Tassel in Brussels. Five years later, in 1898, he bought two adjoining plots of land in the city's Rue Américaine on which to build a house and a studio for himself. Today the house is a museum open to the public and the best place to explore a complete Art Nouveau interior. It is worth noting, however, that the house is an example of what is referred to as "*végétal*" Art Nouveau, in order to distinguish it from the geometric version of the style that was to emerge soon after. Horta's great motif was the tendril, and plant-like forms recur, twisting and coiling, on his façades and throughout the interiors.

The French talk of façades that have been built in "noble materials," such as stone or marble. However, drawing inspiration from the renowned French

Horta's Art Nouveau house
BRUSSELS

architect and theorist Viollet-le-Duc (1814–79), who first advocated the use of exposed iron in domestic architecture, Horta flaunted iron girders and tie-rods boldly and stylishly.

Metamorphosis is a significant concept to bear in mind when considering his work. Thus, the first-floor balcony expands to become a canopy over the front door. The ironwork of the balcony sprouts outward and upward, twisting around the slender colonnettes that curl around the iron brackets supporting the bow window above and continue up the façade. Further up, the plain stone strips that frame the windows expand like the arms of a sofa, and near the top of the façade a butterfly balcony bursts out as if from a chrysalis. Next door, on Horta's studio, both iron and stonework manifest the same sense of growth – the base of the first-floor column emerges through the smooth stonework like the roots of a tree emerging through grass.

Equally novel is the layout of the house. The usual practice in Brussels at this time was to place the main floor at the top of a flight of steps, allowing light into a basement kitchen at the front. Horta moved the kitchen to the back of the ground floor and created a hallway a single step up from the street. "It was I who first drew plans for a ... house with a cloakroom, wc and visitors' reception room in the entrance," he wrote. Three sliding and three

swing doors enabled him to partition off the hall in various ways. "It's like a vaudeville" says the curator, speaking of this curious arrangement of walk-in cupboards that suggests a stage magician's vanishing act. Beyond, Horta shows himself to be a pioneer of two of the great features of 20th-century house design: the split level and the open plan.

At the heart of the interior is a quite sensational staircase that ascends around an open square well; different rooms open off each short flight of steps. Whereas the traditional staircase has a straight handrail and stout corner posts, Horta defies this convention by placing everything on the curve, making mahogany and bronze appear pliable.

In his *Mémoires* Horta wrote: "I designed and created the models for each piece of furniture, for every single hinge and door handle, the carpets and the wall decorations ... my drawings were distorted by my draughtsmen ... I had to correct every change from one scale to another." It was the unconventional nature of his designs, he added, that made this degree of attention to the house's internal detailing and décor necessary.

Among Horta's most virtuoso creations are a bronze column in the hall, which, it transpires, is a radiator, and tendril-like gas lamps that twine around a marble column on the first-floor landing, one of which, situated nearer the music room, has a little

Horta liked to suggest organic growth in his designs. Tendril-like ironwork (right) here embellishes the top of the staircase. Glass roofs and open stairwells are also typical, and bring daylight into the core of the house.

Art Nouveau architects such as Horta would also mastermind the decoration and the design of the furniture. The dining room (below) has a parquet floor with a shaped border in a white mosaic surround that matches the walls.

holder for a box of matches. Not long after their installation, these lamps were converted so that they could be powered by electricity.

The dining room is a remarkable achievement, being faced in white enamelled bricks. Horta had originally intended these for the garden front but decided that the play of light on their shiny surfaces would serve the interior better. Although the tiles' stark uniformity might well have evoked a public convenience, Horta dispelled any such association by introducing gleaming brass edgings and a striped marble dado. Nevertheless, he admitted that even using the finest marble would have been cheaper than these "costly trappings."

Although richly ornate sideboards were a common feature of 19th-century dining rooms, Horta went a step further. He designed a built-in dresser that contained not only a gas fireplace but also a concealed

serving hatch immediately above it, with a metal plate that served as a chafing dish in the adjoining pantry. Access to the pantry is provided by a door to the left of the dresser.

The main bedroom is on the second floor at the back, with the bathroom and toilet tucked away conveniently in cupboards behind the dressing-room mirrors. Perhaps the most unexpected feature of the bedroom is a tiny urinal that folds out from a cupboard beside the bed.

The top landing of the stair is inspired. Horta roofed it in glass, like a conservatory, and by narrowing the flights of stairs as they ascend he sends the maximum amount of light flooding down into the middle of the house from the skylight above. In a final flourish, he sets up multiple reflections by placing large mirrors on opposite walls.

The history of architecture is most often recounted as a history of innovation. However, a fascinating study remains to be written of buildings that look back to the past without being candidly revivalist in style. Many such buildings deceive us into believing that they are older than they really are, either when they stand alone or when they blend cleverly with their earlier neighbours.

A good example is the house of the Italian painter Mario De Maria (1852–1924) in the picturesque and wonderfully preserved hill town of Asolo, a half-hour drive from Venice. The house stands in the Via Canova, which leads out of the town to the studio of the great sculptor of that name. The architectural equivalent of the troubadour style used in paintings depicting medieval times, it is a romanticized version of the Middle Ages, richer and more fanciful than anything else in the town – ornate, colourful and yet at the same time mellow. These characteristics link it to a group of individualistic artists' houses built around Europe, dating from the second half of the 19th century. Examples include the neo-Renaissance house at Cité Malesherbes 11 in Paris, built in 1856 by Anatole Jal for the painter Pierre-Jules Jollivet, and two Art Nouveau properties in Brussels: the studio of the painter Potvin at Rue Charles-Quint 103 (1896), by Paul Hamess, and the home of the painter G de Saint-Cyr, at Square Ambiorix 11 (1900–03), by Gustave Strauven (see pages 128 and 131).

Twin houses
ASOLO

With their stepped gables and Gothic and Renaissance detail, Mario De Maria's house and its twin on the right blend into a largely intact historic town. At the same time the painter succeeded in lending the design a quirkiness that is typically Art Nouveau.

Mario De Maria was born in Bologna, the son of a doctor and art collector who himself was the son of a Neo-classical sculptor. Ignoring his family's desire that he should study to become a doctor, as a young man De Maria first dedicated himself to music then turned to painting. He studied the Old Masters in Vienna and Paris before returning to Italy in the 1880s to settle in Rome and then, in 1892, in Venice. De Maria's paintings reveal a wide-ranging fascination with old buildings, and the most famous, *Il Fondaco dei Turchi*, depicts the arrival, during the 16th century, of an oriental barque in front of the well-known Romanesque building near the city's Rialto bridge. Amid the throng of turbaned figures, the painter Titian can be seen at work.

In 1912 Mario De Maria submitted designs to the Venetian authorities for a studio for his own use, to be built on the Fondamenta della Croce on the island of Giudecca. Called the Casa dei Tre Ochi (the House of Three Eyes), the studio took its name from three large arched windows on the first floor. The diamond-pattern brickwork in the original design was a clear homage to the Doge's Palace. Later De Maria designed a hotel in Cortina in "alpine" neo-Gothic style, and then built his house in Asolo, known as "*Il sogno di Rembrandt*" (Rembrandt's Dream). Like the Dutch painter's canalside house with studio in Amsterdam (see page 49), the Asolo house has a stepped gable. This detail was probably inspired by Mario De Maria's time in the Netherlands and Germany, where he went to study 17th-century painting.

The façade of the painter's house (right) is decorated with a harlequin pattern in blue and beige, echoing colours that are prominent in the Venetian carnival. The window surrounds are in marble and, at the ground floor, iron grilles burst into Art Nouveau foliage.

The panels of the front door (above) are carved with the severe "flame-headed" arches that are found in Venice. Gothic quatrefoils over the door allow a little light into an otherwise intentionally gloomy interior.

Because it stands on one of the main routes out of Asolo, the house has over the years acquired a patina of grime from passing traffic. However, inspection reveals that it is constructed of sumptuous, colourful materials. The exterior walls are decorated with a harlequin pattern in soft blue and beige, and the doors and windows are edged in bands of richly veined marble. Over the front door two quatrefoils, set in marble roundels, let light into the entrance hall. Rich iron grilles protect the ground-floor windows and mean that they can be left open safely on hot days. On the first floor the original octagon and diamond-pattern windows still survive. Between them may be seen suitably medieval heraldic motifs: a coat of arms and a carved knot.

The house has four storeys and a sunken basement that, because the land falls away behind, receives ample light. A few years ago the interior was stripped out and remodelled for a new owner, who told me "I have destroyed everything inside. It was an impossible house to live in – very, very dark." The work was well done, giving an open layout full of light, but it shows that even in Italy, where preservation laws are strict, protection of 19th- and 20th-century interiors is still woefully inadequate. A local architect, Giorgio Zanesco, was in charge, and the house has now been offered for sale. Of interest too is the neighbouring house on the right, also designed by De Maria. This has a matching stepped gable, but the columns of the large loggias are Renaissance in style.

20TH CENTURY
Modern

Although it looks like the hull of a huge upturned boat, this is in fact a row of new houses in Groningen, in the Netherlands, designed by the architect Kas Oosterhuis and completed in 1995. The steady rise of the roof makes each house slightly different from its neighbour. These state-subsidized owner-occupied houses were built in two matching blocks that together contain 26 five-room houses and two six-room houses.

With the dawn of the 20th century architects proclaimed a brave new world that would provide homes with light, warmth, air and sanitation for everyone; with this came the notion of a house as *une machine à habiter*. Much of the promised housing has been supplied by multi-storey apartments, but architects have continued to build terrace houses, in both traditional and modern forms. The latest examples make adventurous use of glass and steel as well as wood shingles and stucco. As the century closes, open-plan airy living is in fashion, based around tall, studio-style spaces, balconies and roof terraces.

Bruno Taut (1880–1938) ranks as one of the great pioneers of 20th-century house design. At two sites in suburban Berlin he and a number of other architects were responsible for more than 10,000 dwellings erected between 1925 and 1930. These apartments and terrace houses (*Reihehäuse* – "row houses") were laid out in model developments that were sensibly provided with community facilities such as central heating plants, laundries, day-care centres and public assembly rooms. Bruno Taut belonged to that rare breed of utopian visionaries also gifted with a practical bent.

Born in Königsberg, north-east Germany, Taut had difficult earlier years, helping to support the family while pursuing his architectural studies. Germany was enveloped in turmoil in the months immediately following its defeat in the First World War, and during this period he was instrumental to setting up a series of radical groups, including the Arbeitsrat der Kunst

Colourful Modernism
BERLIN

On the Onkel Tom Siedlung Taut built the same type of house on both sides of the north–south streets, but broke the uniformity by setting the houses at both ends of each row either forward or back. It is also just possible to distinguish the colour scheme for the façades from Taut's ground plan.

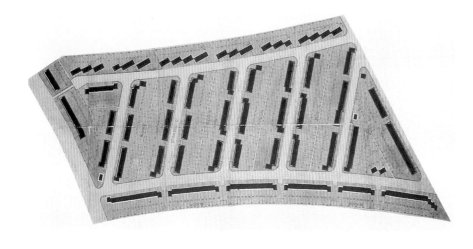

(Works Council for Art) and Der Ring, a group of 25 architects who pressed for new housing policies in Berlin. After three years in Magdeburg as director of the building and planning department, Taut returned to Berlin in 1924 to embark on the design of large-scale housing projects; he carried out the majority of this work for non-profit housing associations.

The two finest examples of his work are at Britz, in south-east Berlin, where apartments fashioned in the stripped-down International modern style are laid out in a spectacular horseshoe around a pond, and at

Zehlendorf, where the Onkel Tom Siedlung (Uncle Tom Estate) nestles amid the pine forests that fringe the south-western edge of the city.

Laid out in 1929–32, the Zehlendorf estate consists of a series of straight streets that have rustic names such as Am Wieselbau (The Weasel's House), Am Fuchspaß (The Fox's Pass), Hochwildpfad (High Wild Path) and Am Lappjagen (The Lapp Hunt). These are sandwiched between two longer gently curving roads, Am Hegelwinkel and Hochsitzweg.

The houses are single-family dwellings laid out in rows, some in groups of just five or six, others in clusters of up to 15. The corner houses are slightly larger and set back from the rest of the row, or occasionally forward. Taut strongly believed that it was of more value to the community to build houses rather than large apartment blocks, and in his book *Die Stadtkrone* (1919) he talks of a god who sweeps away a town of tenement blocks to replace it with houses benefiting from a more humane layout.

Colour was a second key feature of Taut's modern houses. He berated the typical dismal grey houses of the age, and worked out an unusually elaborate colour scheme for the Onkel Tom Siedlung. House fronts facing east are painted a cool greyish green, attractive in the morning light, while fronts facing

Taut's designs were based on a constant play of geometric forms, as in this window (left) where the glazing pattern is reversed from one side to the other. He also liked strong colour; here, for the west-facing façades, he used red for the window, yellow for the inner frame and white for the outer frame.

This row of Type II houses clearly shows that the proportions of all the elements of the lower two storeys are vertical, whereas horizontals dominate in the upper storey.

west are a reddish brown that looks particularly warm in the afternoon and early evening. For the windows he used three colours. On the green fronts, the outer frame was painted yellow, the window frame red and the inner, opening frame white. With the brown fronts the sequence was white, yellow, red. Taut was reacting against the all-pervading white of early Modernism. He wrote: "Of all colours white is the first to get dirty; dust and soot do not combine with white as they do with other colours to soften the original shade or even perhaps to deepen it; white simply turns into a dirt-ingrained dead grey."

Taut usually grouped his houses in symmetrical pairs, with a vertical band of bricks and a drainpipe as punctuation between each pair. The two houses forming the pair were divided by no more than a fine recess in the rendering which has, in the majority of cases, been lost as a result of subsequent repairs.

The Zehlendorf houses are classified by type, and Type II (shown here), embracing a number of minor variants, is by far the commonest. Type II consists of three storeys above a submerged basement that has an internal stair leading to a laundry and cellar. The front door opens into a staircase hall with a kitchen beside it and a living room beyond. This arrangement

applies to the houses on both sides of the streets that run north–south, to preserve symmetry, and therefore only those houses on the east side of the street take advantage of the sun through having a kitchen facing east and a living room facing west. The first floor has two rooms and a bathroom, and the second floor two further rooms.

A special feature of many of the houses is the gracious curving staircase, which has steps that fan out at their corners. The houses are ingeniously planned so that the flight up to the first floor has more space, while the flight continuing to the second floor is more compact.

In an 18th-century terrace house, the size and position of the windows were largely a product of carefully considered proportions. Taut, an apostle of 20th-century Functionalism, which, in brief, sets fitness for purpose above aesthetic considerations, has no such concerns for symmetry and hierarchy. On the street front his windows vary in size, shape and design, according to their purpose. Each one is different, the bathroom being the smallest. It is interesting to note from the plan that the windows of some rooms are not set centrally in the window wall but to one side.

Type II house, Onkel Tom Siedlung

Taut arranged his houses in symmetrical pairs. House fronts facing west were painted a warm reddish brown, those facing east a cooler green, so that they could look best in either evening or morning light. The windows here are picked out in a crisp livery of white, yellow and red.

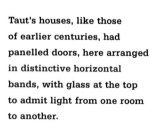

Although the houses were built to a tight plan, Taut contrived just enough space for a graceful stair ascending in a curve that fans out at the bottom. The flight continuing up to the second floor is cleverly designed to be more compact.

Taut's houses, like those of earlier centuries, had panelled doors, here arranged in distinctive horizontal bands, with glass at the top to admit light from one room to another.

KEY

① The entrance porch, with handrail, and a glass panel over the door to light the hall

② A vertical band of bricks acts as punctuation, dividing each pair of houses

③ Taut "horizontalized" the top sections of the houses to make them appear lower

④ The submerged basement with a laundry room at the front and a store behind

⑤ Ventilation grill to laundry

⑥ Entrance hall and staircase. The kitchen is at the front, to the left of the hall

⑦ A glass-roofed verandah overlooks the garden behind the property

⑧ Bathroom with terrazzo floor

⑨ By confining the upper part of the stair to the middle of the house, Taut was able to gain a small extra room on each of the upper floors

⑩ The bedrooms, overlooking the garden. The colour scheme for the interior, as for the exterior, is taken from one of the original properties on the estate

⑪ The chimneys of each pair of houses are grouped together

GROUND FLOOR   **FIRST FLOOR**

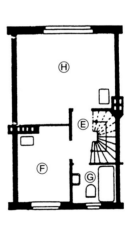

Ⓐ Entrance hall and stair

Ⓑ Kitchen with "X" marking the position of the stove

Ⓒ Living/dining room

Ⓓ Verandah

Ⓔ Landing

Ⓕ Front bedroom

Ⓖ Bathroom

Ⓗ Bedroom overlooking rear garden

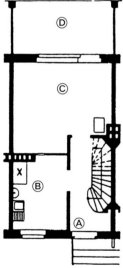

The 1951 Festival of Britain heralded a brave new world after a decade of hardship. Part of it was a Live Architecture Exhibition on London's East India Dock Road, intended to show how the East End, heavily bombed in the Second World War, could be rebuilt as a model community, laid out in the manner of a garden city. The show house was part of the Lansbury Estate, named after George Lansbury, Britain's Labour Party leader from 1931 to 1935, who did much to improve the lot of the poor.

The estate is a mixture of terrace houses, storey apartments and blocks of flats, served by churches, schools and shops. Recent years have seen many

The front door opens into a generously proportioned hall, with the stair descending in a straight line from the landing and making a neat turn at the bottom. The kitchen is on the right, with a large window opening onto the front garden and a door opening into the sideway. At the back the living room, which overlooks the back garden, runs the width of the house. On the inside wall is a fireplace in an unusually large chimney breast. "There were hot-water pipes running up the sides which provided the hot water for the bath and kitchen, the system worked very well," said the tenant, Mrs Underwood. Upstairs there are three bedrooms with built-in wardrobes, a bathroom and a separate lavatory.

Festival of Britain housing
POPLAR, LONDON

"improvements," ranging from new front doors and diamond-pattern glazing to the roughcasting of whole façades. When I visited in July 1997 the least altered row of houses was in Pekin Close: a small, paved square from which cars are excluded. One house still has the open patch of lawn that fronts local-authority houses all over Britain; the others have low-walled front gardens brimming with roses.

Each house has a porch in the form of an "L" with a slightly rhomboid slab canopy – avoidance of right angles is a hallmark of the Festival of Britain style. At the other end of the front is a second door, inside which is a short passage, known as a "sideway," leading to a coal cupboard at the back and allowing the coalman to deliver coal without his boots blackening the floor.

An interesting variant of the terrace house is provided nearby at Nos.30–70 (even numbers only) Saracen Street. These houses, in a darker, plum-coloured brick, look at first like three-storey family dwellings; but for every group of three front doors on the street there is a passage leading to the back with three more numbers above it. Between Nos.32 and 34 the passage leads to 36, 38 and 40, for Saracen Street consists of two-storey houses with flats above. A series of boldly sculptural staircases stands free behind the terrace, with flights cantilevered off a central pier; a short bridge connects the top landing to a balcony opening onto the flats. The architects, Norman & Dawbarn, evidently wished to make a feature of living high off the ground.

Saracen Street retains the feeling of a single terrace built to a unified design. This is largely due to the well-tended front gardens, most of which are edged by neat low hedges. Inside the layout is similar to that of the Pekin Close houses, but the living room is at the front, and at the back are the kitchen and a dining room. On the first floor are three or four bedrooms. The top-floor flats have two bedrooms, a living room, a kitchen, a bathroom and a lavatory.

Walter Bor, one of the planners involved in the layout of the Lansbury, told me: "There was not so much experience in public housing before the war, though there were some good attempts in Liverpool … We said to ourselves, why not try several different types and see how people like to live? So we did terrace houses, four-storey maisonettes, two floors below and two above, and blocks of flats. What is

Shallow roofs emphasize the long, low lines of this terrace of four two-storey houses (below) on the Lansbury Estate's Pekin Close. The windows of the first-floor bathrooms are slightly shallower than those of the adjoining bedrooms, but large enough to admit plentiful light.

interesting, after all these years, is the estate is still by far the most popular in the East End." Perhaps the main reason for this is that the estate still looks like an integral part of the area – the houses are built of traditional brick, not precast concrete panels – and, no less importantly, there is on-street parking. Streets and closes even revived some of the old names: Pekin, Annabel, Elizabeth and Chilcot.

This is no ghetto-like precinct, alienated from its immediate surroundings as many estates of the 1960s and 1970s are. The Lansbury is testimony to the strong sense of community in the East End. This quality was recognized at the beginning and is underlined by the fact that many families have remained on the estate for more than 40 years. Lewis Mumford, the great American writer on urban planning, wrote: "I have not looked at all that Europe has to offer since the war, but I shall be surprised if Lansbury is not one of the best bits of housing and urban planning anywhere … the aesthetic results are remarkably good."

Nos.30–70 Saracen Street (above), two-storey houses with a flat on the floor above, were built in 1951–2 to the designs of the architects Norman & Dawbarn. The flats are approached by way of eye-catching outdoor staircases at the back (right), which each serve three flats, as shown in the plan of the second floor (far right).

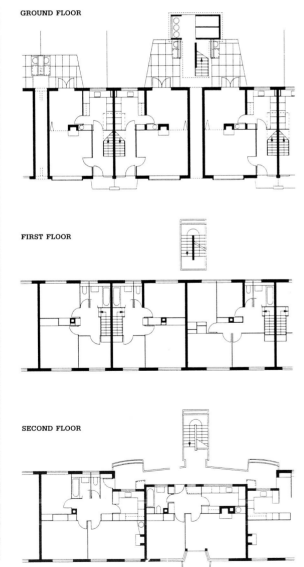

GROUND FLOOR

FIRST FLOOR

SECOND FLOOR

The back of this house (right) overlooks a secluded formal garden with a sunken paved circle in the middle. Away from the street, large windows let in abundant daylight. The spiral fire escapes, each serving two houses, provide additional access to the garden.

These four row houses, which were built during the mid-1970s, are illustrative of the ingenuity and variety an outstanding architect can bring to even the most tried and tested of building types. Their creator, Harry Weese, is perhaps best known as the designer of Washington DC's elegant and spacious Metro stations. Weese studied at the Massachusetts Institute of Technology, and later with Eliel Saarinen. Both before and after the Second World War he worked for a short time with the renowned practice of Skidmore, Owings & Merrill, before setting up in Chicago, in 1947, as Harry Weese Associates.

Weese was among the first of his generation to draw on Chicago's building traditions – by, for example, incorporating bay windows in his Walton Apartments (1956). He was also a pioneer in the rescue and revival of old buildings, sensitively restoring the city's Adler & Sullivan's Auditorium, the Field Museum of Natural History and Orchestra Hall, all in 1967.

These row houses, built in buff-coloured brick, appear both monumental and abstract. Their monumentality comes from the emphatic verticals and

Custom-designed luxury
CHICAGO

horizontals and the mass of brickwork, as well as the deep recession at the top of the houses. The abstract quality derives from the unexpected yet rigorously geometric placing of the windows, almost an echo of Mondrian and the De Stijl movement.

One of the great challenges posed by the modern row house is the integration of a garage, which often ruins the sense of proportion and harmonious composition. Weese resolves the problem by making the front door almost equal in emphasis to the garage and by giving the recessed balcony at the top almost equal dimensions. The play on rectangles continues with the windows between, which are first vertical and then horizontal. The lower windows descend to the floor, and have a safety grille that barely projects from the frontage.

The houses were designed to fit into the historic Old Town Triangle, a quiet residential district with well-established trees, close to a park and to the city centre. On the site had stood a row of three small abandoned houses that had been torn down. As there was no back alley behind the plot, Weese was able to create backyards that seem much larger than they

The layout of the bedrooms on the second floor varies from one house to another, but all have plentiful closet space. The straight flights of stairs that ascend to this level here give way to an internal spiral stair leading to the top floor.

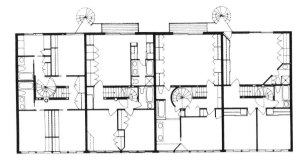

are while affording considerable privacy. One of them has Judas trees, espaliered apple trees and a paved granite terrace. The second is primarily a dog run and the third a miniature farm, while the fourth is landscaped profusely and professionally.

Weese undertook the rebuilding personally, erecting one house for himself and his wife and three for friends, and paid for the houses as they went up. For the Weeses, the move to this house was prompted by the fact that their daughters had grown up and left home, allowing the couple to think afresh about how they wanted to live.

Inside the houses differ markedly, although they are all of the same dimensions. The cupboard arrangement beside the garage varies, as does the layout of the rooms behind: usually guest room, study and bath. The first floor, although effectively open-plan and without doors between front and back, has the kitchen in a different position in each house. Because it is possible to pass through on either side of the staircase people may circulate freely at parties. The living rooms look out through floor-to-ceiling windows onto Willow Street. Dining

and kitchen areas face the garden. Kitchens have a work island, with a storage structure above that slides on ceiling tracks and can be positioned over the island or pushed back by the sink and stove in order to maximize space.

The straight flights of stairs are "stacked" one above the other, and have open treads or risers. On the second floor there is a large bedroom that overlooks the garden; this features an en suite bathroom or shower. Two other bedrooms on this floor share a bathroom (although in one of the houses there are only two bedrooms at this level). The outside spiral staircases, which are shared between two houses, serve as fire escapes and give access to the gardens. At the top another spacious bedroom opens onto a terrace, and one house has a terrace on both sides. Ingeniously, Weese produced ample bathroom and cupboard space within the rectangular envelope, which permitted well-proportioned elevations at both front and back.

The houses were not expensively finished; for example, there are no veneers. Weese achieved value for money by imaginative use of space and clever planning, providing the abundant storage space that most American householders demand. Mrs Weese wrote: "There are so many floors, so many cupboards, enormous private baths with bright windows. The fourth floor seemed superfluous, so with art running rampant through the family, a decision was made to put a studio skylight all across the back, facing north, and a 4 feet by 40 feet [1.2 x 12.2m] closet for storing supplies, canvases, etc."

Weese recognized the kitchen's central role in modern domestic life and integrated it into the living room. This arrangement (right), which includes a work island, makes it easy for the cook to chat with others while preparing food.

The design and proportions of Weese's four Chicago row houses (left) are as carefully considered as the terrace houses of the 18th and early 19th centuries. Windows are no longer set one above the other, but vary in size and shape from storey to storey. At the top there are generous balconies with floor-to-ceiling glass, to take advantage of the view.

Fake, copy and pastiche are labels quickly applied today to any building that attempts to revive traditional styles. Port Grimaud, however, succeeds in avoiding such accusations because it was born of passionate conviction. François Spoerry, the Alsatian architect who designed and built it, became interested in earlier styles of architecture while working in the 1930s for Jacques Couelle, who made a speciality of rescuing fragments of old buildings.

After the fall of France in 1940, Spoerry joined the Resistance, but he was betrayed and found himself sent first to Buchenwald and then to Dachau. In his book *A Gentle Architecture* (1994) he writes: "I forced myself to forget the horror of my present situation and think only of the future. With makeshift drawing materials I tried to sustain my companions by sketching the homes of their dreams, the homes in which they would live as free men after the war."

Lagoon revival
CÔTE D'AZUR

Elevation of a row of Port Grimaud houses. Each building has been designed to be subtly different from its neighbour, as though this were a village that had grown organically over a long period of time. Rooflines change from house to house, as does the pattern of windows.

Spoerry's opportunity to realize his vision came in 1962, when he learnt that on the coast west of St Tropez there was a large marshy site for sale that was failing to find a buyer. When he saw the magnificent panorama of coastline and bay it offered, he pictured a complete village of small fishermen's houses along the shore, from which sailors would take to their boats. It was, he said, "a revelation of the work to which I was going to devote my life."

From the beginning Spoerry's work was a decisive reaction against the anonymity of Modernism; each house is visibly distinct from its neighbour. Each house was also designed to be accessible by both land and sea. There are small gardens or terraces on the water's edge, and the depth next to the properties is at least 10 feet (3m), to enable every kind of pleasure craft to moor alongside. A large car park is laid out at the entrance to the village to discourage the use of cars beyond that point.

The first houses were built directly overlooking the sea, along the natural shoreline, and a new lagoon was then created behind. Every house, says Spoerry, was designed to have a good view over the water, with peninsulas and canals fanning out within the lagoon like the fingers of a hand.

Permission to build was first sought in 1963 and granted in 1966. The first phase consisted of 500 dwellings, soon extended to 900, built on 50 acres (20ha) of quays and surrounded by 40 acres (16ha) of canals. The first houses sold quickly to yachtsmen, resale values rose sharply, and the enterprise flourished. Faced with the threat of a large development of apartment blocks nearby, Spoerry bought up the land and increased the size of his development with a further 800 lots.

Port Grimaud succeeds because it forms a coherent whole and is laid out with genuine flair and unfailing attention to detail. Wherever you walk, vistas appear

This remarkable lagoon village (left), where every house has a mooring space for a boat, is the creation of the architect François Spoerry. Beginning in 1966 on a marshy site on the bay of St Tropez, he used water to create an attractive setting in the way other architects usually employ landscape, grass and trees.

The attention to details, such as the decorative ironwork, and the creation of vistas (below), makes Port Grimaud a place of enormous charm. Narrow pavements along the quays keep you constantly in view of the water.

and groups of buildings compose photogenically. The contrast between the broad expanses of water and the houses tightly packed along the quays is particularly effective. A sense of unity is created by the consistent use of traditional clay tiles, which originally took their tapered form from being slapped into shape on a man's thigh before going into the oven. As specified by Spoerry, these roof tiles are found in a range of soft brown and straw tints that create a sense of mellowness. Roof pitches often contribute to the character of a place; here they are consistently very shallow. A ban on television aerials ensures that the skyline remains uncluttered.

Spoerry collected extensive documentation on the traditional architecture of Provence, Italy and Spain for these houses, but the influence of the islands of the Venetian Lagoon is particularly evident. Although the houses are laid out in rows, each differs subtly from those beside it – higher or lower, occasionally stepped back or forward, with windows of different sizes and shapes, and balconies at different levels.

Occasionally one house is faced in stone, but most are painted in a palette of soft yellows, pinks and greys, with one or two in a deep red or luminous white. Plain façades are enlivened by window shutters painted in contrasting colours. A special feature is the covered balconies at upper level, some inset, others built out to take advantage of the view and the breeze. With its winding canals crossed by arched bridges, Port Grimaud undeniably evokes Venice.

These houses may be simple, but there is no sense of the "penny pinching" that mars so many modern developments. Spaces and proportions are generous, and building materials and finishes are of good quality. The sheer tranquil beauty of the place has won approval even from those usually hostile to architecture that so overtly draws inspiration from the past. The architect Charles Parent has written of Spoerry: "This work is poles apart from mine ... I at first reserved judgement," but after two visits he concluded that "it really has the most wonderful atmosphere – it both works and is pleasing."

For sheer originality, indeed perversity, Piet Blom's architecture is in a class of its own. Single-handedly, he has revolted against the concrete slabs of postwar Rotterdam with new housing that is as fantastic as Gaudí's Parc Güell in Barcelona or Guimard's Paris Métro entrances.

His development at Overblaak, not far from the centre of this Dutch town, turns conventions in architecture upside down. Indeed, his apartment block on that site, Blaaktoren, has almost literally been stood on its head, in that all the window arches point down, not up. But the truly surreal part of the complex is the cluster of cube houses – "pole houses," as the architect calls them. From the outside these are so disorientating that you have to look at them carefully in order to work out how anyone might live in such a place. Nevertheless, Blom's basic concept is very simple: a tilted cube rests on a hexagonal pillar containing the entrance and staircase; it might almost be a modern interpretation of the Netherlands' classic building type: the windmill.

It is the remarkable combination of high-minded experimental living and an unabashed sense of fun that makes the pole-house development such an engaging place. These houses work visually because they have been well thought out. Standing in one of the little courtyards, you look up to the sky and see the roofs meeting in a perfect six-pointed star. Intriguingly, when you look up at them from the

Pole houses
ROTTERDAM

piazza, you feel that they are alive and looking back at you. Their bright-yellow fronts are like faces, the windows suggesting noses and eyes, perhaps with trim Dutch bonnets set above them.

Nor is this impression merely anthropomorphic. As your gaze shifts to the corners of the cubes, the clusters of windows there suggest, disconcertingly, insects' eyes. This is partly because the windows on the upper slope are a matching pair, taller than they are wide, like the eyes of a fly.

Continuing the analogy with nature, the colour of the sloping fronts suggests the soft, smooth yellow underbelly of a crab, while the roof, with its rougher-textured brown shingles, is the shell. The more you peer up, the giddier you become. Your eyes search constantly for a horizontal line.

The next dizzying trick is the fire gangways that run between the roofs of the houses: the "doors" opening onto them lean back at a crazy 45-degree angle. To open the door requires a superhuman push which, if you are unwise enough to hold onto the handle, might fling you down into the piazza.

Almost everyone who visits the development wants to go into one of the pole houses and see what kind of life is offered inside. One enterprising owner realized this and opened his home to the public. "I thought I would just be doing it for a month or two," says Ed De Graaf. "But it has taken over my life and become my job. Now I have 30,000 visitors a year." In fact he has now installed a permanent exhibition in the house and gone to live elsewhere.

Puzzling though they are at first sight, these houses nevertheless follow strict geometric patterns, evident here in the six-pointed star formed by the roofs. The windows are symmetrically arranged in a cross pattern.

The roofs of Piet Blom's cube houses (left) are like no other, with clusters of windows at the top and other windows at the bottom. The cubes are upended, so that every face is sloping. On the left an escape door, with a pointed top, is visible.

The complex was designed in 1978, but a collapse in the housing market delayed the start of building for four years. A new investment partner had to be found, and this investor insisted on a more intensive development that replaced some of the planned 74 cubes with the apartment tower. Eventually, 54 cubes were built, 38 of which are houses and the rest offices, including, originally, an architectural academy that has now been succeeded by a management school. The houses were completed in 1984.

Although this is a private development, with houses for sale freehold, a large part of the funds was provided by the municipality. A substantial part of the expense in building the development was due to two major constructional factors. First, it was decided that the complex was to be built over an eight-lane highway, and second, there was the cost of carrying out deep foundation work because of the marshy nature of the site: "blaak" means "dike." The purpose of building across the highway was to establish an easily used, attractive pedestrian link between the centre of Rotterdam and a large housing estate of 2,000 apartments to the east. It was important that residents should be unaware of the road below and of the fact that they were being coaxed into climbing over it.

Blom's solution was to make the bridge a feature in itself, not only by giving it a beguiling appearance but also by siting small stores along the route, thus creating Rotterdam's answer to the Rialto in Venice. The first tenants to rent the stores did not stay more than a year, so the municipality decided to create instead a shopping precinct selling fashionable goods. As businesses flourished, the occupants of the stores wanted larger premises – the areas are little bigger than small conservatories – and now the spaces are used as small offices and studios.

As a forerunner to the Blaak development, in the early 1970s Blom had built a group of pole houses at Helmond, in the south-east of the country, although only 18 of a planned 180 were constructed. An instant sucess, the Rotterdam cubes were all sold, he says, before they were completed: "They are most popular with young buyers who want something new and different." Five years after completion, more than half the original purchasers remained. The only major problem is that some families have found the houses a little too small. "As soon as the second child is on the way people tend to move away. I have told Mr Blom that next time the houses must be 25 per cent bigger," De Graaf explains.

Inside, the houses are on three floors: living room and kitchen at the first level, two bedrooms and a bathroom at the second and "the heaven house," a hobby room, at the top. Situated right under the slope of the roof, this room seems likely to become a furnace in summer, but windows on four sides, says De Graaf, "invariably catch the breeze, though plants can't stand the draught." All of the windows are double-glazed, and the radiators are connected to the municipal hot-water supply, which keeps the houses warm whenever necessary.

The bedrooms (right) in the pole houses have a view like that of a rear gunner in a Second World War bomber. You can look down on the street below or up to the sky while still in bed. There is no such thing as a square pane of glass here; the windows are all pentagonal.

The upended cubes are held aloft on concrete and brick piers (opposite) that contain the staircases leading to the rooms above. Because the houses are built on a bridge over a major road, residents arrive at their front doors on foot or by bicycle.

As the section (below) indicates, every room has sloping walls, sharply angled upward or downward. The floorplan of the second level shows a room with a double bed and another room with separate beds. The bathroom has a tiled floor in this drawing.

In the living room you have the sense of being in an airplane, because the walls slope in toward the ceiling and also in toward the floor. De Graaf points out that these rooms allow for a novel interaction between public and private space, because sloping windows facing downward give a glimpse of life on the sidewalk below, rather similar to that offered by a glass-bottomed boat.

Furnishing the houses in a conventional sense presents problems, but as they have been sold mainly to first-time buyers, who may not have much furniture of their own, the strong architectural character and built-in features are an asset. The essential items are no more than beds, a dining table and a few chairs. It requires practice to live in such a house, not least because windows can drop open through their own weight, although suction-action pistons slow them down. "Do not open. No refunds for cut-off fingers," said a large sign in De Graaf's house.

As president of the association of owners of pole houses, De Graaf has helped set in motion a major renovation in 1997–8. "We are spending 45,000 guilders [£13,350/$21,350] on each house, but it should carry house prices up to 250,000 guilders [£74,200/$118,700]," he says. The hexagonal pillar supporting each house is of reinforced concrete, as are the floors, but the cube is a wooden frame clad with outer and inner panels that are half cement and half wood fibre, with insulation wool sandwiched between them. The lower panels, which had lost much of their colour, are now a fresh yellow. The brown shingles on the roof, which had dried out, cracked and begun to leak, have been replaced by zinc sheeting covered with white polyester. "We approached Mr Blom about the work, but he wanted to do new buildings, not renovate old ones," says De Graaf. So the owners' association turned to local Rotterdam architects Jobse & Bos.

The victim of wear and tear caused by its numerous visitors, De Graaf's show house is having an interior facelift, including the installation of easy-to-clean granite and marmoleum floors. The colours will be mainly white and grey. "With so many sloping walls, not many colours are needed – it would look chaotic. Just a few objects are enough to provide the accents." The renovation reinforces the futuristic appearance of the houses. "The brown shingles were beginning to look a little old-fashioned."

Piet Blom's pole houses have become a legend in Rotterdam. Indeed, some couples who would have liked to move in when they were first built, but found them too small, are looking at them with renewed interest now that their children have left home.

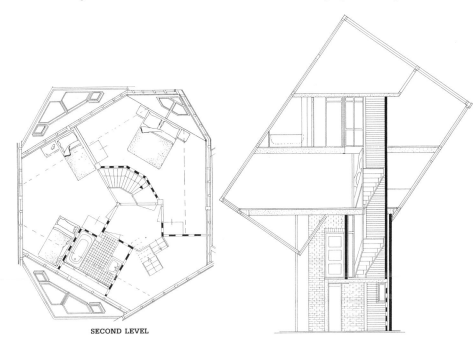

SECOND LEVEL

De Carlo's intention was to create modern housing in a traditional idiom (opposite). By combining two- and three-storey houses, all with the shallow red-tiled roofs that may be seen throughout the Venetian Lagoon, he created a grouping that blends subtly with the landscape.

Curved projections and cylindrical turrets, which contain the stairs, enliven plain, almost abstract geometric volumes (below). The roundness of these features echoes traditional local building styles.

There can be few more sensitive testing grounds for new architecture than the Venetian Lagoon. The Italian architect Giancarlo De Carlo is renowned for grafting the new onto the old, above all in the beautiful city of Urbino. Designing new housing for the Venetian island of Mazzorbo was an even greater challenge. Medieval Mazzorbo was famous for its monasteries, villas and orchards, but its fortunes began to decline in the 16th century as its canals slowly silted up and noble families forsook it for the Venetian mainland. By the latter part of the century the population was less than 500, and much of the land was turned over to vines and vegetables.

Since at least the mid-17th century the island's lifeline has been a long timber footbridge linking it to Burano, a crowded island between Mazzorbo and Venice. Planners viewed Mazzorbo as an appropriate site for housing intended to relieve the pressure on its neighbour, and in 1980 De Carlo was approached and commissioned to design 80 dwellings. Although the obvious response would have been high-density housing, De Carlo's approach was more thoughtful.

The architect followed his usual practice of close study of the local community. He was struck by its fierce devotion to island life. After the decline of the fishing industry, most inhabitants of Mazzorbo chose to commute to the mainland, travelling two hours each way, rather than leave the island. Like Burano, Mazzorbo had resisted the temptation of tourism, and neither had a hotel or boarding house.

De Carlo decided that the first phase of construction would follow the urban intimacy of Burano, the second the more rural layout of Mazzorbo. The main features of Burano were the canal and the paths along the water's edge; the *calle*, a narrow pedestrian alley; and the *campo*, a small square usually opening onto the water on one side.

Modern Venice
MAZZORBO

The site lay between the broad channel separating the two islands and an old canal, which De Carlo reopened to provide a mooring for residents' boats. It was necessary to persuade the city authorities to spend almost $1 million (£625,000) on dredging the site, which was almost as much as the cost of the first 36 houses. The mooring gave the new residents immediate contact with, and access to, the water.

De Carlo has long been passionately committed to the idea of public participation in architecture. Back in 1952, soon after completing a block of flats in Sesto San Giovanni, an industrial suburb of Milan, he spent a Sunday in a café opposite the building, observing how it was used. He wrote: "... the people were all on the access galleries facing the north. They had put out stools and chairs to watch and take part in the spectacle of each other and of the street. The very narrowness of the galleries excited the children who were running their bicycle races along them ... Orientation matters, and so does a view of the landscape and light and privacy, but what matters most is to see each other, to be together."

De Carlo thought that architecture was too important to be left to architects alone. It should be given back to the people, not through forcing architects to relinquish their role, but by increasing popular participation. He believed that since the 18th century

people had been increasingly prevented from shaping their surroundings, and this had resulted in alienation. The enduring dearth of opportunity had led to a loss of traditional building skills.

As a result, many people did not know what sort of homes they wanted, even when they were asked. At the same time architects had become increasingly specialized and remote, pursuing their own formal and stylistic games with scant regard for the user. The architectural press made things worse by rigorously excluding people from photographs of buildings. Architecture, De Carlo insisted, must be reconnected with ordinary citizens.

De Carlo made the significant observation that the Buranese were constantly going to and from the *campi*. They were unconsciously encouraged to do this, he believed, by front doorsteps that rose only an inch or so (2–3cm) from the street. The disadvantage was that these low thresholds made the houses prone to flooding. Mazzorbo's traditionally higher doorsteps, on the other hand, while less of a flood risk, were also less conducive to coming and going.

De Carlo persuaded the authorities to pay for him to raise the whole site by 3¼ft (1m), which allowed him to imitate Burano's lower doorsteps without the risk of flooding. It would have been cheaper to give the houses a high threshold or to raise their ground level by two or three steps. However, the people of Mazzorbo were adamant that they liked to walk onto the street as if they were moving from one room to another; with their support De Carlo convinced the authorities that the extra expense was justified.

The new houses are laid out along a new pedestrian street parallel with the canal, and, following Burano's example, a hierarchy of public spaces is signalled by stone paving for the *calle* and brick for the *campi*. These details were expensive, but they provided durability as well as a sense of familiarity.

The houses are two and three storeys high, and consist of five basic types varied so that no house is the same as its neighbour. De Carlo set out to create a village-like quality where the dwellings have a family resemblance but stand out individually. This is achieved by stepping them forward and back, by alternating taller and shorter fronts, and by juxtaposing flat parapets with gables, which may be end on or side on to the street. Bay windows, balconies and outside steps lend further variety, creating the sense that the façades, to use De Carlo's term, "vibrate."

GROUND FLOOR

FIRST FLOOR

De Carlo avoided monotony by varying the size and shape of windows within each house and from one dwelling to the next. Each house has a simple version of the traditional Venetian chimney with a flattened top to trap flying sparks.

All over the lagoon, older houses have roof terraces, and the architect provided these also. He imitated a specific Buranese tradition of a chimney-stack that stands out from the wall, and introduced further movement into the walls with projecting corners and staircases. He followed the pattern of existing two- and three-storey houses in Burano, avoiding any kind of horizontal division within. This, he explained, was done in order to sustain the vitality that results from having front doors that open onto the street rather than into an inner hallway.

The houses are of three sizes: 495 square feet (46m²), 753 square feet (70m²) and 1023 square feet (95m²). The kitchen, dining room and living room are on the ground floor. The bedrooms are on the upper floors, opening onto the roof terraces. Stores for such items as boating equipment are provided at ground-floor level, close to front doors.

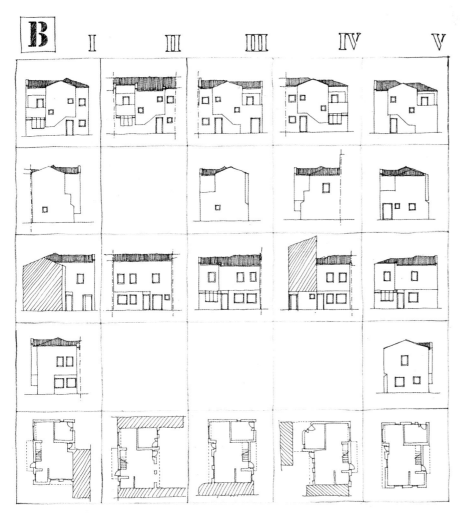

this by building the houses in small groups, often of three, in some cases with a shop giving onto the street. Traditionally, terrace houses form a straight line, broken often by repeating features such as bay windows. De Carlo steps façades back and forward in a less predictable fashion, and creates some clusters in the form of an "L," which in turn gives a sense of enclosure to the small *campi*. So, although the houses lack gardens, each group has a more secluded outdoor space that is less public than the street and where passers-by are less likely to venture.

Before embarking on the design, De Carlo and his colleagues made many drawings of typical details of Buranese architecture. They studied windows and shutters as well as the local version of the Venetian chimney, which was usually rectangular with its own miniature pitched roof rather than the cylindrical pot found in Venice itself. Each of the new houses has one typical Buranese chimney, simplified in design but still recognizably traditional.

De Carlo also noted that on Burano the wall beneath the outside ground-floor windows was picked out in a different darker shade, and copied the idea. This painted "dado," along with the pavement in front of the house, is washed clean almost daily.

His attention to detail is very much informed by the context of the project: "In any part of the world 80 dwellings could be accommodated within a single building and go unnoticed," he says, "but on the Venice Lagoon 80 dwellings are, or should be, 80 houses that together take on a great dimension."

The houses are built of 12.60-inch (32cm) brick, rendered outside and plastered within. Floors are of steel-reinforced terra-cotta. Doors and windows are of standard softwood type, the frames made in the local manner in whitish artificial stone. The windows are equipped with the local external folding shutter.

The appeal of these simple houses is increased by the bold, unselfconscious use of varied colour that is typical of the lagoon – here green, yellow and violet. In earlier times these were the colours used for the boats. De Carlo followed local tradition by using them in different strengths, creating variety and contrast, but not picking out every individual house in this way. He thought that to do so would have been too contrived, while to ask each family to choose colours before getting to know their house and its surroundings would have provided no sound base for a decision. Instead, he took the view that everyone could later repaint their house as they wished.

The Mazzorbo settlement has all the traditional intimacy of small-town or even village streets. A clever balance is struck between traditional terrace houses and more independent, free-standing houses such as many people want today. De Carlo achieves

The terrace house here leaps into the age of high tech. Nicholas Grimshaw and Partners, the architects behind the British Pavilion at Spain's Seville Expo and the Channel Tunnel rail terminal at Waterloo Station, London, like to build with modern industrial materials and products. As Grimshaw has pointed out with some reason, the brickwork on most traditional-looking new houses is no different from wallpaper – it is simply an outer covering.

The Camden houses have provoked powerful reactions. Detractors have compared the houses to a derailed high-speed train, "11 detention centres" and an urban fortress protected against riot or siege. Of course, the appearance of these buildings is nothing if not striking. From the river the gently swelling fronts bring to mind a series of upended caravans,

A strong component of the houses' high-tech look is the long rectangular windows (right) shaped like those in a yacht or high-speed train. Venetian blinds shade the large areas of glass.

High-tech housing
CAMDEN, LONDON

although, set above the waters of the Grand Union Canal as they are, they might be a hydroelectric plant, complete with pistons and moving parts.

Grimshaw explained his approach in a lecture in 1992. Referring to the design elements that gave the lecture its title, "Structure, Space and Skin," he said: "A horse skeleton is all structure ... a bat's wing is definitely structure and skin. A shell combines all three in a rather beautiful unity." He is an intense admirer of Paxton's Crystal Palace, built for Britain's Great Exhibition of 1851. This was a remarkable example of a grand repeating structure enclosing a great space with a skin – in this case of glass – that was a model of prefabrication. Speaking, in the same lecture, about the Camden houses, Grimshaw said: "We gave [them] innovative and carefully considered skins, and raised the quality of the living space with double-height living rooms. The structure is very simple, based on a system of party walls that meet the requirements of British building regulations, which have their origins in the Great Fire of London."

The row of 11 houses – in fact there are ten three-bedroom houses and one house consisting of two flats – were part of a planning deal between the UK supermarket chain Sainsbury's and the north London borough of Camden. Sainsbury's were seeking permission to build a large store on the site of an old bakery; Camden, as a matter of policy, is constantly seeking to increase its housing stock.

Seen from the far bank of the canal, the timber-slatted balconies (opposite) look as if they might drop down like medieval drawbridges to allow visitors to step up from the water. The front doors open off the covered walkway.

Neven Sidor, the architect in charge of this inner-city development, recalls: "Sainsbury's just wanted the store. Six earlier schemes had been produced for the site, all with a chain-link fence along the canal. We had a completely free hand on the houses." Indeed, the estate agents who were to handle the sale told the architects that they should "do something really unusual; it will go."

There was no space for gardens because the houses back onto the service area at the rear of the supermarket. Faced with the challenge of a poor outlook from the backs of the houses, the architects designed this side to present a façade of grey aluminium from which not a window peeps. The white cabin doors might be the access to an electricity substation, but in fact they open into a combined boiler and utility room. The design solution adopted by Grimshaw and Partners was to create a canalside walkway with a controlled gate providing access to the houses. This brought with it a disadvantage – because the gate is a shared access, residents have to walk right past their neighbours' windows.

This brief sense of enclosure is dispelled when you pass through the entrance hall and climb the stairs to the first floor. Here you are in an airy, light artist's studio, experiencing the exhilarating sense of space and openness that is the essence of the best modern architecture. The most prominent feature is the huge wall of glass fronting the dining area and kitchen.

The architects sought to increase the sense of space, light and airiness on every level of the houses. Among the features used to achieve this effect is the porthole window opening from the top-floor bedroom onto the double-height dining area.

At the press of a button, the whole window moves upward and the room suddenly becomes as al fresco as the deck of a yacht, and to complete this impression a nautical mahogany and steel balcony overlooks the canal. The windows are double glazed and electrically operated by a motor at the top.

Dense concrete blockwork is used for the walls of the houses. The bowed fronts facing the canal are based on an aluminium frame clad in horizontal ⅛in (3mm) aluminium panels 3¼ft (1m) high and 11½ft (3.5m) long. These panels, finished with a silvered plastic coating, overlap like enormous tiles. Although modern architecture is sometimes accused of putting design considerations first, these houses have been created with their occupants in mind. The precast-concrete floors, for example, incorporate underfloor heating, so it is pleasant to walk barefoot on the tongue-and-groove beech boards that cover them.

Grimshaw is a keen sailor and often uses both materials and fittings borrowed from boats and the high-tech end of the boat-building industry. One such feature is the slatted decks to the balconies. Privacy is provided by external, electrically operated aluminium blinds which can be raised or lowered whether the window is open or closed. From the two upper floors you can look down on the main living area from a circular internal window or a mezzanine gallery which may be used as a study or sleeping space with its own electronically operated roof light. This has rubber window seals (like those on London buses) that prevent noise or draughts from disturbing the occupants.

Each house came complete with a hefty owner's manual that describes how the mechanisms work and explains what the occupant can do when something goes wrong. On the ground floor is a plant room, housing the boiler, water tanks, an alarm panel and a high-pressure pump to create water pressure all round the house – something the traditional water tank in the loft was supposed to do. Here with the tank safely indoors there is virtually no danger of burst pipes even if the heating is off. It is also in this room that the garbage cans are housed.

The kitchens were equipped in an appropriately high-tech fashion. Each had handsome floor and wall units, an island peninsula with a Neff gas oven and hob and a stainless-steel extractor hood, a Neff microwave, a Corian worktop, and a Franke sink and waste-disposal unit. Spotlights and recessed down-lighters complete the built-in look.

When the houses first came on view, following their completion in December 1988, they enjoyed a rapturous reception from both the architectural press – which was to be expected – as well as the real estate sections of the UK's national press. This enthusiasm was fuelled by the fact that offers were made for all the houses, which were priced at £260,000 ($416,000) and offered on 999-year leases, within two weeks of their going on sale.

However, early 1989 saw the peak of the property boom, and the market started to slump before the sales were finalized. As a consequence, Sainsbury's sold only three of the houses and decided to offer the

The ground floor is entered on the canal side by a secure gate shared by all the residents. This floor has a bedroom, bathroom and utility room. On the first floor is an open-plan living, dining and kitchen area, and a laundry room beside the staircase. On the second floor the main bedroom looks over the canal. The shaded area is a void above the dining area and to the right is a gallery that can serve as either a study or a bedroom.

GROUND FLOOR

FIRST FLOOR

SECOND FLOOR

The steel handrail and glass-panel balustrade (right) are pure high-tech, while wooden treads and white plaster walls add a more traditional domestic note to the staircase.

On the left of this view (below) from the dining area into the living area is the tall glass window. This slides up like a castle portcullis to allow access to the balcony.

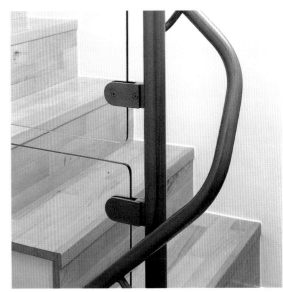

others for rent. When the original buyers came to sell, they had to wait a long time for serious offers. According to an article in the *Daily Telegraph* of December 7, 1996, moreover, none "achieved a price much more than £200,000 [$320,000]."

In 1994 Sainsbury's sold the head lease of the development at auction to Nick Capstick-Dale of UK Real Estate, retaining the freehold. Through this the London-based property investor acquired the seven rented houses for £140,000 ($224,000) each. At first he experienced problems with the management of these unusual properties. "When I took over, every time anything went wrong I had to get five people together before anyone could understand what to do. Part of the trouble was that six out of ten contractors involved had gone bust. It took me four years to get a team who understood the buildings and systems. Now it's all fine."

He continues: "As the houses were mostly on short lets, about half were empty at any one time. There was no camaraderie. Now half are sold and the place is full of people."

Capstick-Dale is very enthusiastic about Grimshaw and Partners' design: "They're great places to give parties. The 30-foot [9m] ceilings and sense of open space can't be bettered. People use the gadgetry, especially the sliding windows, all the time."

He is so keen that he is looking for a nearby site on which to build more innovative new houses in this popular area of London. But he would do things slightly differently and says so with brutal frankness: "The ground floors are a waste of space. No one ever enjoys staying in one of those downstairs bedrooms. They haven't got decent views over the canal because of the high-level windows set toward the top so people can't look in as they walk to other houses. I would turn the houses round. It's depressing to walk along a gangway to your front door. If I did anything I would put the front door in Sainsbury's car park. To open the front door there and look through to the water would be a staggering sight."

The modern house has always been an easy target for satire. Osbert Lancaster, in his cartoon history of architecture *Here, of all Places*, describes glass-walled houses where the householder "was looked on as a potential exhibitionist ready to perform the most intimate acts beneath the interested scrutiny of any neighbour with a good pair of fieldglasses." Grimshaw guards against such intrusions not only with blinds but also with a form of "L" plan which sets the balcony back out of sight of neighbours.

Far from being fazed by the unusual design and high-tech gadgetry of these imaginative houses, owners and residents alike have embraced their possibilities and grown passionately attached to them.

Thiis unusual development of row houses was completed in 1992. It stands in downtown San Francisco, at 443 Fulton Street, quite close to mighty City Hall. These older parts of San Francisco are criss-crossed with mid-block alleys, introduced in the 1850s and 1860s by speculators seeking to pack more houses onto the original city blocks. Many of these lanes have become very pleasant places to live, not least because of their largely pedestrian character. Fulton Grove, however, was no more than a parking lot, 200 feet (61m) long and 95 feet (29m) wide, when it was acquired by two enterprising property developers, Donald Klingbeil and John Heckel, in 1989. Through their company, Urban Frontier, they set about reviving an old form in a modern idiom.

The developers chose a leading local architectural practice, Solomon Inc, which supplied designs for 20 town houses and two flats, arranged so that a bridge forms over either end of the road. Daniel Solomon considered that the first challenge was to provide security, space for cars and private gardens. The area surrounding Fulton Grove, he says, "is quite a tough neighbourhood, so we're proud it does not have gates, and is used by local people and children as a short cut. It could have been a walled enclave but it functions on the 'eyes on the street' principle and has been virtually free from crime and vandalism."

Klingbeil and Heckel set out hoping to buck the old property adage that what matters is location, location and location; their concept was to provide a better standard of design and finish outside the prime areas. In deciding to build houses rather than apartments Soloman was influenced by a friend's row house in London, which impressed him with its ingenious use of space. The new houses were aimed toward the lower end of the housing market, and with this went an obligation to provide two of the units at slightly subsidised rates.

Economy of construction was critical, and the houses are faced in a prefabricated cedar shingle known as Shakertown. The backs are simply plywood,

These shingle-clad town houses, completed in 1992, have built-in garages at the bottom and large, airy studio living rooms above. A striking rhythm is created by the bold projecting bays, which increase in scale and monumentality towards the top of the buildings.

Mid-block alley houses
SAN FRANCISCO

The positioning of large windows in the studio living rooms (right) alternates from house to house. Where they are placed in the side walls of the bay in one property, they will be in the front wall of its neighbour. This avoids the possibility of being directly looked into where buildings are in close proximity.

The floor plans (below) show a garage, small hall and bedroom at ground level, with a master bedroom and bathroom above. At the top is an open-plan living room and the kitchen, which is set into a recess at the back and gives a view over the city.

GROUND FLOOR

FIRST FLOOR

SECOND FLOOR

The site plan for Fulton Grove is contained in an extremely confined area; in just half an acre (0.2ha) twenty houses and two flats have been built. The project's success has largely been due to the placing of living rooms in the upper levels (below), where increased ceiling heights create a sense of spaciousness.

painted dark green to fade into the city. For the road surface Solomon and his project architect, Lev Weisbach, chose inexpensive man-made cobblestone rather than asphalt and designed the drainage so that no kerbs were needed; indeed, the gentle undulations give a mellowness to the place. Street detail has also been handled with care: eucalyptus trees have been planted at regular intervals, and special attention has been paid to street lighting, which is fixed on the buildings. "It gives a golden glow, very different from the harsher light in nearby streets, making the place special," says Solomon.

Compared with the row houses of earlier centuries the plots are shallow, essentially only one room deep with a small backyard; the houses, therefore, are three storeys high. At ground level a built-in garage takes up half of the available space. Alongside it is an entrance lobby and a small back room. The master bedroom is on the floor above, with a spacious walk-in cupboard for hanging clothes, and a "split" bathroom: a room with bath, shower cubicle and basin opening directly off the master bedroom, and a separate lavatory opening off the landing. The living room, a lofty space with abundant skylights, fills the top of the house. The kitchen is ranged along the back wall.

Issues of privacy are important when building at a density of 44 houses to the acre (18 houses/ha). If you look carefully at the double-height oriels on these houses you will see that, although they are placed exactly opposite each other, the arrangement of the windows alternates. Where a large window faces directly across the street at the upper level, it has small windows below it. This pattern is reversed in the houses opposite and on either side, so the larger window is below and the windows in the upper floor are placed in the cheeks of the oriel. Each house is thus both private and well lit.

Inside, the houses are all space and light, but outside there's a touch of austerity. "We've taken the scale and proportions of the Victorian city, but shed the embellishments. It's a reductive interpretation," says Solomon. Fulton Grove may be a far cry from San Francisco's 19th-century Painted Ladies (see pages 118–21), but the show of strength is a valid response to the demands that are being placed on town house architecture in today's cities.

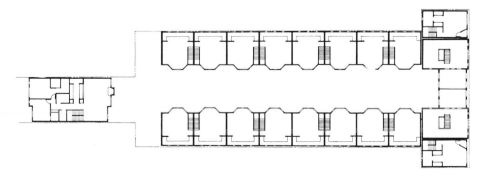

Peaceful though the scene appears today, Broadwall Street – on the south bank of the River Thames between Waterloo and Blackfriars Bridges – was at the centre of one of the fiercest planning battles of the 1970s, with local groups fighting for homes and facilities against a consortium determined to create a new office quarter. The office development had the backing of the architectural establishment – Richard (now Lord) Rogers was the architect.

However, the locals not only won but in 1984 acquired the whole 13-acre (5.5ha) site. Coin Street Community Builders was born. Beginning with a development of 46 family houses and 10 flats facing Stamford Street, they then transformed Gabriel's Wharf into workshops for artists and craftsmen, and refurbished Oxo Tower Wharf, creating shops, workshops, flats and, at the top, a smart new restaurant.

The brief for Broadwall Street was for ten family houses with gardens, five two-bedroom flats and ten one-bedroom flats. One solution would have been to place the flats above the houses, but the architects, Lifschutz Davidson, convinced the clients that most of the flats should be in a nine-storey tower, with 11 three-storey terrace houses alongside.

"The trick was to make them slightly wider than the minimum – just over 15 feet [5m]," Alex Lifschutz says. "This allowed us to place the stairs and the bathrooms in the centre, giving bedrooms and living rooms the full width of both fronts." In this way it was possible to avoid the typical 19th-century back extension and it allowed the architects to make a feature of both entrance and garden fronts.

The big architectural gesture was to turn the gables end-on to the street, reverting to a practice that was followed in Britain from the 12th to the 17th century.

Light and flexible space are the guiding principles of this terrace designed by Lifschutz Davidson (below). The west-facing fronts overlook a new public park, and the gable ends project imaginatively over the glazed façades. The twin stainless-steel pipes allow residents to use a solid-fuel stove wherever they decide to have the living room.

Riverside housing
SOUTHWARK, LONDON

Plans by the architects show three arrangements of the interiors of the houses. The first house is for a family with five children, each of whom has a bedroom. Two couples live in the second house, comprising two maisonettes, one with a master bedroom on the first floor, the other with the bed on a gallery below the roof. The third house has a street-level flat for the grandparents, a separate living area on the first floor for the other members of the family, and three bedrooms on the second floor.

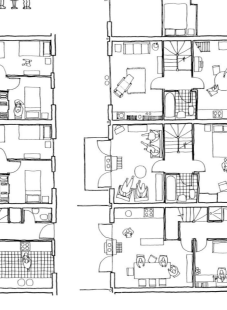
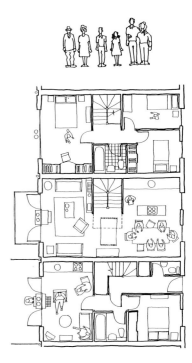

HOUSE FOR FAMILY WITH FIVE CHILDREN   TWO MAISONETTES   FAMILY HOUSE WITH INTEGRAL FLAT

The street front faces onto the backs of warehouses, but the architects coped with this by shifting the whole row back to accommodate private parking spaces and a raised walkway in front of the houses. This provides separation from the street and easy wheelchair access by way of a ramp at the end.

The backs of the houses look west over small enclosed private gardens and a new public park, so they receive the full benefit of the sun at all times of the year. There are large balconies at first-floor level. "We stipulated that each unit should have a balcony that could take four chairs and a table. It's worked and people enjoy chatting over balconies," says Iain Tuckett of Coin Street Community Builders.

Inside, the houses are planned for flexibility. The ground floor can become a self-contained granny flat, the top floor a refuge for teenage children. Tom Keller's house, No.8, is arranged to accommodate a family with two children. On the right is a kitchen opening into a living/dining room looking into the garden. The stair is a "winder" rising without a break to the first floor. Here there is a sitting room opening onto the balcony, and a bedroom toward the street. Apart from the vinyl floor in the kitchen, all the floors are of timber boards laid on timber joists.

The most notable feature of each house is the top room overlooking the park. By leaving out the ceiling, the architects were able to create a double-height space with glass filling the west wall right up into the gable. A ladder stair can provide access to a bed on a balcony. Behind is an ample attic, boarded to provide dry, dust-free storage.

In earlier centuries architects would have used columns or pilasters to add dignity to a façade. In this function-conscious age, Lifschutz Davidson has updated tradition by running gleaming pairs of stovepipes up the garden fronts to achieve a similar effect. Window frames and external timber boarding are of Iroco hardwood, while the red brick is Danish. On Broadwall Street, all that needs painting is the metalwork of the balconies.

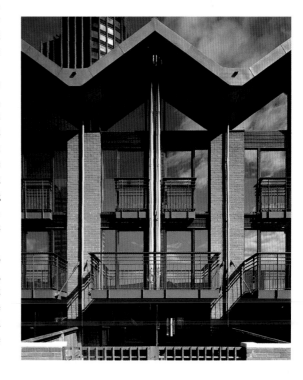

The garden fronts are almost entirely of glass. By glazing the area within the gable, the architects allowed residents to choose whether to have a tall, studio-like space open to the roof or to insert a sleeping gallery offering a panoramic view from the bed.

To some these striking houses are a fine example of airy, open-plan living; others see them as a high-tech version of a shanty town. Either way, this development shows that the simple terrace house can be reinvented endlessly. "There's nothing like them," says the architect, Martin Münzenmaier of Schaudt Architekten, with justification.

The eight single-family houses stand near the German-Swiss border, in Jungerhalde, a prosperous suburb of Konstanz. The city authorities, wanting to encourage a pattern of development denser than that of the large, detached houses being built in the area, held a competition, which Schaudt Architekten won. Although the site was originally earmarked for just one house, these architects were to revive the German tradition of row housing.

The project architect of the new houses was Martin Cleffmann. Münzenmaier, who worked with him, explains that "all were sold off-plan, that is before construction began." Building costs were about 15 per cent lower than for comparable new houses in the locality, but the overall prices also reflected the fact that the city provided the land at low cost. Many of the savings were achieved by using prefabricated industrial materials and a time-saving skeletal steel frame. Building on the site commenced in 1992 and was completed the next year.

An ever-increasing number of private clients are interested in creating adventurous detached modern houses, but the purchasers of terrace houses have proved more conservative. So, despite the fact that the Jungerhalde houses sold readily, the architects found themselves having to fight all the way in order to preserve the essentials of their design.

Although the Konstanz development is clearly a unified composition, the individual houses vary sufficiently to avoid repetition or predictability. Some have gently arched roofs like those of Dutch barns, others simple monopitch slopes. Window patterns

Glass and steel row
KONSTANZ

Walls of floor-to-ceiling glass mean that this fully internal bathroom (right) is filled with natural light; they are only slightly frosted, however, so the user is not completely concealed. The lines of glass "planks" echo those of the larch boards that have been used for the floor.

In the minimalist bathroom, exposed pipework provides easy access for maintenance. The generous washbasin has no built-in soap dish; instead, a bottle beneath the shelf dispenses liquid soap.

The south-facing garden fronts of these houses (left), with their balconies and small private roof terraces, allow the occupants plenty of fresh air. The deep roof overhangs provide essential shade in summer for the large areas of glass.

also differ radically from one house to the next. The overall composition is made striking by the boldness of the roof overhangs and the eye-catching use of metal and glass. An intriguing rhythm is also created by the glass lean-tos, which have roofs sloping in the opposite direction to the main monopitches. Each house is 33 feet (10m) in depth, has three storeys above ground and is built on a plot 20 feet (6m) wide.

The party walls are of solid brick, which prevents noise from passing between houses. The remainder of the structure is glass, galvanized steel and, for the roof, aluminium sheeting. Metal roofs are notorious for being noisy in heavy rain (and almost unbearable in hail), but here roof insulation reduces the sound to an acceptable level. Steel bracing rods strengthen the walls and roof, and each house has a solid concrete basement entirely below ground, with a store and utility room containing the heating.

Upstairs, layouts vary – some occupants sleep on the ground floor, others on the first and second floors. Some houses have the kitchen and dining room on the ground floor, others combine the two in one large open-plan living room on the first floor.

One of the houses, Jungerhalde 15, Cleffmann took himself. Spurred on by the authorities' demands for alterations that would dilute the strength and clarity

of the initial concept, he rebelled against "boredom by decree" and obtained permission to construct one "exemplary" house as planned. A major feature of his house is that, instead of a traditional enclosed stair, there are flights of steel steps that stand free of the walls. "It is very important for us to create a sense of openness between floors," Cleffmann says. Very young children feel closer to their parents in an open-plan layout, but the price is a loss of privacy, as well as the greater noise and reverberation that come with steel stairs and wooden floors. These floors, formed by laying oiled and waxed larch planks over steel joists, also form the ceilings of the spaces below. An advantage of this arrangement is that the floors can be cut back to open up double-height spaces.

Cleffmann's bathroom, set like the others in the middle of the house, away from windows, has floor-to-ceiling blocks of cast glass, measuring 8 feet (2.5m) by 8 inches (20cm) by ⅓ inch (8mm), so that it receives borrowed daylight and at night glows like a lamp. In the tall, studio-like space at the top of the house is a gallery with a tent to sleep in.

Other owners have opted for traditional rooms with walls, but all the houses enjoy very large areas of glass that are double-glazed for warmth. Average heating costs, says Cleffmann, are no higher than those for traditionally constructed houses in the neighbourhood. This is largely due to the excellent insulation. The warmth absorbed by the glass on sunny days in winter compensates for some of the heat lost on cold dark days. In summer the temperature can rise to 95°F (35°C), but the boldly projecting roofs on the south side give shade during the hottest parts of the day. On each floor there are at least two windows on the south front, and when these are open at the same time as windows on the north a cooling breeze is drawn through the house.

The large areas of glass on the south wall provide a magnificent panorama, creating the sense of fluidity between inside and outside that is the essence of Modernism. This feature has made some residents feel uncomfortably exposed, and in response they have introduced fences, greenery, blinds and net curtains. Nevertheless an abundance of light is the touchstone of these houses, with their floor-to-ceiling glass in each end and a band of clerestory windows along the side at the top. The area of glass on the north elevations is considerably lower than that on the warmer south side. A small south-facing roof terrace is inset

at the top of each floor, thus providing one virtually private space for each dwelling. Each house also has a generous south-facing balcony at first-floor level, opening off the living room. This connects with the garden by means of an external stair. On the other side, across a small, slightly sunken garden court, is a carport with open sides and an aluminium roof. Owners have customized these, introducing side walls to enclose the space entirely.

Most of the houses have been sold to families with two or three children. Because they are single-family dwellings rising no higher than 26 feet (8m) they do not require the fire doors and fire lobbies specified for apartment houses, which militate against open-plan living. Each floor has its own direct means of escape – instead of conventional windows there are glazed doors opening directly onto balconies or roof terraces. The fact that these are single-family houses has also allowed Cleffmann, in his own home, to display the slim elegance of the steel frame, which elsewhere would have had to be covered with fire-retardant material, completely obscuring the clean profiles of the steel. Fire protection between houses

The house that was designed by Martin Cleffmann of Schaudt Architekten for himself (right) explores the limits of open-plan living. He dispensed with almost all internal walls and made one floor visible from another by using a staircase that hangs free from the wall.

The view from the first-floor living room to the glazed entrance (below) shows the staircase with its open steel treads, designed to allow the interrelation between floors that Cleffmann values.

This view of the second floor shows the exposed structure of standard steel "I" beams, galvanized and bolted together. The bed is in a tent beneath the curved metal roof and is reached by a barely visible retractable stair. This arrangement frees the space below for use as a study.

On the ground floor of Cleffmann's house there are three bedrooms and a bathroom. The first floor is an open-plan living and dining area with a kitchen by the window. On the second floor the tent bed, indicated by dotted lines, is raised up on the steel structural sections above the study area.

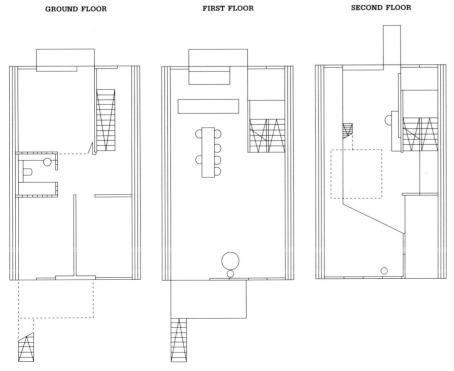

GROUND FLOOR   FIRST FLOOR   SECOND FLOOR

is provided by solid brick walls offering the statutory minimum of 90-minute's resistance. The open design of the staircases, with gaps between the treads, caused concern that small children climbing the steps could slip through. This was resolved by inserting a rod to reduce the size of the gap.

Living in terraces, say the architects of this development, is popular because people want their own house rather than an apartment. Because land is so expensive in and around Konstanz, few people can buy a plot for a detached house, and terrace houses remain the next-best option for most. At present it is clear that prospective purchasers would have preferred more conventional and solid-looking houses. The big question is whether the sense of space, light and sheer style that these houses offer will gradually win more admirers. Without a doubt they are among the most original and adventurous of modern houses, potentially initiating a new era of design.

Glossary

Acanthus Leaf ornament used on capital of Corinthian column, in cornice or as circling scroll motif.

Anthemion Classical ornament resembling a honeysuckle flower.

Arch-headed A window or opening with a curved head.

Arcade Series of arches supported on columns or piers, often forming a covered walk in front of shops.

Architrave The lowest third of a classical entablature.

Ashlar Blocks of stone, hewn square and smooth to fit closely, laid in horizontal courses with vertical joints.

Attic Top storey within a roof, or storey set above the main cornice of a façade.

Balustrade Series of vertical posts used to support a staircase handrail.

Bargeboard Carved or shaped board set within a gable.

Base Moulded foot of a column or pilaster.

Battlements Defensive, and later ornamental, parapet or top of façade.

Bay window Projecting window of one or more storeys; may be semicircular, bowed, three-sided (canted) or rectangular.

Buttress Vertical projecting support used to stabilize wall or resist lateral thrust of an arch, roof or vault.

Cantilever Horizontal projection, such as a flight of steps, apparently self-supporting but held in place by the weight of masonry on one side.

Capital Head of a column or pilaster.

Casement Side-hinged window, used especially in France and other mainland European countries. By contrast, vertically sliding sash windows were used in England and Holland from late 17th century.

Caryatid Stone pillar in the form of a draped female figure, used to support an entablature.

Cast iron Iron cast in a mould to a predetermined shape.

Chamfer Vertical or horizontal indent on a beam or pillar.

Clerestory Row of high-level windows used to light the upper part of an internal space.

Coade stone Durable artificial stone used for ornamental details. Made in Lambeth, London, 1769–c.1840, to a recipe now lost.

Coffering Pattern of sunken panels (coffers), square or polygonal, used to decorate a ceiling, vault, arch or dome.

Colonnade Row of columns supporting an entablature.

Corinthian Tallest of the classical architectural orders, with acanthus-leaf capital and plain or fluted column shaft.

Cornice Ornamental projection along the top of a façade, or moulding around the edge of a ceiling. Also upper element of a classical entablature.

Corps de logis Main part of a building, as distinct from wings, stables, pavilions etc.

Cour d'honneur Formal entrance courtyard immediately in front of a substantial town or country house.

Cove Broad concave moulding, used, for example, to form a curved junction between wall and ceiling.

Crosswall Structural wall between two flanks or party walls of a terrace, or row, house.

Crown glass Old form of window glass that gives distinctive rippled reflections.

Cupola Small external or internal dome.

Dado Lower portion of a wall, faced or coloured differently from the upper part and extending from floor to table height.

Dado rail Moulding set along the top of a dado.

Dentil Small square block used along cornice.

Dogleg (stair) Parallel flights rising alternately in opposite directions.

Doric Simplest and stoutest of the classical architectural orders, with a plain cushion capital. The shaft of a Greek Doric column is often fluted and has no base.

Dormer Window projecting from the slope of a roof.

Downpipe Vertical pipe on outside of building to carry rainwater down from roof.

Eaves Projecting edge of roof.

Enfilade Series of grand rooms with doorways in line, commonly used in French baroque palaces.

Entablature In classical architecture, a lintel carried by a row of columns, consisting of architrave, frieze and cornice. Used inside or outside a building to emphasize a wall or storey, or carried by a colonnade.

Fanlight Window resembling an open fan, usually set over a front door to light an entrance hall.

Fluting Vertical grooves on a column or pilaster.

Flying stair Stair cantilevered out from the walls or suspended free of them.

Frieze Middle section of a classical entablature – may be plain or ornamented. Also band of ornament around a room, usually immediately below the cornice.

Gallery Long room or passage, or balcony overlooking an internal hall or staircase hall.

Giant order or giant column Column rising through two or more storeys.

Glazing bar Wooden or metal bar framing glass within a window frame.

Inglenook Recess, with a seat, at the side of a large fireplace.

Ionic Classical architectural order with volutes, or spiral scrolls, on both side of the capital.

Jetty In a timber-framed building, the projection of one storey over that below. When a building is jettied out on two adjoining sides a dragon beam is set diagonally to carry the joists of the storeys above.

Joist Beam supporting the boards of a floor (or other floor covering). Also used as attachment for ceiling below.

Keystone Central stone of an arch, often larger or more emphatically treated than the others.

Lintel Horizontal beam of stone or wood set across an opening.

Mansard Roof with a double slope in which the lower slope is steeper than the upper.

Mezzanine Low storey between two other floors, usually ground and first; also known as an entresol.

Monopitch Roof with single slope.

Mullion Vertical division separating lights, or glazed parts, of a window. Mullions and transoms are often used together.

Multi-storey Of five or more storeys.

Ogee Double curved arch with arcs bending first one way and then the other to meet in a point at the top.

Order Style of column used in classical architecture. The principal orders, Doric, Ionic and Corinthian, were revived in the ancient Roman forms during the Renaissance and in their Greek forms in the late 18th century. The Tuscan order is a simpler version of Roman Doric. The Composite capital combines Ionic volutes with the Corinthian acanthus foliage. Column shafts may be plain or fluted. Full columns are free-standing; attached or engaged columns are partially embedded in walls; and half-columns are placed against walls or piers.

Oriel Window built out from a wall, in the form of a large window rising from the ground or a projecting upper window.

Overdoor Painting or relief above a door in a room.

Ovolo Rounded moulding, usually formed of a quarter-circle.

Palladian Architectural style inspired by the Italian neoclassical architect Andrea Palladio (1508–80), author of the widely used *Four Books of Architecture* (1570).

Panelling Wooden facing applied to internal walls; also called wainscoting.

Parapet Wall at top of façade, used to conceal roof or to prevent falling.

Party wall Wall shared by two adjoining buildings.

Pediment Triangular gable as used on the front of a classical temple, often set over doors and windows. May also be arched (segmental) or broken.

Piano nobile Principal floor of a classical building, above a ground floor or basement (French: *bel étage*).

Pier Large masonry brick or stone pillar or support, often carrying an arch.

Pilaster Flat version of an engaged classical column.

Pointing Exposed mortar jointing of masonry and brickwork. Modern cement used for brickwork differs from traditional lime mortar.

Porch Enclosure or protection, usually projecting but sometimes recessed, for a doorway.

Portico Projecting covered entrance, usually supported on columns.

Quoin Dressed stone or brick used externally, usually with others, to emphasize the corner of a building or the surround of a door or window.

Rafter Sloping roof timbers used to support the roof covering.

Rendering External coat applied to a wall as protection against weather; often used as a substitute for stone.

Reveal Inner face, or cheek, of a door or a window. May be splayed (angled back) to allow in more light.

Rococo Architectural style current c.1720–1770s, using "S" and "C" curves and *rocaille*, a decorative technique using shells and rock.

Rubbed brick Brick rubbed to a very smooth surface, mostly used for door and window openings.

Rustication Emphatic treatment of masonry, often used for ground floor or basement. In France, channelled rustication is often favoured over blocked rustication, where each stone stands out from its neighbour. Vermiculated rustication has a texture akin to worm-casts.

Sash (window) Vertically sliding window with two sliding frames, one sliding up, the other down (occasionally the upper sash is fixed). Sashes are set in a sash box, which itself may be partially set into the wall. In Britain, Holland and North America sashes have counterweights (out of sight in the sash box) attached to sash-cords, or occasionally chains, which allow the sashes to be left open at any level.

Scagliola Composition with smooth lustrous texture, used since Roman times to imitate marble.

Setback An outside wall stepped back.

Sgraffito Decoration, usually in plaster, in which a wet top coat is incised to reveal a coat of a different colour below.

Solar Private upper chamber of a medieval house for family use, usually at upper end of great hall.

Spandrel Roughly triangular sections between arches supporting a dome.

Strapwork Technique used in the late 16th and 17th centuries (and revived in the 19th century) to produce decoration like interlaced leather straps or carved fretwork.

String course Horizontal moulding (often plain) used along a façade, sometimes to mark a division between storeys.

Stucco Fine plasterwork used internally and externally to coat walls and form decoration.

Tie-rod Bar, usually of iron, used to tie outer walls together, sometimes long after erection of building. Also used to brace two sides of a large internal roof span. The ornamental ends of tie-rods are often a feature of façades.

Timber-framing Building style in which walls are formed of connected vertical and horizontal timber beams, with the spaces between them filled with a non-structural material.

Toplight Window or glazed opening set in roof and often used to admit light into a space – for example, a staircase – without windows.

Transom Horizontal division separating lights (parts) of a window.

Truss Frame, usually triangular, carrying a roof.

Undercroft Room or rooms, usually vaulted and often underground, beneath main floor of medieval building.

Vault Arched stone or brick ceiling, which may also be plastered. A tunnel or barrel vault is a continuous arch, usually semicircular, segmental or, in medieval times, pointed. Tunnel vaults intersecting at right angles are known as a groin vault.

Voussoir Wedge-shaped stone used, with others, to form an arch.

Winder Spiral staircase, with treads wider at one end than at the other, in a rectangular compartment.

Bibliography

GENERAL

Girouard, Mark. *The English Town* (London and New Haven, 1990)

Lancaster, Osbert. *Here, of all Places* (London, 1959)

Muthesius, Hermann. *The English House* (London, 1979)

Muthesius, Stefan. *The English Terraced House* (London and New Haven, 1983)

AMSTERDAM

Spies, Paul and others. *The Canals of Amsterdam* (Amsterdam and The Hague, 1993)

BATH

Fergusson, Adam. *The Sack of Bath: a Record and an Indictment* (Salisbury, 1973)

Ison, Walter. *The Georgian Buildings of Bath* (London, 1948 and 1980)

Woodward, Christopher. *The Building of Bath* (Bath, 1993)

BERLIN

Kloss, Klaus-Peter. *Siedlungen der 20er Jahre* (Berlin, 1982)

Portuguesi, Paolo. *Die Bauwerke und Kunstdenkmäler von Berlin: Bezirk Zehlendorf, Siedlung Onkel Tom* (Berlin and Florence)

Vier Berliner Siedlungen der Weimarer Republik (exhibition catalogue of Bauhaus-Archiv, Berlin, 1984–5)

BOSTON

McIntyre, A. McVoy. *Beacon Hill: A Walking Tour* (Boston)

Moore, Barbara and Gail Weesner. *Beacon Hill: A Living Portrait* (Boston, 1992)

Weinhardt, Carl J. Jr *The Domestic Architecture of Beacon Hill 1800–50* (Boston, 1973, reprinted from the Bostonian Society Proceedings, 1958)

BRIGHTON

Bingham, Neil. *C.A. Busby: The Regency Architect of Brighton and Hove* (London, 1991)

BRUSSELS

Borsi, Franco and Hans Wieser. *Bruxelles, Capitale de l'Art Nouveau* (Brussels, 1996)

Demanet, Marie and others. *Les Sgraffites à Bruxelles* (Brussels, 1996)

Vandenbreeden, Jos and Françoise Dierkens-Aubry. *The 19th Century in Belgium: Architecture and Interior Design* (Tielt, Belgium, 1994)

CHICAGO

Weese, Kitty Baldwin. *Harry Weese Houses* (Chicago, 1987)

CHESTER

Brown, A.N. and others. "Watergate Street" in *Chester Archaeological Society Journal* (vol. 69, 1988)

CLUNY

Kräftner, Johann. *Bürgerhäuser* (Munich and Vienna, 1982)

Grandchamp, Pierre Garrigou and Michael Jones, Gwyn Meirion-Jones, Jean-Denis Salvèque and others. *La ville de Cluny et ses maisons* (Paris, 1997)

DUBLIN

Craig, Maurice. *Dublin 1660–1860* (Dublin, 1969)

FLORENCE

Fanelli, Giovanni. *Firenze: architettura e città* (Florence, 1973)

Martucci, Roberto and Bruno Giovannetti. *Florence: Guide to the Principal Buildings* (Venice, 1997)

Preyer, Brenda. *Il Palazzo Corsi-Horne* (Rome, 1993)

HAMBURG

Mallgrave, Harry Francis. *Gottfried Semper: Architect of the Nineteenth Century* (London and New Haven)

Wolfgang, Rudhard. *Das Bürgerhaus in Hamburg* (Tübingen)

KONSTANZ

Bleck, Jan. *"Future Terrace"* in *Architectural Review* (June 1997, page 32)

KRAKOW

Marczynski, Fr. *Le vieux Cracovie: Rues, Portails, Vestibules* (Krakow, 1908): *La Maison de Ville à la Renaissance* (Paris, 1977)

LONDON

16th and 17th centuries

Leech, Roger H. *"The Row House in Late Sixteenth- and Early Seventeenth-Century London"* in *Archaeological Journal* (vol. 153, 1996)

Mowl, Timothy and Brian Earnshaw. *Architecture without Kings: The Rise of Puritan Classicism under Cromwell* (Manchester and New York, 1995)

18th and 19th centuries

Cruickshank, Dan and Neil Burton. *Life in the Georgian City* (London, 1990)

Cruickshank, Dan and Peter Wyld. *London: The Art of Georgian Building* (London, 1975)

Girouard, Mark and others. *The Saving of Spitalfields* (London, 1989)

Simmonds, Henry S. *All about Battersea* (London, 1879)

Summerson, John. *Architecture in Britain 1530–1830* (London, 1953 and later editions)

20th century

Pawley, Martin. *"Market Leader,"* article on housing by Nicholas Grimshaw & Partners in Camden Town in *Architects' Journal* (October 4, 1989)

Porter, Stephen (ed.). *Survey of London, Vol. 43*; see chapter on Lansbury Estate (London, 1994)

LÜBECK

Hübler, Hans. *Das Bürgerhaus in Lübeck* (Tübingen, 1968)

MAHON

Martorell, Josep. *Guia d'Arquitectura de Menorca* (Barcelona, 1980)

NEW YORK

Lockwood, Charles. *Bricks & Brownstone: The New York Row House, 1783–1929* (New York, 1972)

PARIS

General

Pérouse de Montclos, Jean-Marie (ed.). *Le Guide du Patrimoine: Paris* (Paris, 1994)

Sutcliffe, Anthony. *Paris: An Architectural History* (London and New Haven, 1993)

16th and 17th centuries

Babelon, Jean-Pierre. *Demeures Parisiennes sous Henri IV et Louis XIII* (Paris, 1965, 1991)

Babelon, Jean-Pierre. *Paris au XVIe siècle* (Paris, 1986)

Ballon, Hilary. *The Paris of Henri IV: Architecture and Urbanism* (New York, 1991)

Gady, Alexandre (ed.). *De la Place Royale à la Place des Vosges* (Paris, 1996)

Le Muet, Pierre. *Manière de bien bastir pour toutes sortes de personnes* (Paris, 1623, 1647)

Thompson, David. *Renaissance Paris: Architecture and Growth, 1475–1600* (London, 1984)

18th century

Gallet, Michel. *Paris Domestic Architecture of the 18th Century* (London, 1972)

Krafft, J.-Ch. *Plans, coupes, élévations des plus belles maisons et des hôtels construits à Paris et dans les environs* (Paris, 1802)

Scott, Katie. *The Rococo Interior* (London and New Haven)

19th century

Calliat, Victor. *Parallèle des maisons de Paris construites*

depuis 1830 jusqu'à nos jours
(Paris, 1850)
Calliat, Victor. *Parallèle des
maisons de Paris construites
depuis 1850 jusqu'à nos jours*
(Paris, 1864)

PHILADELPHIA
Moss, Roger W. *Historic Houses
of Philadelphia* (Philadelphia,
1998)
Murtagh, William John. *"The
Philadelphia Row House"* in
*Journal of the American Society
of Architectural Historians*
(vol. XVI, 1957)
Tatum, George B. *Philadelphia
Georgian: The City House of
Samuel Powel* (Middletown,
Connecticut, 1976)

PORT GRIMAUD
Parisot, Serge-Henri. *Port-Grimaud et
la Côte des Maures* (Paris, 1972)
Spoerry, François. *A Gentle
Architecture* (Chichester, 1994)

POTSDAM
Mielke, Friedrich. *Das Bürgerhaus
in Potsdam* (Tübingen, 2 vols.,
1972)
Seiler, Michael and Jörg Wacker.
Insel Potsdam (Berlin, 1991)

ROTHENBURG OB DER
TAUBER
Denkmäler in Bayern: Mittelfranken
(Munich, 1986)
Mayer, Eugen. *Das Bürgerhaus
zwischen Ostalb und oberer
Tauber* (Tübingen, 1978)

RENNES
Derveaux, Daniel. *Les Vieux Logis
de Rennes* (St Malo, 1946)
Irvoas-Dantec, Dominique. *Rennes*
(guidebook, 1996)

ROUEN
Gasperini, Alain. *Rouen: Les Maisons
à Pans de Bois* (Rouen, 1982)
Quenedey, Raymond. *L'Habitation
Rouennaise* (Rouen, 1926)

SAN FRANCISCO
Delehanty, Randolph. *In the
Victorian Style* (San Francisco,
1991)
Pomada, Elizabeth and Michael
Larsen. *Painted Ladies: San
Francisco's Resplendent
Victorians* (New York, 1978)

VENICE
Gianighian, Giorgio and Paolo
Pavanini. *Dietro i Palazzi:
tre secoli di architettura
minore a Venezia 1492–1803*
(Venice, 1984)
Goy, R.G. *The House of Gold:
Building a Palace in Medieval
Venice* (Cambridge, 1993)
Goy, R.G. *Venetian Vernacular
Architecture* (Cambridge, 1989)
Goy, R.G. *Venice: The City and its
Architecture* (London, 1997)
Zucchi, Benedict. *Giancarlo De
Carlo* (Oxford, 1992)

Where to visit

AMSTERDAM
Rembrandt House,
Jodenbreestraat 4–6, 1011 NK
Amsterdam, Netherlands. *The
17th-century painter's house and
studio. Under reconstruction in
1998.*
Museum Van Loon, Keizersgracht
672, 1017 ET Amsterdam,
Netherlands. *Furnished family
house.*

BATH
1 Royal Crescent, Bath, BA1 2LR,
UK. *Show town house run by
Bath Preservation Trust.*
The Building of Bath Museum,
Countess of Huntingdon's Chapel,
The Paragon, Bath BA1 5NA, UK.
*Not a town house but a museum
with a wealth of information on
the subject.*

BOSTON
Nichols House Museum on Beacon
Hill, 55 Mount Vernon Street,
Boston, Massachusetts 02108,
USA. *Furnished town house of
1804, bequeathed as museum by
last of family to live here.*

BRIGHTON
Regency Town House, 13 Brunswick
Square, Hove, East Sussex BN3
1EH, UK. *Town house being
restored by the Regency Town
House's Trust. Tours available
throughout the year; pre-book on
01273 206306 until renovations
are complete.*

BRUSSELS
Horta Museum, 25 Rue Américaine,
B-1060 Brussels, Belgium.
*House of Art Nouveau architect
Victor Horta, designed for himself.*

FLORENCE
Palazzo Horne. *Early-16th-century
house, restored by an English art
critic, which became a museum
after his death in 1916.*

LONDON
Charles Dickens House, 48 Doughty
Street, London WC1, UK.
*Late Georgian house where the
19th-century writer lived.*
Linley Sambourne House, 18
Stafford Terrace, London W8, UK.
Late-19th-century home of

*illustrator and Punch cartoonist,
with interiors preserved much
as he left them. Managed by the
Victorian Society.*
Sir John Soane's Museum, 13
Lincoln's Inn Fields, London
WC2, UK. *Remarkable house,
studio and museum of the
Neo-classical architect, preserved
as it was at the time of his death
in 1837.*

NEW YORK
Old Merchant's House, 29 East 4th
Street, New York, NY 10003, USA.
*Red-brick Federal-style row
house of 1832, which opened in
1936 as a historical society
museum.*
Theodore Roosevelt Birthplace,
28 East 20th Street, New York,
NY 10003, USA. *Reconstruction
(1923) of the brownstone in
which President Roosevelt
was born.*

PARIS
Maison de Victor Hugo, Place des
Vosges 6, Paris 75004, France.
The 19th-century writer's house,

*furnished with mementoes of his
life but with little of the 17th
century, when it was built, in
evidence.*

PHILADELPHIA
Powel House, South 3rd Street,
Philadelphia, USA. *Handsome
18th-century town house,
preserved as museum.*

ROTTERDAM
Pole House, Overblaak 70, 3011 MH
Rotterdam, Netherlands. *House in
group by the architect Piet Blom,
on show to the public.*

SAN FRANCISCO
Haas-Lilienthal House, 2007
Franklin Street, San Francisco,
CA 94109, USA. *Furnished house
run by the Foundation for San
Francisco's Heritage.*

VENICE
Casa di Goldoni, Calle dei Nomboli
2793, Venice, Italy. *15th-century
Gothic house, preserved as
birthplace of 18th-century comic
playwright Carlo Goldoni.*

Index

Acknowledgments

Author Acknowledgments

At Mitchell Beazley, my thanks to Alison Starling, with whom I first evolved the idea of this book; Anthea Snow, my guiding editor at every subsequent stage; Anna Kobryn for quantities of diligent picture research; Viv Brar for shaping the look of the book; Adrian Morris the designer; Stephen Guise, who has helped take the book to press; and Richard Dawes, who has edited the text with as much knowledge, precision and patience as an author could hope for. At SAVE Britain's Heritage, thanks to Richard Pollard, and before him Emma Phillips, Sophie Andreae and Marianne Watson-Smyth. To my American friend Calder Loth, for guidance and help of many kinds. For help and advice with the cutaway drawings, special thanks are due to Richard Goy and Marco Zordan for Venice; to François de La Ferrière for the Place des Vosges; to Nick Tyson for Hove; to Charles A Markis for New York; and to Ulrich Borgert for Berlin. For help with individual places and buildings, my thanks as follows – Amsterdam: Harry Reijnders and Edzerd Brons, Titia Vellenga, Herman F Willems. Asolo: Giorgio Zanesco. Bath: Christopher Woodward. Berlin: Ulrich Borgert. Brussels: David Stevens, Françoise Aubry. Chester: Peter de Figuereido. Chicago: Jerrold McElvain, Kitty Baldwin Weese, Chicago Public Library. Cluny: Susan Content, Philip Dixon, Michael Jones, Gwyn Meirion-Jones, Roger H Leech. Dublin: Mary Bryan. Hamburg: Frédéric Ulferts. Hebden Bridge: Ann Kilbey, Peter Thornborrow. Hove: Nick Tyson. Konstanz: Martin Münzenmaier. Litomerice: Josef Stulc. London: Jim and Wynn Alloway, H Godwin Arnold, Douglas Blain, Walter Bor, Dan Cruickshank, Philip Davies, Donald Findlay, Michael Gillingham, John and Eileen Harris, Haskoll & Co, Jackie Hawkins, Dulcia Keate, Roger H Leech, Alex Lifschutz, Roger Mears, Neven Sidor, Spitalfields Trust, Steve Pilcher, Paddy Pugh, Iain Tuckett, Peter Watts. Lübeck: Dr Peter Kallen. Mahón: Drew Galloway, Josep Martorell. New York: Mosette Broderick, Charles A Markis, Mimi Sherman. Paris: Vincent Bouvet, Robert Dodd, Alexandre Gady, John Hardcastle, Isabel Duhan, Martin Meade, Edith de Richemont, François de La Ferrière and Daniel Duché, Mme Cloué, Anne-Frédérique Roubaudi, Eléanore Toussaint du Wast. Philadelphia: Dr Roger Moss, Bill Murtagh. Potsdam: Brian Hanson, Richard Röhrbein. Rennes: Dominique Irvoas-Dantec. Rotterdam: Ed R De Graaf. Rouen: Alain Gasperini. San Francisco: Anne Bloomfield, Randolph Delehanty, Donald Klingbeil, Philip C Rossington, Daniel Solomon. Sterzing: Gion Rudolf Caprez and Agostini & Zanella. Sydney: Clive Lucas. Venice: Architetto Andreotti, Richard Goy, G Romanelli, Marco Zordan.

Key

Arcaid: **A**; Architekturwerkstatt Helge Pitz-Winfried Brenne: **AHPB**; AKG, London: **AKG**; British Architectural Library, RIBA, London: **BAL**; Centry Hill Press, Boston, MA: **CHP**; D'Arts, Amsterdam: **D**; Douglas Keister: **DK**; Derry Moore: **DM**; Ernst Wasmuth Verlag GmbH & Co, Tübingen: **EW**; Giancarlo De Carlo, Milan: **GDC**; Hilbich: **H**; Huw Thomas Associates Architects, Winchester: **HT**; Harry Weese Associates: **HW**; Joe Cornish: **JC**; Jo Reid and John Peck: **JRJP**; Lifschutz Davidson, London: **LD**; Reed Consumer Books Limited: **RCB**; Marcus Binney: **MB**; Nicholas Grimshaw & Partners, London: **NG**; Nicholas Kane: **NK**; Oosterhuis Architekten, Rotterdam: **OA**; Reiner Blunck, Tübingen: **RB**; Richard Bryant: **RBr**; Robert Harding Picture Library: **RHPL**; Royal Institute of British Architects: **RIBA**; Richard Sexton: **RS**; Solomon Inc, San Francisco: **SI**.

Picture Acknowledgments

Front jacket Richard Davies; **back jacket t** RCB/NK; **back jacket b** GDC; **endpapers** D; **back flap** Anne Binney; 1 RCB/NK; 2 DK; 5 RB/Schaudt/Cleffmann; 6 Service Régional de l'Inventaire Général de Basse-Normandie/Cl P Corbierre, Inventaire général (from *Petits Edifices, Normandie*, A Vincent et Cie, Paris); 7 Service Régional de l'Inventaire Général de Basse-Normandie/Cl P Corbierre, Inventaire général (from *Petits Edifices, Normandie*, A Vincent et Cie, Paris); 8 Collection of the New York Historical Society; 9t Jean-Loup Charmet/Musée Carnavalet, Paris; 9br RIBA/BAL; 10t RIBA/BAL; 10b Dean & Chapter of Wells; 11t RHPL/Phil Robinson; 11b Krzysztof Dydynski; 12 RCB/NK; 13t HT; 13b HT; 14 Tony Stone Images/Denis Waugh; 15 Travel Ink/Jill Swainson; 16t Scope/Jean-Luc Barde; 16b Centre d'Etudes Clunisiennes/Jean-Denis Salvèque; 17l Scope/Jean-Luc Barde; 17r Jean-Denis Salvèque; 18 RCB/NK; 19l RCB/NK; 19r RCB/NK; 20t RCB/NK; 20c RCB/NK; 20b RCB/NK; 21r Architetto Marco Zordan, Venice; 22t Corbis UK Ltd/Sean Sexton Collection; 22b Peter De Figuereido/Chester City Council; 23 Chester City Council/Graham Holme; 24 Scope/Philip Gould; 25t MB; 25b MB; 26l MB; 26r MB; 27t Wojciech Gorgolewski, Airphoto GORPOL, Krakow; 27b MB (from *La vieux Cracovie: Rues, Portails, Vestibules*, Fr Maczynski, 1908); 28 Edition Tappeiner; 29t Touristmusverein Sterzing; 29b University of Innsbruck, Austria (from a student's publication c.1920–30); 30t MB; 31 Corbis UK Ltd/Dave G Houser; 32 Dr Peter Kallen; 33t Dr Peter Kallen; 33b EW (from *Das Bürgerhaus in Lübeck*); 34 JC; 35 JC; 36 Bridgeman Art Library, London/New York/Palazzo Vecchio, Florence; 37t MB; 37b MB; 38 Index, Florence/Cantarelli; 39t MB; 39b Index, Florence/Cantarelli; 40t RCB/NK; 40b Photographie Giraudon/Musee Carnavalet, Paris; 41l RCB/NK; 41r RCB/NK; 42tl RCB/NK; 42cl RCB/NK; 42bl RCB/NK; 43r François de La Ferrière, Architecture intérieure, Paris; 44t RCB/NK; 44b RCB/NK; 45t RCB/NK; 45bl RIBA/BAL; 45br RIBA/BAL; 46 D; 47t D; 47b D/Rijksmuseum-Stichting, Amsterdam; 48l D; 48r D; 48t D; 49 RHPL; 50t Museum van Loon, Amsterdam/Maarten Brinkgreve; 50b Gemeentearchief Amsterdam; 51l Caroline Jones; 51r Museum van Loon, Amsterdam/Maarten Brinkgreve; 52 RHPL/Bildagentur Schuster Krauskopf; 53t Kunstverlag Edm von König, Dielheim; 53c EW (from *Das Bürgerhaus zwischen Ostalb und Oberer Tauber*); 53b EW (from *Das Bürgerhaus zwischen Ostalb und Oberer Tauber*); 54bl English Heritage Photographic Library; 54br English Heritage/courtesy Richard Lea; 55t RCB/NK; 55b English Heritage/courtesy Richard Lea; 56l MB; 56r MB; 57 Editions d'Art Jos, Le Doare, Chateaulin; 58 RCB/NK; 59l RCB/NK; 59r RCB/NK; 60l RCB/NK; 60r RCB/NK; 61t Peter Aprahamian, London; 61b Angelo Hornak; 62 Ladislav Bezdek; 63t Ladislav Bezdek; 63b courtesy of The State Institute for Heritage Preservation, Prague; 64 Corbis UK Ltd/Adam Woolfitt; 65 JC; 66 RCB/NK; 67t RCB/NK; 67b RCB/NK; 68 RIBA/BAL; 69t RCB/NK; 69b RCB/NK; 70t Image Bank/Romilly Lockyer; 70b The Building of Bath Museum/Helena Webster, Oxford; 71t Edifice/Jackson; 71b RHPL/Julia Bayne; 72 RCB/NK; 73t EW (from *Das Bürgerhaus in Potsdam*); 73b RCB/NK; 74t RCB/NK; 74b RCB/NK; 75t RIBA/BAL; 75bl RCB/NK; 75br RCB/NK; 76t RCB/NK; 76b RIBA/BAL; 77t RCB/NK; 77b Anthony Richardson and Partners, London, ARP/Matthew Weinreb; 78t RCB/NK; 78b RIBA/BAL; 79 RCB/NK; 80t Stephen J Whitehorne; 80b The Slide File; 81 Image Bank/Matthew Weinrub; 82 Image Ireland/Geray Sweeney; 83l Stephen J Whitehorne; 83r Bill Doyle, Dublin; 84 MB; 85t MB; 85b MB; 86 Edifice/Lewis; 87l *Journal of the Society of Architectural Historians* (from "The Philadelphia Row House," William John Murtagh, Dec 1957; vol. XVI no.4); 87tr Edifice/Lewis; 88t Tom Crane Photography Inc; 88b Tom Crane Photography Inc; 89t Tom Crane Photography Inc; 89b *Journal of the Society of Architectural Historians* (from "The Philadelphia Row House," William John Murtagh, Dec 1957; vol. XVI no.4); 90t The Bostonian Society (from *The Domestic Architecture of Beacon Hill 1800–1850*); 90b RCB/Nicolas Goodall; 91 RCB/Nicolas Goodall; 92 CHP/Southie Burgin; 93tl CHP; 93tr CHP; 93b CHP/Southie Burgin; 94 RCB/NK; 95l RCB/NK; 95r RCB/NK; 96tl RCB/NK; 96acl RCB/NK; 96bl RCB/NK; 98 Rick Woods; 99l Grant Compton, Brevard, NC; 99r Rick Woods; 100t Edifice/Nabarro; 100b RHPL/K Gillham; 101 Corbis UK Ltd/Dave G Houser; 102 Roger Miller; 103 Roger Miller; 104t Frédéric Ulferts; 104b Hamburger Staatsarchiv/Keimer & Keimer; 105 Frédéric Ulferts; 106 RCB/NK; 107t Angelo Hornak; 107b Bridgeman Art Library, London/New York/Museum of the City of New York; 108 RCB/NK; 109t RCB/NK; 109b RCB/NK; 110t RCB/NK; 110cl RCB/NK; 110b RCB/NK; 111r The Theodore Roosevelt Birthplace, New York; 112t RCB/NK; 112b RCB/NK; 113 RCB/NK; 114t DM; 114b DM; 115 DM; 116t RCB/NK; 116b London Borough of Lambeth Archives Dept/Godfrey New Photographies; 117t Peabody Trust, London; 117b RCB/NK; 118t A/Annet Held; 118b A/Annet Held; 119 RS; 120 RS; 120l RS; 121t DK; 121b DK; 122t RCB/NK; 122b *Survey of London* (volume XLII: "Southern Kensington: Kensington Square to Earl's Court"), The GLC/The Athlone Press; 123 RCB/NK; 124l RCB/NK; 124r RCB/NK; 125t RCB/NK; 125b RCB/NK; 126t JC; 126b MB; 127t JC; 128t AKG/H; 128b AKG/H; 129l AKG/H; 129r AKG/H; 130l AKG/H; 130r AKG/H; 131t RIBA/BAL (from *L'Emulation*, 1905); 131b RIBA/BAL (from *L'Emulation*, 1905); 132 A/RBr; 133l AKG/Erich Lessing; 133r A/RBr; 134 RCB/NK; 135l RCB/NK; 135r RCB/NK; 136 OA/Hans Werlemann; 137 OA/Hans Werlemann; 138t RCB/NK; 138b AHPB; 139 RCB/NK; 140t RCB/NK; 140cl RCB/NK; 140b RCB/NK; 141 AHPB; 142 RCB/NK; 143r *Survey of London* (volume XLIII: "Poplar, Blackwall and The Isle of Dogs. The Parish of All Saints"), Royal Commission on the Historical Monuments of England/Norman & Dawbarn Architects/The Athlone Press; 143t RCB/NK; 143bl HW; 144tr HW; 144b HW; 145t HW; 145b Kitty Weese; 146t RHPL/C Martin; 146b Grange Bateliere SA, Paris & Istituto Geografico De Agostini SpA, Novara; 147 MB; 148 Tony Stone Images/David Hanson; 149 Corbis UK Ltd/Farrell Grehan; 150 Corbis UK Ltd/Farrell Grehan; 151t Kijk-Kubus/Show-Cube, Rotterdam/courtesy Ed de Graaf-Blaakse Bos; 151b Kijk-Kubus/Show-Cube, Rotterdam/courtesy Ed de Graaf-Blaakse Bos; 152 GDC; 153t GDC; 153b GDC; 154 GDC; 155t GDC; 155b GDC; 156 A/RBr; 157 A/RBr; 158t JRJP; 158bl NG; 158bc NG; 158br NG; 159r A/RBr; 159b JRJP; 160 SI; 161t SI; 161c SI; 161b SI; 162 LD/JRJP; 163t LD; 163b LD; 164t RB/Schaudt/Cleffmann; 164b RB/Schaudt/Cleffmann; 165l RB/Schaudt/Cleffmann; 165r RB; 166l RB/Schaudt/Cleffmann; 166r RB/Schaudt/Cleffmann; 167t RB/Schaudt/Cleffmann; 167b Schaudt Architekten, Konstanz.

De Heeren Gragt

De Heeren Gragt

Leidse straat

De Heeren Gragt

Leidse Gragt

De Heeren Gragt

Huyde straat

De Heeren Gragt

Wolve - Straat